A WORLD A

M000208639

A Memoir of Jewish Life
in Nineteenth Century Galicia

JUDAISM AND JEWISH LIFE

ACADEMIC
STUDIES
PRESS

A WORLD APART

A MEMOIR OF JEWISH LIFE
IN NINETEENTH CENTURY GALICIA

Joseph Margoshes

Translated from Yiddish
by Rebecca Margolis and Ira Robinson

Boston
2010

ISBN 978-1-934843-63-5 (paperback)

Book design by Yuri Alexandrov

Published by Academic Studies Press in 2010
28 Montfern Avenue
Brighton, MA 02135, USA
press@academicstudiespress.com
www.academicstudiespress.com

CONTENTS

INTRODUCTION

In 1936, Joseph Margoshes (1866–1955), a writer for the New York Yiddish daily *Morgen Zhurnal*, published a memoir of his youth in Austro-Hungarian Galicia entitled *Erinerungen fun mayn leben* ["Memoirs of My Life"], which is presented here for the first time in an English translation by Rebecca Margolis and Ira Robinson. In it, we enter the world of Margoshes' youth in Galicia, then part of the Austro-Hungarian Empire. Even from the perspective of the mid-1930s when he wrote this memoir, the Jewish Galicia he evoked had been changed almost beyond recognition as a result of the events surrounding the First World War, and was shortly to be completely obliterated by the Holocaust.

Eliezer Joseph Margoshes was born in 1866 in Lemberg (Lvov/Lviv) into a family with a distinguished rabbinical ancestry (*yihus*), as described in an appendix to these memoirs, and into a society in which that *yihus* counted for much. After his father's death, he moved to Tarnow. He received a traditional Jewish education in Bible and Talmud, as well as grounding in the German language and European culture. He married into a family of wealthy landowners and spent his early married years administering agricultural estates in Western Galicia.

Because of severe personal financial reverses, compounded by a serious agricultural depression in his country, he first emigrated to America in 1898. He evidently found adjustment to America difficult, because he returned to Europe in 1900. However he came back to America in 1903, this time to stay. At the time of his second arrival in New York, he established what would be a lasting connection with New York's then burgeoning Yiddish daily press. He started working with the *Tageblatt*, with which he was affiliated until 1911. In that year, he began work in the Bureau of Jewish Education, which had been established by the New York Kehilla movement, led by Judah L. Magnes, and helped edit the Kehilla's *Yearbook*. In 1914, he became a writer for the Yiddish daily *Der Tog*, where he worked until 1921. From that year and for the rest of his life, he wrote for the *Morgen Zhurnal* (which merged with *Der Tog* in 1954), while also contributing to many other Yiddish newspapers and periodicals.

He was a founding member and first secretary of the Y.L. Peretz Writers' Association, the union of Jewish writers in New York. He was prominent, in the 1920s, as one of the founders of the American branch of YIVO. He was also noted as an avid collector of books, amassing a personal library of some 20,000 volumes.

As a journalist, Margoshes became well-known for numerous series of articles on topics related to Jewish history, thought, and folklore. Examples of such series include "Maimonides," the Ten Tribes," "Great Figures in the World of Hasidism" and the "Belzer Dynasty." He was also engaged in an extensive study of the history of Jewish journalism in America. The *Erinerungen* originated in just such a series of journalistic pieces in the *Morgen Zhurnal*, and constitutes his only published volume.

In telling the story of his life, lived in a world that had passed away, and that he doubted would ever be revived, Margoshes provides the reader with important insights into numerous areas of the Jewish life of Austro-Hungarian Galicia. We read of Orthodox and Enlightened Jews and their conflicts, Jewish urban and rural life, the multifaceted relationship between Jews and their gentile neighbors, and much more.

Margoshes was an eyewitness to the beginnings of an organized Orthodox Jewish political movement in Galicia. He provides important insights into the inner workings of the nineteenth century Galician Jewish press. He is an important witness to the Jewish presence as estate owners and in the livestock trade of Western Galicia. This book is an important evocation of an entire Jewish society and civilization, and bears comparison with his contemporary Yehiel Yeshaia Trunk's masterpiece, *Poyln* as a vivid evocation of Jewish life in late nineteenth century Poland.

Ira Robinson and Simcha Fishbane

For Leytshi:
My life's partner,
Mother of our children,
In eternal love
And gratitude.

Author's Forward

I not have recorded these pages because I consider myself a great and important personage who has accomplished all sorts of great things. Rather, I have done so because it is human nature for one who has reached his later years to want to look back and take stock of his life.

I have lived in a different generation and under completely different circumstances from my own children and many of my friends and acquaintances. I thus hope that it might interest them to read the memoirs of my past.

I
FAMILY MEMOIRS

The meaning of my family name, "Margoshes" is not entirely clear to me. However, according to what I heard from my older brother Mendel, the word must be Spanish in origin. According to his claim, there is an old legend in the family that we stem from a Judeo-Spanish family that, after the Spanish Expulsion in 1492, was cast away all the way to Poland. Our family lived in the city of Apt (Opatov/Opatow) in Great Poland for several hundred years. The family then migrated from there and settled in Brod (Brody) and in Lemberg (Lvov/Lemberik/Lviv). In later generations Margosheses also settled in in Nadverne, Eastern Galicia, and in Jassy, Romania.

According to what my relative, Rabbi Eliezer Lipa Gartenhaus, "The Mikolayev Rabbi" (currently in New York), told me, we stem from great *gaonim*. He can enumerate our entire lineage all the way back to the Maharshal (Rabbi Solomon Luria, the author of many Talmudic works). Luria lived 350 years ago and was Rabbi of Lublin, and is considered one of the first and most important *gaonim* in Old Poland.

My great-grandfather, Reb Eliezer Margoshes, died in 1807, according to his headstone in the old Lemberg cemetery. In his youth, he was a revered community leader. He was the General Secretary of the last *Vaad Arba Aratzos* (a sort of Jewish parliament that existed in the Polish provinces for about three hundred years, and was abolished in 1764). This was a very important and esteemed position because the General Secretary kept the Vaad's books and minutes, and executed all of the decisions that were made at the semi-annual meetings during the great fairs.

His son, my grandfather Reb Joseph Margoshes (d. 1840), was a highly accomplished and educated man, and possessed great facility in the Latin language (in which all important legal documents were written at that time). He used to write Latin deeds for the courts. Moreover, he was also very affluent. He was also one of the heads of the Lemberg *Kahal*. From the Austrian Kaiser Ferdinand I, he received the privilege of building Austria's "first royally privileged" Rosolia factory, which produced an assortment of sweet liquors. The factory existed for quite a few years. Many empty bottles with the company's label could be found lying around in our attic at home. Because of the beautiful and colorful labels on these bottles, I used to play with them as a child. In his later years, my grandfather took on as his partner Reb Mordecai Dubsh [Marcus Dubos]. Dubos was a well-known *maskil* and scholar: he used to work for the Hebrew journals of that period and often corresponded with Shadal (Shmuel David Luzzato) and the other great rabbinic scholars. Reb Mordecai became wealthy from the Rosolia factory. At his death in 1874, he left an estate of half a million gulden, a fantastic sum of money over 60 years ago.

The Margoshes family has always been learned, and *maskilic* to boot. This can be ascertained from the acknowledgments in Moshe Mordecai Yovel's Hebrew natural history in three parts, *Limmudei Ha-Teva* (Czernowitz, 1836) that was dedicated to the Jewish philosopher Reb Nachman Krochmal. Its list of "the honorable and distinguished men who have committed to purchase the book at a price of two Rhenish thaler from me, the author" includes the following signatories from my family: Reb Yehoshua Fleker (my mother's father), Reb Joseph Margoshes, Marcus Dubos, Reb Nisn Margoshes, and my father, Reb Shmuel Margoshes.

My uncle, Reb Nisn Margoshes, who I still had the opportunity to know as a small boy, was a great rabbinic scholar, and highly respected in the Lemberg community. He was a very wealthy man and was deeply involved with Jewish communal affairs. In his later years, he became profoundly deaf and thus had to withdraw from his communal activities. Together with his two sons-in-law, both esteemed men of wealth, Reb Shlomo Sprekher and Reb Avraham Yitzhak Menkis, he undertook the publication of holy books on a very large scale. First, they published all of *Shas* with the *Alfas* in such a splendid edition that it continues to be greatly sought after by book-lovers, who pay handsomely for it.

When Reb Nisn later withdrew from all business affairs, both sons-in-law, Shprekher and Menkis, published many books, including several editions of *Shas*. Sprekher then entered into business with his brother, Yaakov (a son-in-law of the world-renowned *gaon*, Rabbi Zvi Hirsch Chajes). He founded a large wholesale iron business and became extremely affluent. The company still exists to this day, with Reb Jonah Sprekher, the wealthiest man in Lemberg, as owner. As for Menkis, he went on to publish many holy books at his own expense. "Menkis's *Shas*" remains a work of renown and is highly valued by rabbinic scholars. In addition to his great learning, Menkis was also a *maskil*. He founded and published the first Hebrew weekly in Galicia, *Habesor*. He published the newspaper over a period of about two years and then handed it over to his sister's son, the eminent and important *meylets* and rabbinic scholar, Reb Joseph Cohen Zedek, who later became editor of other Hebrew newspapers and journals.

As the evidence shows, writing and occupation with the printed word is an old "family disease" for me and two of my sons (Dr. Shmuel Margoshes and Herman Morgenstern, both with the *Tog*.)

2

My Mother's Family

The lineage and roots of my mother's family is less familiar to me. However, according to what was told to me by my Bubbe Yutele (deceased at age 86), we stem from the revered *gaon*, Rabbi Alexander Shor, author of *Tvuos Shor*, a famous book on the laws of ritual slaughter. She once showed me a book that was published in Zholkve (Zholkiew, Zhovkva). Facing the title page were two pictures: on top was an old Jew, a man devoted to the Torah, and underneath was a big ox with long horns. The caption read: "a firstborn bull in his majesty" (Deuteronomy 33: 17). When I was older, I went to a lot of trouble to get my hands on that book with the picture again. It had been reprinted several times, but always without the pictures. Perhaps this family copy contained the only existing exemplar of the drawing.

My grandfather, Reb Chaim Yehoshua Fleker, was at that time a worldly, highly educated person. He was a cloth merchant who would often travel to Vienna for his extensive business dealings. He had 13 children, of whom I knew eight. The sons were all "Germans" (that is: they wore short, modern clothing). The daughters were all educated and read the German classics.

Only two of his children were *frum*. One was his eldest son, my uncle Reb Zalman Leib, who was a *maskil* and wrote Hebrew poetry. He was also a great rabbinic scholar, and a famous printer and publisher of holy books. The second *frum* person in my grandfather's family was my mother, Sore Rivke (Rivele), may she rest in peace. Although she was an educated and extremely well-read woman, she was very *frum*. In her youth, she had been married to a man by the name of Safir of Tarnopol. She did not live with him very long because soon after the wedding he began to dress in short jackets and behave "German-style." She divorced him and only married my father, who was a widower, several years later. He had been married to the daughter of his oldest brother, Reb Nisn Margoshes, and had two sons with her.

7

My grandfather, Reb Chaim Yehoshua (who died in 1858), was, as stated earlier, a maskil. He supported the Hungarian rabbi, Rabbi Yehonatan Alexanderson, when he came to Lemberg to gather subscribers for his book, *Tomekh Kavod* (including a German section, "*Ehrenrettung*" [Rehabilitation]). The Hungarian rabbis had persecuted Alexanderson because of his *Haskalah* and had him removed from his rabbinate. My grandfather was among his first subscribers, and backed him with a significant sum of money.

My grandfather had a brother-in-law, a brother of my grandmother's, who was an extremely frum and respected Jew: Rabbi Avigdor Tshortkover. Although Rabbi Avigdor Tshortkover was not a Hassidic rebbe and did not head a Hassidic court, he had quite a few followers in Lemberg and had his own minyan in the family home where he lived with my grandfather: number 13 Golokhovski Place, facing the big house of Count Skarbek. The minyan was always packed, and Rabbi Avigdor would sit all day in his talis and tfilin and devote himself to Jewish communal affairs. One of my grandfather's sons-in-law, an uncle of mine, Reb Wolf Haberman, was also a "German." He was the son of Rabbi Nachman Krochmal's sister in Zholkve. When I was still a child, his only son was already a renowned medical doctor.

3

MY FATHER

My father, Reb Arye Shmuel Margoshes, was born in Lemberg in 1814 and died at the age of 66 in 1880.

He was an educated person in the field of Jewish studies, and also possessed a fair amount of secular education. He was highly savvy about worldly affairs, and a great expert in provincial government laws. Prominent lawyers would often seek his counsel on important legal issues. He earned a large proportion of his income from these services because many people hired him for their important cases. His "clients" knew that if Reb Shmuel Margoshes took on their case, they had as good as won. He kept two to three legal secretaries on hand to take dictation.

When the world-renowned *gaon*, Rabbi Joseph Shaul Ha-Levi Nathanson, author of the *Shoel U'meyshiv*, was appointed Rabbi of Lemberg, my father, who was at that time already in his forties and a very busy man, became one of his students. He was one of a group of Torah scholars that included: Reb Shmuel Goldberg, Reb Abraham Nissan Zis, Reb Hertzele Morgenshtern, the later *Rosh*

Beys Din, Reb Uri Wolf Salat, and a few others. My father is often mentioned in the responsa of the *Shoel U'meyshiv*.

In his youth, my father had been a very wealthy man. He owned the family home on the then-aristocratic Sikstuska' Street as well as three big houses "on the hill," which were called "Margoshes' Houses." They were occupied by the poorer classes, mostly Jews, with whom my father was always lenient when it came to the rent. Like virtually all of the wealthy Jews of Lemberg at the time, my father played the stock market. During the great crash of 1873, he lost most of his wealth. The banks foreclosed on the houses, and he never recovered. He still maintained a middle class household, but it wasn't like before.

No one from my father's family was a Hassid, and no one had ever visited a Hassidic court. I also strongly doubt whether at that time my father, who in his youth had had *maskilic* leanings, was a devotee of any *rebbe*. His growing closeness to the Belzer Rebbe, and subsequently to other Hassidic rabbis, began, in my opinion, in 1867-8, when he left the Shomer Yisrael (Guardians of Israel) Society and, with other Jewish scholars, began to consider the founding of a separate, Orthodox society.

The Shomer Yisrael Society had initially been founded by young *maskilim* with the goal of propagating education among the Lemberg masses. My father had been one of its initial founders. However, over time, a number of doctors and lawyers without any Jewish education slipped into the group. Their sole motivation was to gain respect and to establish careers for themselves. Over time, these petty lawyers became the ringleaders of the group and their assi-milationist spirit became more and more pervasive. The more *frum* members thus left, and began to think about founding an Orthodox society to combat the assmiliationist tendencies of the Shomer Yisrael.

In 1867, the Shomer Yisrael came up with a scheme that they proposed to the Imperial Ministry in Vienna: a Rabbinical Seminary would be founded in Galicia, and only those rabbis who graduated from this seminary would be recognized by the state. The *frum* Jews regarded this as a terrible decree, especially after the Shomer Yisrael concocted a parallel plan to introduce reforms to the *khadorim* and Talmud Torahs. The Ministry in Vienna, which at that time was very inclined towards the "Germanization" of Galician Jewry, and tearing it away from Polish influence, was enthusiastic about these projects. It sought to use the opportunity for its own political ends.

As far as I know, that time in 1867 marked my father's first public appearance as a community leader. He continued in this role until his death in 1880. At my father's behest, five of the community's most important movers and shakers gathered in the house of the Rabbi of Lemberg, Reb Joseph Shaul Nathanson. Together they issued a letter to all of the rabbis of the biggest Jewish communities in the land. It advised them to protest the Shomer Yisrael Society's project, which was well on its way to being implemented as soon as possible. This letter was sent to the world-renowned *gaon*, Rabbi Shlomo Kluger, the "Broder Maggid." This Shlomo Kluger was, incidentally, one of the greatest *gaonim* of his time, author of 28 published books, in addition to 84 books that remain to be published on all subjects of the Jewish Torah, as well as another 60 books on the *khumesh* alone. The letter is still in existence today, and has been reprinted in the book, *Toldot Shlomo*, by his grandson, Rabbi Yehudah Aaron Kluger. *Toldot Shlomo* was published in Lemberg through my cousin, the renowned printer and publisher, Reb Eliezer Margoshes, the son of the uncle mentioned above, Reb Nisn Margoshes, in 1888.

Because *Toldot Shlomo* is difficult to locate today, I am including the whole letter as a tribute here. It is, in my opinion, an important historical document about the cultural war in Galicia:

A letter to Lvov [Lemberg] informing them that the sect of modernisers there is increasing its wrongdoing in requesting that the government investigate the judgments of the Babylonian Talmud, upon which all the House of Israel depends. They agree to equality of rights (*gleichberechtigung*) being given to the Jews. They also advocate building a seminary for rabbis and teachers who destroy God's vineyard. Therefore he should alert the heads of the community who tremble at God's word that they should write letters of protest and express their disagreement that money come from their purses in any manner to support such educational institutions. He should transmit the protests to the Minister in Vienna.

With the help of God, May He be Blessed

Vienna, at first daylight, Friday, the eve of the Sabbath portion *Va-yishlah*, 5640 [November 28, 1879].

Peace and Blessing to our friend, a friend among friends, the Rabbi, the sharp-minded, the outstanding leader, the Hassid, Our teacher the rabbi Shmuel Margoshes, may his light shine, in Lvov, may God protect it,

My friend, it is time to act for God and to stand for our lives to save our holy Torah from the hand of the sect of modernisers who are about to destroy, annihilate and eradicate [the Torah] in your city. For the wicked are like the tossing sea, etc. [Isaiah 57, 20] and they do their deed in darkness. You should know that they have made a petition and sent it to the Wahlen Club. They speak bad things about the Holy Babylonian Talmud, which is for us an established foundation. They say that it is right and proper to ask the Noble Government to keep a sharp eye on the nation of the Children of Israel to see whether their conduct according to their Talmud is in agreement with the equality of rights (*gleichberechtigung*), which was given to the Jews.

My father was a fine stylist and had elegant penmanship to boot. He conceived and, by his own hand, wrote these letters to the rabbis. However, out of respect and deference, he signed his name last.[1]

[1] Because of importance of the matter I present here the letter of the gaon our Teacher, Rabbi Yosef Shaul Nathanson, may his righteous memory be a blessing.

Letter of the Rabbi, the distinguished *gaon*, the generation's prodigy and its glory, our teacher, Rabbi Yosef Shaul ha-Levi Nathanson. May his righteous memory be a blessing, head of the rabbinical court of Lvov and the district, and with him the Rabbis the great *geonim*, and the renowned magnates mighty in the world, the authorities, supervisors and good men, and the heads, the distinguished individuals of the holy community of Lvov. This is the exact text [of the letter]:

Blessed be God,

                    Sunday of [Torah] portion *Tsav*, 5627 Lvov [March 17, 1867]

Peace and all good, Selah. To his honor the rabbi the *Gaon*, the great, fortress and tower, exemplar and glory of the generation, unique in his generation, light of the exile, holy elder, the crown of Torah, our teacher the Rabbi Shlomo Kluger, may his light shine and radiate, the Rabbi and head of the [Rabbinical] Court of Brody, may God protect it.

We have a matter of God. Doubtless you have also known what has come from the lofty place the Ministry of Religion to the governor's office, and from there to all the district concerning the education of young children and to prevent their studying the oral Torah [Talmud] until the age of twelve years, and even then only after they have studied four classes in German. And also that no permission is to be given to be a *melamed* unless he obtain a license from the governor's office that he has already studied four classes of German and the science of pedagogy. Woe to us that this has happened, and we have no one to support us except our Father in Heaven and the merit of the multitude who will arise and plea for mercy for this to change the hearts of the high officials upon us for good. Therefore to action, quickly arouse yourselves and prepare yourselves for counsel and prayer. Say not "there is yet a vision for a set time" [Habakkuk 2, 3]. For brethren, we surely know that this matter is very immediate, and if we delay we will be found to have sinned. Do not form separate groups. Rather, all of us together will request the high officers concerning this thing, and enlighten their eyes that this is in truth the sacrifice [*akedah*] of the holy religion, which they did not at all consider. Quickly let your words, which God will give to your hearts, race to us in order that we may know what to do and we will be one unity. Do not delay for this is a time to act for God. We will do that which we are able to do and God will do what is good in His eyes, may He finish the matter for us for the good. We ask from your honorable Torahship to write to every city that will respond to your voice all the things we have written to you.

These are the words of those who speak from the depths of the heart and the bitterness of heart, and look to the salvation of God that He should have mercy upon us for the sake of the honor of His Name and for the sake of His Holy Torah.

The words of those who seek your welfare with love. May you have length of days and years is the wish of the soul of the young

Yosef ha-Levi Nathanson, head of the [rabbinic] court in Lvov and district

The young Yerachmiel ha-Levi Ish-Horovitz

Yaakov Naftali Hirtz Bernstein, Parnas and leader of the congregation of Lvov

Yitzhak Aharon Segal Ittinga

Yeshaya Aryeh Leib Ish Horovitz

Yaakov Yitzhak Yutes, author of the book of responsa, *Oholei Yaakov*, and *Mikra'ei Kodesh*

The young Aryeh Shmuel Margoshes.

The letters appear to have had the desired effect. The major rabbis, together with their communities, sent their protests to Lemberg City Hall (*Stadthalterei*) and the "decrees" regarding the *khadorim* were rescinded. However, the Shomer Yisrael did not give up agitating for them.

In order to attain influence over the Jews of Lemberg (about 20,000 at that time) as well as across the whole land, the Shomer Yisrael Society began to publish a fortnightly newspaper called *The Israelite* in 1868. For over four years, the newspaper was published in a kind of Galician "German" written in Yiddish letters. However, in its fifth year of publication, the newspaper moved over to pure German, with German letters. During the later great disputes, or election campaigns, supplements were added to the newspaper in a beautiful, clear, modern Hebrew. (This newspaper was published for over 20 years, eventually once a week. Today it is hard to come by. I have bound volumes of ten years' worth, with two or three of them in Yiddish.) It is no surprise that the publication of the Shomer Yisrael's own newspaper and the frequent agitation for "progress" was like a thorn in the side of the more *frum* Jews. They began to think about founding a counter-society with the eventual intention of publishing their own organ to fight against the Shomer Yisrael, and to defend Orthodox interests.

4
REB MORDECAI PELTZ

My father, who embodied the entire spirit of this *frum* "counter-movement," and who was devoted to it with body and soul, sought someone to help him in his work. He found that person in Reb Mordecai Peltz in Lemberg. Reb Mordecai Peltz (his real last name was Enser) was a fascinating individual, and it is worth dwelling on him a little.

Reb Mordecai's father, Rabbi Moses Tzvi Enser (1804–1871) was one of the most important of the Lemberg *maskilim*. He was a close friend of Rappoport and Nachman Krochmal, and a frequent contributor to the Hebrew anthologies of the time. He was a Hebrew teacher and supported himself by giving lessons ("*Stunden* [hours]" is what we called it then) in rich Jewish homes. He was also the author of a Hebrew grammar called *Ha-metsaref*, or *Massoret Moshe*, in two parts (printed in Zholkve in 1854).

What led the son of a *maskil* and fervent *misnaged* to become a Hassid, I do not know. But from 1877, when Reb Mordecai Peltz became a frequent presence in my father's house, I can recall him as a broad, tall, and sturdy man with a high *spodik* on his head. At that time, he was already a "private secretary" of the Belzer Rabbi, Rabbi Yehoshua Rokeach, as well as his political attaché.

Reb Mordecai owned his family home together with several other partners. One was "Viertel Revisor [Quarter Auditor]" Ginzberg (the city of Lemberg was, for law enforcement, divided into four quarters, with the Rinek, as a separate district). Because of this family home, Reb Mordecai was involved in litigation for years, in particular with his relative, "Viertel Revisor" Ginzberg, who was, from what I can recall, a *maskil* who was constantly speaking about Torah, but a very difficult person. My father, who was, as they called him, an "unofficial" lawyer (as I have already described above), represented Peltz in court. He was a frequent guest in our house and I, a boy of 11 or 12 and a fairly sensible human being, (not like American children, who don't know their left from their right) had the opportunity to get to know him well.

This big Hassid, with the old *spodik* and big *gartl* around his broad body, was a highly educated person. He knew Hebrew, German, Polish, and French well. He was proficient in world history, and especially in geography. I remember how he once was debating with my older brother, Yehoshua Margoshes, at the time a very accomplished young man of 18 (at his wedding, Yehoshua received the title of "*Moreinu* [Our Teacher]" from the Rabbi of Lemberg, Rabbi Tzvi Hirsch Orenstein) who spoke several languages, about a certain river: was it located in South or North America? When they verified in *Meyers Konversations Lexikon*, it turned out that the Hassidic Reb Mordecai Peltz had recalled the exact details of this river much better than my accomplished brother, who considered himself a big expert in geography.

When the president of the Kaiser Ferdinand Bahn (Imperial Railway, which ran from Krakow to Vienna), Counsellor von Sacher, was running for the Vienna Reichstag (Parliament) as representative of several Galician districts and the Belzer Rabbi supported him politically, Reb Mordecai Peltz acted as the sole facilitator between them. The aristocratic Vienna counselor was not ashamed to be seen strolling with Reb Mordecai, clad in his *spodik* and long cloak, in the Vienna Prater (fairground).

What became of the Peltz Family Home, I do not know. However, in his later years, Reb Mordecai had no interests outside of the new Machzikei Hadas (Fortifiers of Faith) Society, and the Belzer Rabbi gave him a generous allowance. When his first wife died, he remarried a wealthy woman from Belz. He resided there until his final years and remained the Belzer Rabbi's advisor and confidant. Although Reb Mordecai was an educated person, he did not want to give his children any secular education. His two sons were Hassidic boys with long *peyes*, but big ignoramuses, even in Jewish studies.

The eminent Reichstag deputy, Rabbi Dr. Joseph Samuel Bloch, recounts in his memoirs that when he was running for the Reichstag in the Galician districts of Kolomea (Kolomyya, Kolomyja), Sniatyn and Butshatsh, Reb Mordecai Peltz came to him in Vienna and requested the sum of 5,000 gulden. Not, God forbid, for himself, but to give to the Austrian government as "security" so that the newspaper, *Machzikei Hadas*, would be permitted to be published every week and not have to appear under two names (one week as *Machzikei Hadas* and the next as *Kol Machzikei Hadas*). This would save the publishers a great deal of anxiety and quell their constant fear of denunciation. Reb Mordecai claimed that for this 5,000 gulden, he would support Bloch in the election, and that his support was worth a lot more than this paltry sum. When Dr. Bloch refused, rejected the "offer," and would not raise the money among the rich Vienna Jews, Reb Mordecai threatened to rally for his opponent, Maizels. Maizels was a very wealthy man and a grandson of the renowned *gaon*, Rabbi Berish Maizels, former rabbi of Krakow, and later of Warsaw. According to Bloch's account, Reb Mordecai Peltz died suddenly in Krakow before the elections took place. Although he does not provide a date, he believes it to have been in December of 1890. From the tone Bloch uses to discuss Reb Mordecai's death, it appears that he understood the death as divine retribution. However, the Hassidic *rebbe*, Rabbi Meir Rokeach, the esteemed "Kozlov Rebbe" (currently in New York), who knew Reb Mordecai very well, told me otherwise: Reb Mordecai died in Lemberg, not Krakow, and in 1892 (5652 by the Jewish calendar) and not in 1890. He recalled how the *Machzikei Hadas* newspaper printed a long eulogy under the heading, "The Loss of a Hassid."

According to a friend of mine, Reb Chaim Aaron Hafner (who was a Hassid and a resident in the Belz Hassidic court in his youth, and went on to become a *maskil* and the "editorial assistant" to the *Haivri* in Brody), Reb Mordecai Peltz would, in the last years of his life while he was living in Belz, *stand* (not sit) while studying holy texts. It often happened that Reb Mordecai would position himself in front of a lectern in the evening and become so absorbed in the *Gemara* that when Hafner would awaken in the morning on his hard spot on the study house bench, he would see Reb Mordecai still standing with one foot propped on a bench reading the *Gemara*. He was so absorbed and focused that he was oblivious to what was going on around him and to the fact that it had long become daylight outside. Reb Mordecai had a sunny disposition and did many favours for Jews, including *misnagdim* and prominent opponents. I heard a great many stories about him. It would, however, lead me too far afield if I were to recount them here.

This very talented person, who also, incidentally, possessed a great eloquence and a talent for speaking, chose my father as his assistant in the founding of a new, *frum* society to vigilantly uphold Orthodox Judaism in Galicia, and to weaken the progressive tendencies of the Shomer Yisrael. Because of this goal and the influence of Reb Mordecai Peltz, my father became a devotee of the Belzer Rabbi as well as the other Hassidic *rebbes*. The Belzer Rabbi was very pleased with this new devotee. He had good human intuition and soon understood the great prize that he had won in my father becoming a Hassid, in particular as my father had a fine reputation as one of the most important and highly respected figures in Lemberg, and possessed significant influence in the city.

5

THE BELZER RABBI

I am not writing a history of Hassidism, in which the Belzer Rabbi played a very significant role. However, in order to know who the Belzer Rabbi was, and what a strong personality he was, I will sketch out a few of his character traits. I knew him well: he was a guest in our home on several occasions, for a week and sometimes longer. After my wedding, I was his guest and, because of my father, I was very well received.

The Belzer Rabbi, Yehoshua Rokeach, was the eldest son of the world-renowned Belzer Rabbi, Rabbi Sholem Rokeach. Rabbi Sholem Rokeach was the founder of the Belz Rabbinic dynasty, which exists to this day, currently in its fifth generation. After his father's death in 1855, he maintained the Belz Rabbinate for about 40 years until his death in 1894. During that entire period, he was considered one of the most important rabbis of his generation. Still, the Belzer Rabbi, always insisted that his adherents call him "rabbi," not "*rebbe*," for in his modesty, he did not deem himself worthy of being a *rebbe*. He had tens of thousands of Hassidim in Galicia, Poland, Hungary, and the surrounding provinces. On Rosh Hashanah, between 5,000 and 6,000 Hassidism would gather in Belz. Virtually the entire small and muddy city of Belz lived off the Rabbi's "court" and off the Hassidim who came to visit. This amounted to several hundred visitors in an average week, and many more during holidays.

The Belzer Rabbi was a tall, broad, and sturdy man with a densely bearded face and very long eyebrows. In this massive body flickered a strong, fiery spirit that was not intimidated by anything. He never wavered and held fast to his beliefs, which he regarded as the only truth. He believed very strongly in himself, and was deeply convinced that he was a higher being with a direct connection to the heavenly realm.

I was once in Belz when a Jew gave him a *kvitl* with a *pidyon* (in Belz fairly small *pidyones* were allotted; twenty kreuzer sufficed), and asked for advice about an involved issue. The Rabbi responded and advised him according to what he deemed correct. The man left, or better said, was shoved out of the way by those who were standing behind him and also wanted their turn. However, as soon as the man considered the matter, he began to doubt that the Rabbi's advice was correct. He soon returned to the Rabbi and pushed his way back to his chair. The Rabbi recognized him immediately and asked him: what did he want now? The fearful man found himself shamefaced and barely able to stammer that he wanted to ask the Rabbi whether it might be possible to give him a different and better piece of advice because the previous one was, it seemed to him, not practical enough. As soon as the Belzer Rabbi heard this, he stood up to his full height and called out in his strong and ringing voice:

"What do you mean? *I* have given you advice. A heavenly revelation ordered *me* to speak!"

A large audience was always assembled in his "court." When the noise and the commotion would become intolerable and the voices and screams would reach high heaven, the Rabbi would suddenly open the door and let out a loud shout, *"Sha!"* for everyone to fall silent immediately. For a while, a deep silence would fall over the whole "court." Everyone held him in great awe and trembled with mortal fear. He was always a true standard-bearer. All of his days, he stood on guard and made sure that Belz and its surrounding *shtetlekh*, where his influence was enormous, should not diminish their age-old observance, God-forbid, and that even the tiniest of bit of progress or spirit of the times should not be able to steal in.

In Belz and in the *shtetlekh* in much of the surrounding area, Jewish men and women still walked around in clothing that had not been worn in the rest of Galicia for a very long time. The males, who were almost all Belz Hassidim (with a very few exceptions),[2] wore old, worn fur caps on their heads. Their shirts were never buttoned at the collar, much less fastened with a tie or even a cravat. In the winter, they wrapped their throats in a kind of cotton scarf. Their pants, always dirty, were tucked into once-white socks and a pair of slippers or cow-hide boots in cold weather. Their bodies were swathed in coarse, cotton

---

[2]   Next to Belz there is a little town with the name of Hivnev (Ugnev in Polish). It is a small train station not far from Belz and a round trip cost 26 kreuzer.

Once, on Erev Yom Kippur, I was traveling to Belz. When the train arrived in Hivnev, the station was packed with Jews. All of them were dressed up in their *shtreimlekh* and satin (more torn than whole) *bekeshes*. Every one had his little bundle containing just his *talis* and a bit of food, a bit of chicken to snack on after the fast. From the Belz train station, they immediately headed off on foot (from the train into town was quite a trek) to the synagogue, and right after Yom Kippur, they headed back by train. According to what the Jews of the time recounted, they numbered, old and young, about 400. In Hivnev on Yom Kippur, only women, extremely elderly, sick people, and children remained.

16

bekeshes. Cloth or "fabric" could not be worn; that was an action of a partisan of the Enlightenment. These *bekeshes* were always fastened with thick *gartlekh.* A true Belz Hassid never walked slowly. He always rushed and was in a constant hurry, although he hardly ever had a reason.

The women likewise wore clothing from their grandmother's era: full, long, grey *jubkas*, gowns like shrouds and caps on their heads. They did not even dare know about modern fashion and "licentious" clothing. In Belz and the surrounding area, there were simply no tailors for this sort of clothing. In Belz, Hivnev, Most and the other nearby *shtetlekh*, the women, young and old, had to wear a kind of veil called a "Belz veil." Wearing one's own hair was out of the question; this sort of loose woman would have simply been stoned. Even thread or silk wigs could not, God-forbid, be worn on their shaved heads.

In all of the above-mentioned places, no "German" could be found, for love or money. The only exceptions were the young barber, a visiting apprentice tailor, or that sort of person. Even the mailman was a Jew in a *spodik* with a non-Jewish assistant to deliver the mail on Saturdays and on holidays. All of the other Belz Jews wore the ancient Jewish costume. A respectable person would not have dared to wear "German clothing." The education and worldly knowledge of these people can easily be surmised: They did not miss it, and could not even have wished for another lifestyle.

For his first 25 years as Rabbi, the Belzer Rabbi contented himself with the influence that he had in Belz and its small, surrounding communities. However, when Reb Mordecai Peltz became his confidant and later his private secretary and chief advisor, and when the abovementioned business with Shomer Yisrael took place in nearby Lemberg, the Belzer Rabbi sensed that this was the right time to fully exert his extensive influence over Orthodox Jewry in more distant and larger cities in Galicia.

My father, together with Reb Mordecai Peltz and other important personages in Lemberg, had worked out a plan to found a major society under the name of Machzikei Hadas with a head office in the capital city of Lemberg. Every city and *shtetl* across the country, whether large or small, would house a branch so that any Jew with a spark of Jewishness in him could become a member and pay an annual membership of only three gulden (25 kreuzer) a month. However, it took several years for this simple yet practical plan to be realized.

The Shomer Yisrael Society in Lemberg, whose membership included Jews across Galicia, and which consisted of many doctors, lawyers, bankers and *maskilim*, as well as miscellaneous members, almost all of them "Germans," strongly disapproved of the new society. Until that time, the Shomer Yisrael Society had felt "in the saddle." At that time, there were not as many doctors and lawyers as today. They were thus very respected and influential. They gradually began to take over the Jewish communities and become Jewish representatives and spokespeople.

Kosher meat almost never entered their homes. They were generally far removed from Judaism, and often laughed at it publicly. And yet, they became the Jewish representatives. They took it upon themselves to introduce new ordinances to the Jewish communities, and wanted to establish new customs and ways of life according to "Nusakh Ashkenaz," the fashion of the reformers in "progressive" Germany. These *maskilim* and assimilationists began to get their hands on more than just individual Jewish communities (in the smaller *shtetlekh*, they had not yet gained a foothold): they had ambitions to represent the entire Jewish people in the political arena, in the Lemberg Landtag (State Parliament, Sejm) and in the Vienna Reichsrat (Imperial Assembly).

In that era, the leaders of the province of Galicia were adopting a more liberal outlook. Jews were granted full rights as citizens and they were allowed to vote as well as to be elected as deputies to the Galician Landtag and the Austrian Reichsrat. The Jewish assimilationists—the wealthy bankers, the successful doctors and lawyers—now perceived a wide-open world and great arenas in which to fulfill their ambitions. They had never sought to utter a single Yiddish word, and were completely estranged from the Jewish people and its religion. Now these same men employed every means possible to become the Jewish representatives. When some of them attained their goals, they used their elevated posts and mandates for their own personal gain. The Jews and their religious, social and economic interests were completely irrelevant to them. Orthodox Galician Jewry observed these developments, grasped them all perfectly, but could not help itself. Its powers were divided, scattered to the four winds. It could not even try to oppose the Jewish representatives and spokespeople, who were tightly knit under the organization called Shomer Yisrael.

This is how such a calamity befell the "Germans" that they did not even have the ability to react: the Orthodox Jews awoke from their long slumber and united in order to fight and to throw off the yoke of the "Germans"! Naturally, everyone who belonged to Shomer Yisrael and who had cause to fear the existence of this new organization "girded their loins" and conspired, first in secret and then in open warfare, against the Orthodox Jews and their association.

At that time in the Austrian provinces, the founding of any organization or society, even a *khevre mishnayes*, required authorization from a local government office. Associations with separate branch offices like the planned Machzikei Hadas required dealing with a higher body in the Austrian capital of Vienna. When my father, together with Reb Mordecai Peltz and the other founders, had completed the preparations for their new association, the "Machzikei Hadas," they presented their request for authorization, as the law required.

The Shomer Yisrael soon became aware of these developments, and began a secret war against a society that did not even exist yet. First, they spread the slander that the founders of the new association were a band of "sinister characters" who had joined forces with the fanatical goal of hindering the course of "precious civilization" and culture among the Jewish people, and that they wanted to keep the Galician Jews in the dark forever in order to more easily use them for their own, selfish ends. Because the members of Shomer Yisrael included individuals who personally knew the authorities in whose power it was to decide the fate of the planned organization, they did not spare any effort or means. They employed the full force of their influence to ensure that the request of the Machzikei Hadas be denied.

The pace of courts and bureaucratic offices crawls to begin with: as the old saying goes, "the wheels of justice turn very slowly." This has always been particularly true of backwards Galicia. Aside from this factor, the authorities, the "Golden Buttons," now had an incentive to delay the request for as long as humanly possible. And who could tell them what to do? It thus took several years until the matter passed through all the necessary channels, and the founders of the new organization were forced to concede with great heartbreak that their hope was very far from being realized.

Aside from their secret slander and their appeals to the authorities, the Shomer Yisrael embarked on an open battle against the Orthodox Jews in general, and the few important personages that comprised the founders in particular. Their newspaper, the *Israelite*, was at the time being published in German, the bit of Yiddish that had once been there having long since been tossed out. They spared no expense and began to publish Hebrew supplements. Both editions, the German and the Hebrew, tirelessly cursed the Orthodox Jews and the planned organization, whom they called "*Mazikei Hadas* [Spoilers of Faith]" instead of "*Machzikei Hadas* [Fortifiers of Faith]." They also attacked some of the founders in a mean-spirited way, personally insulted them, and went as far as to attempt to harm their personal interests.

The Orthodox Jews did not yet have their own organ—a newspaper or an open tribune—in which they could respond to the abuse and accusations. They thus had to make do with publishing leaflets and posters that were written in Yiddish or German, as well as Hebrew. This "literature" was written by my father and Rabbi Hertzele Goldenshtern, who was a fine Hebraist and a major expert in this type of incendiary literature. Goldenshtern was, incidentally, the author of small brochures, "*Shever Poshim*," "*Shevet Legev Kesilim*," and several other leaflets in 5629 (1869), when the great dispute was taking place between the Hassidic communities of Sanz and Sadigora about Rabbi Ber of Leova, who went astray. I also played a role in the battle against Shomer Yisrael: I regularly helped to distribute leaflets, and carried the articles concerning the struggle to be typeset at the printer's.

6
IGNATZ DEUTSCH

The handful of people who worked uninterruptedly toward the founding of the new Machzikei Hadas Society did not rest. Notable among them were my father together with Reb Mordecai Peltz, and with them the Belzer Rabbi, who also covered most of the expenses. However, they found almost all of the doors to the authorities sealed shut because the movers and shakers of Shomer Yisrael had exerted their influence to ensure that the organization of these "sinister characters," the Machzikei Hadas, would never be authorized. It is possible that the "Germans" would have succeeded, and that the few individuals on the *frum* side would have eventually burned out and given up working towards their ideal. However, a certain Ignatz Deutsch from Vienna came to the assistance of the Machzikei Hadas, and the Orthodox Jews were thus victorious. They received, directly from the Imperial Ministry (over the heads of the Galician Stadthalterei), authorization for their own, *frum* newspaper, and were also granted the right to found their planned association with branch offices in all Galician cities.

Who was this Ignatz Deutsch, and where did his great power come from? Ignatz (Yitzhak) Deutsch was born in the Hungarian city of Pressburg around 1809. He stemmed from an old, aristocratic Jewish family. In his a youth, he studied at the Pressburg Yeshivah and was a student of the world-renowned *gaon*, Rabbi Moshe Sofer, the "Chasam Sofer."

He later settled in Vienna, where he became a great merchant. He grew wealthy and became a banker. He soon developed a reputation as a highly capable person, and an honorable man. The most important nobles became his clients. Almost all of the princes and princesses of the imperial court entrusted their huge fortunes to him, and he managed these funds to their full satisfaction for years and years. His royal clients brought Deutsch to the attention of Emperor Franz Joseph, who honored him with the title of "Kaiser-Königlicher Hof Wechsler [Imperial Court Banker]." This meant that he managed imperial (not government, but private) monies.

Ignatz Deutsch was a very *frum* Jew and Orthodox Jewry, in particular Hungarian Jewry, found substantial support in him. Thus, for example, he petitioned the government to permit young Jews who spent four years at the Pressburg Yeshivah to be exempted from military service, as was the case with several universities in the Austro-Hungarian Empire. Also, if someone from among these Yeshivah students was willingly drafted into the military, he would serve for only one year as a "volunteer" and leave with the rank of officer. If the Rosh Yeshivah issued a certificate to a young man stating that he had spent four years at the Yeshivah the government was prepared to exempt him from general military duty. Thus the Pressburg Yeshivah was recognized by the government as a public theological institution, and this was thanks only to Deutsch's efforts. How long this lasted and whether it continues to exist to this day, I do not know. Deutsch also did a lot for Eretz Yisroel. He petitioned the government for permission to collect money from across all of Austro-Hungary on behalf of Eretz Yisroel institutions and for *Haluka*, something that had earlier been forbidden.

The book, *Igrot Sofrim* (Vienna, 1928), which contains letters from members of the brilliant Eiger and Sofer families, and whose author, the old *gaon* Rabbi Shlomo Sofer, knew Deutsch very well personally, recounts the following interesting episode:

One time, Deutsch had carried out some sort of major business transaction that had reaped large profits for the imperial family, and Emperor Franz Joseph wanted to reward him for it. He sent one of his high officials to Deutsch, offering him the coveted and esteemed title of "baron," which would elevate him to noble status. Deutsch, however, declined. He requested that the Emperor be thanked, and let it be known that since his parents were simple but honest Jews, he would not permit himself to be superior to them. There was one thing, however: the biggest reward for him would be if every time he lobbied the government with an appeal on behalf of his Orthodox brethren, the request be carried out to the greatest extent possible. It was to this *frum* and upstanding man that the Galician Orthodox Jews therefore turned.

My father, together with his constant companion, Reb Mordecai Peltz, traveled to Vienna to see Deutsch and had a long talk with him about their battle with the assimilationist Shomer Yisrael. Deutsch promised to assist them, and he kept his word. He interested one of his clients from the imperial court (it seems to me that her name was Princess Carolina) in the matter. Before many weeks had passed, my father received authorization to publish his newspaper from the Austrian Kultusministerium [Ministry of Religion]. Two months later, the foundation of the Machzikei Hadas Society was also approved by the same Ministry, including the right to create branch offices in cities across Galicia. The Orthodox won and the "Germans" of the Shomer Yisrael were left with mud on their faces.

Two years later, when the newspaper and the Society were in full swing, Deutsch celebrated his seventieth birthday with great pomp and circumstance. In honour of the festivities, many Hungarian rabbis and communal leaders traveled to Vienna for the occasion. My father, as Vice President of the Machzikei Hadas and editor of its newspaper, was also present and made a fine speech. The newspapers, especially the Yiddish/German and Hebrew ones, wrote a great deal about this event and some of them also provided a list of all the guests in attendance. Two years later, Ignatz Deutsch died. I am not certain, but it seems to me that he did not have any children and his relatives inherited his large estate.

7
THE KRAKOW RABBI

When my father and Reb Mordecai Peltz had received authorization for their newspaper and a "secret" promise that they would soon receive permission for their new organization, the crucial question surfaced: whom to select as Head of the Society, as "*Nassi*," [President]? It soon became apparent that a post like President of the Society would be an honourary position only, without much work involved. The primary management would remain in Lemberg in the hands of the other officials.

If it had only been a local association that served just the city of Lemberg, there would have been no question that my father, or another of the important Lemberg personages, would have been selected for the post. However, because the new association was to have (and later did have) branch offices in cities and *shtetlekh* across Galicia, the head would have to be a person with a great reputation, a national figure whom everyone knew and who commanded respect.

The most logical association head was the Belzer Rabbi, Rabbi Yehoshua Rokeach. First of all, he was rabbi of tens of thousands of Hassidim and had a major influence over them. Secondly, he had always been a standard-bearer who devoted a great deal of money to communal affairs. His flaw was that he was a *rebbe*.

At the time in Galicia, there were several other great rabbinic dynasties that ruled with force and exerted a major influence on their followers: the sons of the Riziner Zadik, Rabbi Yisrael: the Sadigorer, the Tshortkover, the Husiatiner and their brother-in-law, the Vizhnitzer Rebbe with his Kossov family; the Ropshitser dynasty, the Sanzer Rebbe's children and grandchildren, Zhidachev, and several other dynasties. Together they had over 100,000 followers in Galicia alone, in addition to which they wielded significant power in other provinces and countries. However, these *rebbes* sat quietly, each one in his own "court," and mixed very little into wider public affairs. Each was occupied with his own path and prayed on behalf of those who appealed to them for help. Each in his own corner (or "court") understood what great harm the "Germans" were causing Galician Orthodox Jewry. They often moaned and groaned about "*shkhinoso be galuso*" [the *Shekhinah* in exile] and "*hisgobrus ha kelipos*" [strengthening of the husks], heaven forfend, but they did nothing about it.

If the Machzikei Hadas Society had been founded with the unwavering involvement of the Belzer Rabbi as President, then the other rabbis, and especially their Hassidim, would have perceived this as trespassing onto their territory. They would have been suspicious that the whole purpose of the project was to expand the Belzer Rabbi's influence at the expense of the other *rebbes*. In addition, the Galician Jews (approximately 800,000) did not consist solely of Hassidim.

There were, in particular in the larger cities, large numbers of *misnagdim* and ordinary *frum* Jews. There were also a lot of educated people who did not think much of *rebbes*. Although they were against the "progressive" Shomer Yisrael, they would never have joined an organization with the Belzer Rabbi at its head.

If not a *rebbe*, the Head at the very least had to be great rabbi who was familiar to everyone. The eyes of the founders thus turned to Rabbi Rabbi Shimon Sofer, the Krakow Rabbi. Rabbi Shimon Sofer was born in 1821 and died in 1883. He was the son of the world-renowned *gaon*, Rabbi Moshe Sofer of Pressburg, the "Chasam Sofer." He was one of the greatest *gaons* of his generation and one of the strongest opponents of the reform that had already begun to steal into Hungary during that period. On his twenty-first birthday, Rabbi Shimon Sofer was appointed rabbi in the old community of Mattersdorf, Hungary. In 1860, he was named rabbi in Krakow, where he remained until the end of his life.

I had several opportunities to see him up close. Each time that he was in Lemberg, he stayed at our house. I, who was at the time a boy of 10–12 years of age, was his "right hand man." This meant that he would send me to the post office to mail letters, or to run errands. Once, in 1878, when he was at the big Rabbinical Assembly of which he was president, I had the rare privilege of overhearing him discuss a bit of Gemara and Tosephos. He pinched my cheek, and said with a smile, "Good boy!" Before he left Lemberg after the Rabbinical Assembly, he gave me a gift: a big painted wooden box (probably for snuff). This box remained in my procession for a number of years. My own children played with it until they eventually broke it. The Krakow Rabbi was an unusually attractive person with a handsome face and rosy cheeks. He carried himself like a true aristocrat and did not like to get excited.

As can be seen from the exchange of letters between him and my father and the other founders of the Machzikei Hadas (published in the aforementioned book, *Igrot Sofrim*, he initially had little desire to place himself at the head of the organization, which had confrontational and aggressive tendencies. He was a quiet person who used to write Hebrew poetry and enjoyed a calm and peaceful existence. As far as I understand, it was the potential great honor of standing at the head of all of Galician Jewry that tempted him. He was especially enticed by my father's and Reb Mordecai Peltz's promise that, with the help of the new association and the influence of the Belzer Rabbi and the other Hassidic rabbis, he would be elected as representative to the Austrian Reichstag. This was an honour that was otherwise never—not before and not since—extended to an Orthodox rabbi. This promise was kept.

In 1879, Rabbi Shimon Sofer was elected as Reichstag representative in the Galician electoral districts of Kolomea, Sniatyn and Butshatsh (which had large Jewish electorates). He held this mandate for just about four years until his death in 1883. During this entire period, he allied himself with the Polenklub [conservative political party] and voted in solidarity with them. He never once took the floor in a debate, and did not make a single speech for the common good. Although he was born in Hungary and spoke a pretty fluent German, he probably felt that he was no great orator in the language, so he opted to remain silent and allow Poles to represent Jewish interests. When he died, the President of the Reichstag made a warm and gracious speech about him at a public meeting. (It was printed at the end of the book, *Chut Hameshulash*).

The election of the Krakow Rabbi to the Austrian Reichstag made a tremendous impression on the entire Jewish world, and Galician Jews anticipated salvation. It gave them enormous pleasure to see even a single Rabbi achieve the major honour of sitting among so many great personages, clad in a fine *calpac* amid such esteemed gentlemen. The poor things did not know that the *calpac* was part of historic Polish dress, and that many Poles, especially extreme nationalists, would wear these same *calpacs* at their meetings.

The Krakow Rabbi's election to the Reichstag inspired many sensational stories and legends. I will relate two of them here: When Emperor Franz Joseph once asked the Krakow Rabbi why he never voted with the rightist Zentrum party, the Krakow Rabbi responded without hesitation:

"Because Jews have no *rights*." One Saturday the Reichstag was in session. The Emperor was present and he gave the Krakow Rabbi a fine cigar. Thanking him for the gift, the Rabbi stowed the cigar in his pocket instead of immediately smoking it as was customary, and as some of those present, who had also received cigars, were doing. When the Emperor pointed this out to the Rabbi, he responded with a clever smile,

"This gift from your majesty is so important to me that I cannot allow myself to let it go up in smoke." Galician Jewry believed these stories with all of their hearts and derived great satisfaction from them.

* * *

Although his presiding over the Machzikei Hadas brought him honor and satisfaction, Rabbi Shimon Sofer also had to endure a lot of disrespect and personal insults. Obviously the people from Shomer Yisrael were very distressed that a highly prominent man like the Krakow Rabbi would place himself at the head of their opponents. They soon began to attack him in their mouthpiece, the *Israelite*. In particular almost every issue the newspapers published during the Reichstag election campaign included material on him, some of it insulting.

The publishers of the Hebrew newspaper, *Haivri* in Brody, went even further. Among those who participated was its contributor, the great scholar who later turned senile, YaHa"Sh [Yehoshua Heshl Shor]. Ever since the founding of Machzikei Hadas, this YaHa"Sh had published his epigrams called "*Rishfei Esh* [Sparks of Fire]." They were penned in a stilted, erudite Hebrew with rhymes, but full of bile and venom as well as personal insults. The *Haivri* (this was its title one week, and the second week it was called *Ivri Anokhi* because of the regulation that I have already discussed above) had a run of several hundred copies. It was not allowed into Russia for some time, and was printed on cheap paper. As a result, its issues are very hard to come by today. The New York Public Library holds several years' runs, but in such poor condition that they cannot even be bound. They lie between hard covers. What can be salvaged from them is hard to say.

The Krakow Rabbi was depicted as a man of limited learning. His political enemies, the Shomer Yisrael Society and the *Haivri,* openly wrote that without the merit of his ancestors as a son of the illustrious Rabbi Moshe Sofer, he could never have been appointed to such a high rabbinical post as that of the Krakow Rabbi. They would constantly throw it in his face that he, a man in his sixties, had not published a single *seyfer,* as was, and still is, the convention among great rabbis.

In the heat of the dispute, the *Haivri* printed the following "announcement," which was supposed to give the impression of being a serious, factual item:

A plea to the great rabbis of our time!
I have received a request from a rabbi in Russia, who is assembling and publishing the responsa of the great rabbis of today, to gather the responsa of *Harav Hazadik Moreinu Harav* [Our Righteous Rabbi and Teacher] Rabbi Shimon Sofer, Rabbi of Krakow. He wants to publish them.
So that the work on this *mitsve* is not done gratis, I shall pay a price for each responsa: 10 florins for each item that amounts to 1,000 printed lines, and 30 gulden for those that reach 2,000 printed lines.
Copies will not be accepted. They must be written in his own hand. The letters and the responsa should be sent to Israel Moshe Segal in Krakow, or to the editorial offices of this newspaper.

This "announcement" was printed in *Haivri* on February 6, 1880 as well as in several subsequent issues.

It goes without saying that "Israel Moshe Segal of Krakow" did not exist. It later turned out that that the author was the well-known *maskil* and book vendor, Aaron Faust of Krakow, who had his own personal accounts to settle with the Krakow Rabbi.

8
THE NEWSPAPER

When the Machzikei Hadas newspaper was launched, and more than ever once it was published, it opened up a new world for me.

It was decided, probably because of a shortage of funds, not to rent an office for the editorial offices for the time being. Instead, one of the rooms in our house, the "green room," was used. This was, however, only a pretext for the sake of my mother, who had always liked things tidy and well appointed. However, in truth, all five of our rooms (except for the bedroom) were always as packed with people as if it were a railway station. People with various projects were constantly coming and going. I was always kept busy: going to the printer's, to the post office, on other "literary" errands, or helping with something in the editorial office. Although I was at the time only about 10–12 years old and quite a mischief-maker at that, I made an effort to behave myself. I was present during all conversations and meetings, and everyone spoke freely around me.

As soon as the authorization for the newspaper arrived, three editors were selected: the abovementioned Hertzele Goldenshtern, my brother Yehoshua, and a wealthy young son-in-law, Joseph Joel Philip. This Reb Philip was a fine German writer. Of equal significance, he was extremely well versed in all matters relating to the operation of the Lemberg *Kehilah,* with which the newspaper was in constant strife.

The first three issues of the newspaper were printed in the same manner as all of the world's newspapers: at a printer's. However, the next three issues were lithographed: handwritten and then transferred from the plate at a lithographer's. I do not know the real reason behind this, but I suspect that it was due to financial constraints. Two other justifications were offered to the public: first, a printed newspaper is not kept for long and is soon thrown away or used to wrap profane things. Thus, it could easily happen that, God forbid, the holy texts published there would be degraded, which would, of course, be a great sin. Secondly, the publishers of this newspaper were providing a practical incentive for all Jewish youths to...develop nice handwriting. The newspaper was penned using goose quills in several scripts: round, half round, a kind of script where the letters appear very thin, where only the corners of the letters *nun* and *kof* are thick, and other types of lettering. The writers of these scripts were my brother Yehoshua, co-editor of the newspaper, and a young man by the name of Gedalia Yitzhak Arokh ["long"], who was, like his name indicated, a tall, skinny youth. He also helped to write news articles and other minor items. For his efforts, he received the princely sum of five gulden a week. I still have in my possession several copies of the three lithographed issues of the newspaper. There was usually a run of 800 copies.

When the *"Zeitung für das Wahre Orthodoxische Judentum,"* as it was called, was in its seventh issue, authorization for the establishment of the Machzikei Hadas Society arrived. In the seventh issue, the newspaper began to be called *Machzikei Hadas,* but the German title remained the same. The founders acknowledged that, given the altered circumstances, a much greater circulation could be anticipated. This was the case later, when the newspaper appeared in runs of up to 3,000. The impractical, lithographed paper was no longer appropriate, and they returned to the printer.

In order to justify to the world the prohibited printing of a newspaper with holy letters, my father made inquiries with the then-Rabbi of Lemberg, Rabbi Tzvi Hirsch Orenstein. He conveyed the difficulties inherent in a lithographed newspaper, and the Rabbi declared it proper provided that every issue include a cautionary note in large type that warned readers to treat the newspaper with respect, to conserve the pages and to have them bound at year's end, just like any holy book. This advisory note appeared for as long as the newspaper existed. Nevertheless, bound volumes of the *Machzikei Hadas* are very rare and almost impossible to come by today. I believe, however, that this has to do with the World War, which destroyed the entire area where the newspaper was distributed.[3]

The newspaper was initially a mixture of Yiddish and Hebrew. Only later did it become a purely Hebrew newspaper. I do not, however, wish to devote too much space to the content of the newspaper here. I would just like to point out that several young people who contributed to the newspaper later became renowned in other areas. They include my childhood-friend, Dr. Yehuda Leib Landau, the renowned poet and current Chief Rabbi of Johannesburg, South Africa. He was a very proficient contributor and saw many of his Hebrew poems and articles published.

While my father was alive, the newspaper was run out of our home. This is also where all of the meetings of the association were conducted. Only after my father's death, and with the expansion of its activities, was a two-room office rented at Number 14 Krakauer Platz in the house of Rabbi Yaacov Yutes, facing Count Skarbek's house, in the heart of the Jewish quarter. Now I became much busier running back and forth, especially with errands for my two brothers, Mendel and Yehoshua, who were very devoted to the association and to the newspaper itself. Mendel took over some of my father's business dealings and writing, and people were often waiting to see him.

---

[3]   Until 1900, the entire Austro-Hungarian Empire had a law in place that stated that every weekly newspaper had to deposit a sum of 3,000 gulden with the government as collateral that it would not break the press laws. There was also a requirement that every weekly had to feature a proof of payment or stamp for one kreuzer on each issue.

Jews, however, found a way around this (non-Jewish publishers of weeklies also did this): two newspapers were published with similar sounding names, but in truth they were one and the same. The government knew about this, but if no one informed on the newspapers, they turned a blind eye.

In Galicia and Austria there thus existed newspapers with double names: for example, *Hamevaser* and *Hanesher*, *Ivri* and *Ivri Anokhi*, *Hashemesh* and *Hakharsa*, *Machzikei Hadas* and *Kol Machzikei Hadas*, *Der Karmel* and *Der Veker*, and quite a few others that I cannot recall right now.

9
HOSPITALITY

Ever since I can recall, our home was always full of people.

As I have already indicated several times, my father was an "unoffical" lawyer. As such, he ran a whole administrative office out of his home. He always kept a legal secretary on hand, sometimes two or three. People were always coming for counsel about their court cases. Among them were quite a few *shtetl*-Jews and leaseholders who were involved in cases with nobles.

In addition, Hassidic *rebbes* and Hassidim would often stay with us. When the Krakow Rabbi or the Belzer Rabbi came to Lemberg, they were nearly always our guests for the entire period that they were in town. These were the regular guests who stayed with us for the whole time that they spent in Lemberg: the Belzer Rabbi's brothers, Reb Moshe and Reb Zundel (one of them, I can't remember which, was blind), when they came to collect funds from the Hassidim; the Belzer Rabbi's children (Reb Shmuel, the Skoler Rabbi, Reb Naftoli, the Makarover Rabbi, and Reb Yisachar Ber, later the Belzer Rebbe). Other rabbis were our guests as well, for example, the Zhidachever: Reb Elye and Reb Sender Lipa, the sons and followers of the great rabbi, Reb Ayzikl Zhidachever. Reb Avromshe Mikulover (a son-in-law of the illustrious Reb Meyerl Premishlaner, who was deemed a great miracle worker, also stayed with us. Other guests included Reb Berish, the son of Reb Mordkhele Nadvorner. When he hid from the military through an entire winter, he stayed with us the whole time. He then went on to become a *rebbe* of great stature.

In 1876 (5636), the great book of responsa by the world-renowned *zaddik* and *gaon*, Rabbi Chaim Halberstam of Sanz, *Divrei Chaim*, was published in Lemberg. For this project, two of his grandchildren, the Bardiover Rabbi, Rabbi Moyshele [Moshe] Halberstam, and the Ushpiziner Rabbi, Rabbi Shloymele Halberstam (later a great *rebbe* in Vizhnitz and then in Bobov), stayed in Lemberg for several months and supervised the publication of the book.

We gave them a large room where they stayed the entire time with an assistant of theirs. Both rabbis soon took a liking to my 10-year-old self, and often used me for small errands, in particular to the telegraph office. They often had to consult with Sanz whenever they thought that they might not have interpreted something in the manuscript correctly. Sometimes they came together, sometimes alone; one would often travel elsewhere, at which time I would have to accompany the other during his trips by carriage to the distant print shop.

A very interesting incident happened between me and the Ushpiziner Rabbi, Rabbi Shloymele, which shows how powerful a memory he had.

28

It was six years after he had stayed with is in Lemberg. My father had passed away, and I was living with my mother in Tarnow together with my brother, Yehoshua. Reb Shloymele was at the time a *rebbe* in Vizhnitz (several miles from Tarnow) and had a considerable Hassidic following that he had taken over from his deceased Sanz grandfather. After Shavuot, he came to Tarnow and stayed with the well-known gentleman and Sanz Hassid, Reb Yosl Schiff. Almost all of the Sanz Hassidim in town went to welcome him and bring him *kvitlekh* and *pidyones*.

I, at the time a youth of about sixteen, did not go to see him at that time. However, Friday evening, when a large crowd of Hassidim gathered for *Kabbalas Shabbos* at the home of Reb Joseph, I was among them. Three large rooms in the house had been put at the Rebbe's disposal. The crowd in attendance was kept in the first room, located right behind the kitchen. The door to the other two rooms designated for the Rebbe was half closed. I had intended to greet Reb Shloymele right after *Kabbalas Shabbos*. I did not, however, want to do so as part of the large crowd, so I stole into the second, unlit, room and waited there for the Rebbe to pass through on his way to the brightly lit front room. When the praying concluded, the Rebbe, with his *talis* over his head, entered the second room followed by a fair number of Hassidim. Walking through and tapping with his hands along the walls of the barely-lit room, he bumped right into me and called out,

"Who is this?"

I was so surprised that a single, foolish, word came out:

"Me!"

Despite the fact that he had not seen me for six years, and that I had developed from a 10 year-old boy into a young man of 16, and although he was covered to over his head in his *talis*, and there was no way that he could have seen me in the half-darkness, the single word, "me," was enough for him to immediately recognize me:

"Yoshe, is it you?" he called out. When I answered, "yes," he took me by the hand and brought me with him into the front room. Once the Kiddush had ended, he quizzed me about what I was doing in Tarnow, my mother's health, how my two brothers were doing, Mendel in Lemberg and Yehoshua in Tarnow. Over the entire duration of *Shabbes*, at all three meals, he was extremely friendly to me and showed me a lot of affection. Mid-week I was back there with my brother, Yehoshua. My mother did not want to go: She did not think much of Hassidic *rebbes*. She was raised by *misnagdim* and enlightened people. As I was to be married that summer, he blessed me, wished me all the best, and expressed the hope and the wish that I would become one of his followers. Unfortunately, I never saw him again. I was more drawn to Belz and sometimes also to Shinieve, or to Rabbi Alter of Dembitz of the Ropshits dynasty, who was extremely savvy about worldly affairs.

I also had the opportunity (or perhaps the honour) to personally meet the rabbis who did *not* stay with us when they came to Lemberg. This was because my father considered it his sacred duty to visit every *rebbe* who came to town, and acted upon it. Every time he went to visit a *rebbe*, he took me, and often my brother Yehoshua, along. My oldest brother, Mendel, was long married and independent. He was, however, also a young Hassid: a son-in-law of the Brody Rokeach clan, a distinguished Hassidic family that was closely related to the Belzer Rabbi. He often visited all of the Hassidic *rebbes* who came to Lemberg of his own accord, and took me along, in order to instruct me in *mitsves*!

IO

THE TALNER REBBE

The most important *rebbe* in Russia at that time was Rabbi Dovidl Talner (Twersky), the son of Rabbi Motele Chernobyler. Precisely because he was the greatest and had the largest following of Hassidim, he had to endure an enormous amount of persecution by the Russian government. He therefore decided to settle in Galicia in the city of Brody, which lies very close to the Russian border. He resided there for over a year. As soon as he arrived from Russia, he spent about three weeks in Lemberg. When he returned home, he was in Lemberg for another two weeks. Both times, he stayed with us at Number 3 Sikstuska Street.

Our house had two stories, aside from which there was also the one-story building in the yard with a walled *sukkah* on the roof. We always lived on the second floor. The first floor was occupied for many years by a wealthy local Hassid, Reb Shimon ben Reb Z. P. Rappoport. This Reb Shimon, a dignified and handsome Jewish scholar, was a son-in-law of the wealthy Russian Sussman family from Ostrow. He was a Talner Hassid and would travel twice a year from Lemberg to see Rabbi Dovidl. When his *rebbe* came to Lemberg, Reb Shimon offered him his entire apartment, although he himself had six small children. He was a widower at the time.

The large household that accompanied the Rebbe made it impossible for everyone to live in Reb Shimon's home, which consisted of five rooms with a kitchen. The Rebbe's son-in-law, Reb Meyerl Kodorov, with his wife and children therefore lived with us on the second floor, along with a young Rebbetzin from their family.

The Talner Rebbe also had two grandchildren with him, boys of my age. I soon befriended them and we became pals. These two boys, who came from the *shtetl* of Talno, had never in their lives seen a big city like Lemberg, so I became their guide and escort around town. And because the Talner Rebbe lived opulently and did not skimp when it came to the grandchildren, we would go sightseeing every day, always in a different area of town. We were accompanied everywhere by Zishe the Cabby, a young man with his own cab and a good horse. All of the rabbis and Hassidic *rebbes* who visited Lemberg would ride with him, including the Belzer Rabbi and his family. This was because Zishe was an honourable man and there was, God forbid, no *shatnez* to be found in the upholstered seats of his cab.

The two boys, my friends, grew up to be famous Hassidic *rebbes*. Reb Nokhemtshe, who was the only child of Reb Dovidl's son, Reb Motl, took over his grandfather's vast *rabistvo* [rabbinical post] after his death, and later lived in Tulchin. The Talner Rebbe of Attorney Street, New York, is one of his sons. The other is Reb Motele Khodorov, who went on to become a son-in-law to the Vizhnitzer Rebbe, Reb Borukh Hager from the well-known Kassow dynasty. He calls himself the Tolner-Vizhnitzer Rebbe and lives in the Bronx, New York. I have seen the latter here several times. Whenever we meet, we recall Lemberg and relive our memories from over half a century earlier.

* * *

At that time, when the first Rabbinical Assemblies were being held in Lemberg, some of the most important rabbis were our frequent guests. Rabbi Shimon Sofer, the Krakow Rabbi, was our guest for a week. Our house was like a railway station from early in the morning till late at night. People came and went and I was always very busy and on the go.

II
MY FATHER'S DEATH

My father was a sick man in his later years. He suffered from a chronic stomach condition. However, he paid it no heed and carried on with his daily tasks as usual, in particular for the Machzikei Hadas and its newspaper. Both were developing at a steady pace and occupied all of his time. He worked for days on end, especially at night.

In winter of 1880, he became really sick and was bedridden. However even in bed, his constantly busy spirit would not let him rest. He often dictated letters as well as entire Yiddish or Hebrew articles for the newspaper to my brother, Yehoshua, or to someone else.

At dawn on Friday, January 30 (17 Shevat, 5640), he left for a better world at the age of 66. He left behind three sons: Mendel, from my father's first marriage, age 32, Yehoshua, age 20, and myself, the baby of the family, who had just turned *bar-mitsve* three months earlier. My sister, Henna, had died several years earlier at 17. I recall her as a tall, pale, and weak girl with two long, black braids.

As I described earlier, my father's wealth had already dissolved in 1873 with the Vienna stock market crash. The bank had foreclosed on the large house "on the hill." Only the house on Sikstuska Street, in which we lived, remained. But even this did not belong to us; there was a bank mortgage. However, my father had made certain counterclaims against the bank about some conditions of the mortgage and because of this, there was a lawsuit that dragged on for years, even after my father's death.

My brother, Mendel, who went on to become a well-known "unofficial" lawyer and a major legal expert, was in court for 10 years with the bank after our father's death. He lived in the house and paid rent until the bank finally came to an agreement with him. My brother Yehoshua and I did not benefit much from this as neither of us needed it at the time. Nevertheless, a little money remained from my father, about 3,000 gulden, and close family friends together with the accountant of the Machzikei Hadas, Reb Yehoshuele Lipsker, settled the estate among the heirs: I, the unprovided-for orphan, received the largest portion, a whole 1,000 gulden. My mother, the sickly widow, also received 1,000 gulden, and my two brothers got the rest, which amounted to about 600 gulden each.

We lived in Lemberg for another year. My brother, Yehoshua, had left for his wife's birthplace of Tarnow several months earlier. He opened a big glass and porcelain store, which he ran until his death in 1931. My mother and I no longer wanted to remain in Lemberg and we moved to Tarnow, where we lived with Yehoshua.

* * *

My father's death made a great impression on the Orthodox Galician world, where he had been considered one of the true "*oskim be-tsarkhei tsibur be-emuna*" [faithfully involved in the needs of the community]. All of the newspapers, the *Hamagid*, and the other Jewish-German periodicals in Vienna and abroad, wrote about him in a positive way. It goes without saying that this was the case in the *Machzikei Hadas* newspaper. Over a period of several months, every issue featured a poem or an article about my deceased father. One of these was by my young friend, Yehudah Leib Landau, the current Chief Rabbi of Johannesburg, South Africa.

The famous *meylets*, MaVa"H of Vienna, an old friend of my father's, published a long, florid eulogy in the *Machzikei Hadas*, where every word began with the letters *shin* or *mem* (the intials of Shmuel Margoshes). This particular eulogy was reprinted in the *frum* newspaper, *Halevanon*, which was published in Mainz, Germany by Reb Yekhiel Brill. The true editor of this publication was the well-known Orthodox rabbi, Dr. Marcus Lehmann, publisher of the *Mainz Israelite* and the author of the historical Jewish stories that still appear today in all Yiddish newspapers.

On the other hand, the rival newspapers, especially *Haivri* and its contributors, old YaHa"Sh [Yehoshua Heshel Shor], dragged my dead father's name through the mud ceaselessly for weeks and weeks. This was the case even though YaHa"Sh was a relative of ours on my mother's side, a grandson of the "*Tvuos Shor.*" The *Israelite*, the organ of the Shomer Yisrael, maintained some decency. And because it appeared in Lemberg, they were quite simply ashamed to sully my father's name to the extent that the *Haivri* did in Brody. It will most certainly be of interest and perhaps even contribute to the Jewish cultural history of Galicia to become further acquainted with these two individuals, YaHa"Sh and Jacob Werber, and to see what battle tactics they employed.

12

YaHa"Sh

I shall provide a short biography and overview of YaHa"Sh, and also present some of the "*Rishfei Esh* [Sparks of Fire]" that he printed in *Haivri* about my father and the *Machzikei Hadas*.

YaHa"Sh, or Yehoshua Heshl Shor, as he was known in full, was born in Brody in 1814 and died at the age of 81 in Brody in 1895. He stemmed from a very wealthy and distinguished family. His wife also stemmed from illustrious lineage: she was a granddaughter of the world-renowned Rabbi, Yechezkel Landau, the "*Noda Biyehudah,*" Chief Rabbi of Prague.

As a young man, YaHa"Sh became an adherent of the haskalah and carried on a correspondence with the great *maskilim* of the day. In honour of his wedding, ShaDa"L [Shmuel David Luzzatto] published and dedicated the first edition of Rabbi Yehuda Halevi's Hebrew poems (or *Diwan*) under the title of *Betulat Bat Yehuda*. Later, YaHa"Sh developed into a sharp critic of the Jewish Torah, and especially of the Talmud, to the point that he ridiculed and mocked everyone. To this end, he published the famous Hebrew journal, *Hakhaluts*. During a period of 37 years, all of 30 issues appeared. In the early years, several of the most important Jewish scholars worked with him. They included Avraham Krochmal, [Moritz] Steinschneider, Pineles, my uncle, Marcus Dubos, and other free spirits. However, the later issues of *Hakhaluts* became more and more barbed and aggressive, and all of its previous contributors distanced themselves from him. He thus filled the journals himself and ceaselessly cursed and denigrated everyone who had helped him earlier.

YaHa"Sh was an extremely affluent man with an estimated value of several hundred thousand gulden, but he was an even bigger miser. He only had one son who died young. Although he had poor family members (including his brother, the Hebrew poet and author, Naftali Mendel Shor, who used to sign himself using the last letters of his name, Y-L-R), he let them starve and did not offer them any support. In his later years, YaHa"Sh withdrew entirely from human company. He lived alone in his big house, and would not even let anyone enter for rent collection. He was served by a single old woman; every day she cooked him a big pot of porridge, which he ate with milk. The Jews of Brody did not want to have anything to do with him, and even the few *maskilim* of the city would not cross his threshold.

When he died, he left his entire estate, about 150,000 gulden, to the Vienna Rabbinical Seminary, which was being founded at the time. He also left his vast library of many thousand rare *sforim*, books, and manuscripts in numerous languages.

The older he grew, the more embittered and aggressive he became. He unleashed his bile and venom in his stilted rhymes that he published each week in the *Haivri* under the heading of "*Rishfei Esh*." I shall provide several examples below. He poured his wrath not only on the Orthodox Jews and their Machzikei Hadas, or on the Hassidic rebbes, but on anyone he would get his hands on. This included the Shomer Yisrael and the maskilim, however with less bile and venom than he poured on the Orthodox Jews and their representatives.

13

JACOB WERBER, THE MASTER OF *HAIVRI*

The *Haivri* was founded in Brody in 1865 by Reb Baruch Werber, a *maskil* and an old-style Jewish scholar. He was also the author of a commentary on Ecclesiastes, which has been published twice.

The *Haivri* was actually founded as a rival to the *Hamevaser* in Lemberg, whose publisher was the esteemed *meylets*, Reb Joseph Cohen Zedek. Cohen Zedek and Werber were close relatives and both originated from the city of Brody. Initially, Boruch Werber was one of the main contributors to this relative's newspaper. However, later they fought and Werber became an editor himself. He wanted to show Cohen Zedek that he was just as capable. If he was not much better, then he was certainly no worse.

Whoever has the opportunity to see the two newspapers, both extremely difficult to find today, will be amazed at how much dirt and coarse language these two Jews used against each other in public. There is virtually no human crime of which one of these relatives did not accuse the other. I know neither the root of, nor the difference between, the two newspapers. Both cursed each other, and the same contributors—*maskilim* and scholars—contributed to both newspapers for free. It did not occur to anyone to charge money for these sorts of things, and it would have been an insult, even to the poorest.

When the *Hamevaser* ceased publication due to an enemy denunciation, the *Haivri* remained the only Hebrew newspaper in Galicia. Efforts were made to publish other Hebrew newspapers, but to no avail. All of these newspapers were in the *maskilic*-bourgeois spirit, and a man like YaHa"Sh, a free spirit and ridiculer of everything that is holy to Jews, would not have been able to gain access to them. He, who was at that time involved in his research into Jewish history and critical scholarly investigation of religion, would not have wanted anything to do with them either.

Only when YaHa"Sh grew older and his spirit weakened—when he had become senile—did he began to approach the *Haivri*, which was published in his hometown of Brody. Reb Baruch Werber was no longer living by that time, and his only son, Jacob Werber, then only about 17 years old, took over as editor. The young Werber later went on to study law, always spoke Polish, and would not utter a single Yiddish word. He was no great expert in Hebrew or other Jewish studies. According to my friend, Chaim Aaron Hoffner, who was his editorial assistant, he remained the editor and refused to give up the newspaper after his father's death because his mother, a highly sensitive woman, strongly urged him to hold on to it because the editorship would snag him, her only son, a fabulous, rich match. Unfortunately, her hope did not materialize. Jacob Werber was a sickly and weak boy, and he died at 31. After his death, his mother attempted to publish the newspaper under outside leadership. This arrangement only lasted a little over half a year, when the *Haivri* closed forever.

The issues of the *Haivri* are, as stated above, very rare. I shall reprint several of YaHa"Sh's "*Rishfei Esh*" epigrams, as well as what the newspaper printed after my father's death. The *Haivri* from February 6, 1880, eight days after my father's death, reprinted the following news:

35

To the Head of the "Upholders" in Lvov
Please give me your ear and hear,
Why are you with the Rabbi of the evil Hassidim?
You should be entirely with the noble *maskilim*.
It is already written in the book of the first man:
Shmuel will be called wise,
He will not be called rabbi.

Soon after my father's death, YaHa"Sh authored the following:

I am depressed from the head, I am depressed from the arm
Woe to me for my fracture, dreadful is my wound
Comfort me not with vanity, therefore I said
Is there a hurt like my hurt, a trouble like my trouble.
Woe is me, I have been broken by a double fracture!
I am depressed from the head, the head of the upholders of Lvov,
Our Master Samuel, second to the great scholar
For he has left us life and has ridden on a cherub
and flown away [Psalm 18, 10] to enjoy the good of the world that is coming
He turned and went away to the pleasures of factions
To harvest the fruit of the preparation of his work with joy
And us—he has left to groans and worries.
Woe is me, he is a reed and he has become as a reed.

It goes on like this for 24 lines. He concludes:

For whom do I cry, and shed my tear
Shall I bewail the dead who is called a living man?
Our Master Samuel my "upholder," my noble and my shepherd
Who stops the people that they do not backslide to opprobrium?
Shall I cry over a living man who is called a dead corpse
A guardian of hard heart, a strong face and strong forehead
Who hurried to the bad each and every time
And his great sin is preserved for eternity?

When MaVa"H published his flowery eulogy on my father (as detailed above), YaHa"Sh did not like it at all. He expressed his fury in the following *"Rishfei Esh"* (*Haivri*, February 27, 1880):

All the praises and acclaim
In the Book of Praises [Psalms]
None is missing
Have all come together
And have become his portion

For the vice president of the society
Samuel Margoshes
Who possesses a sensitive soul
Great in might, large in strength
Thus he will call with the throat—
Possessor of double misfortune
The innkeeper of our teacher the rabbi,
All the callers will be astonished
About a man greatly exalted
Not known by the people
And with holy feeling
He will sing a new song
A great miracle was there!

The *Machzikei Hadas* newspaper, in turn, did not keep silent and attacked YaHa"Sh because he lacked the tact to let a dead man rest and to refrain from continuing to sully his name. YaHa"Sh thus defended himself in one of his "*Rishfei Esh*" (*Ivri Anokhi*, March 5, 1880):

How Many Joseph ben Shimons Are About in the Marketplace!
I am angry at the upholders
For they are seeking a pretext against me [2Kings 5, 7]
And they annul the words of the righteous
And this is a sin to be judged!
Did I not say from the beginning
And did not speak in secret:
"Do not rejoice at the death of the upholder"
Until I swallow my spittle, salvation will arise
And they will falsify in their secret counsel,
And express with their tongue
And not know shame
That I rejoiced at their notable event
The death of the upholder of their religion
Master Samuel Margoshes!—
For I truly know in my soul
The greatness of the holy society
The valued corner, the chief stone
Over all the nations together
For an excessive love is destined for it
And every man finds in it
Hassid, venerable *zaddikim*
How many Simons and Samuels there are in the marketplace!

I have recorded other "pearls," but I think that these few are enough to provide a sense of what sorts of rusty arms were used to fight against Galician Orthodoxy and what many *maskilim* delighted in.

14

MY CHILDHOOD

I, Eliezer Joseph Margoshes, was born in Lemberg on November 16, 1866 (Thursday, the eighth day of Kislev, 5627).

My mother, Sore Rivke (Rivele) had, ever since I can recall, been a weak woman and was under constant medical care. She had three children aside from me: a daughter Henna, who died when she was 17 and who I remember as very sickly, and my brother Yehoshua, named after my mother's father Chaim Yehoshua Fleker, who was just about seven years older than me. I was the baby of the family.

My father also had children from his first wife, Rokhele. She was the daughter of his eldest brother, Reb Nisn Margoshes. They had two sons: Mendel, and another older son, Joseph, who died before I was born. I am named for him, and after my grandfather, Reb Yosl. As a "remedy" for being named after a brother who died young, I was given an additional name: Eliezer after my abovementioned great-grandfather, the General Secretary of the *Vaad Arba Aratzos*.

This brother Joseph, my predecessor, was a highly accomplished boy. When he died at 19, he already knew six languages and was also a great Hebraist. When I was a boy of about 10 and constantly fiddling with *sforim*, I came upon quite a few of his "writings" in German and Hebrew in one of the bottom drawers of a book-cabinet. There was also a handwritten newspaper with the name of *Apirion* that was full of Hebrew poems, and flowery rhetoric that he had compiled for one of his friends. It seems to me that this friend was the later-renowned Hebrew poet, Aaron Dornzweig, who died very young. I also found a title page that was painted in beautiful water colours. Whether he did it himself or it was the work of someone else, I don't know.

In this drawer I also found a complete translation of one of Philipson's longer stories, *"Die Maranen."* He called it *"Haanusim Be Sfarad."* This was, incidentally, the same title under which this same story appeared years later, published by the esteemed author, Abraham Abba Rakovski, and it was reprinted several times. When I was a little older, I had this book bound and kept it for several years after I got married until it got lost somewhere. Woe for the loss!

My mother would never let me fiddle with these remaining "writings" when my father was home. She knew that if he saw it, an old and never-healed wound would reopen. For this same reason, my mother would not allow me to play with the assorted needlework that remained from her daughter, even though I was beloved by her and she indulged me in everything. She kept everything locked in a special drawer of her commode and never let me near them. After my mother's death, these family keepsakes were destroyed or lost. My brother's wife had no feeling for these kinds of family mementos.

As long as my father was alive, he observed the Yahrzeit of his deceased eldest son. The Yahrzeit fell on the last day of Chanukah, "*Zot Chanukah.*" For the occasion, my father would throw a big annual party at his house to which he invited his good friends and all of the gentlemen from Reb Vovtshi's Kloyz, where we lived. There would be 70–80 people at the party. The guests included those who had known well this very accomplished young man who had been a great expert in Gemara and Poskim. Quite a few years later, my brother Mendel, who followed in my father's footsteps, observed his older brother's Yahrzeit and threw a party on the last day of Chanukah, although on a much smaller scale.

15

MELAMDIM

I don't have much to recount about the *melamdim* that I had in my youth. One thing that I realize now is that they knew very little themselves and were therefore incapable of accomplishing anything substantial with their students, even though their pupils included boys with good heads on their shoulders. The custom was that every good-for-nothing beggar and loser became a *melamed*. Even in Lemberg, a community of over 20,000 Jews including many learned people, the situation was not much better.

I learned the *Alef-beys* [the alphabet] and "*trop*" [cantillation] with Reb Israel Kitsch (Rohotin, father of the renowned book printer, Haim Rohotin). He was the *khazan* and *shames* of the Sikstuska *Shul* and he had his apartment in the *Shul* courtyard. He was a quiet man and a very fine person. The *Rebbetzin* was a respectable old woman. However, his Jewish learning, and especially his "pedagogical wisdom," were pretty flimsy. I studied with him and his helpers for some time, and spent most of my time playing in the courtyard, next to the public synagogue.

This continued until I grew older and I was taken away to a *khumesh* Melamed named "Blind Moshe." He was also no great instructor: he was an older man and his diction was also not too sharp. Nonetheless, when Tuesdays came or, at the latest, Wednesday, I already knew the two to three *parshes* with a few Rashi commentaries that he had studied with us. He and my earlier rabbi, Reb Israel Kitsch, almost never hit their students. At most, when we made some trouble or committed a more serious crime, we were put "in the corner." That is, while the other children learned, the guilty boy was placed in a corner and two "*giborei yisroel* [Heroes of Israel]" with blue "swords," or twigs, in their hands, would guard him so that he did not run away. This particular punishment generally lasted 15 minutes "by the clock." But when the six or seven year-old boy would bawl, the *rebbe* would "pardon" him and order his "heroes" to release him a lot earlier than 15 minutes. "Blind Moshe" also lived in a big courtyard and there was a lot of place to run around and play. I do not recall who my friends were in these two *khadorim*. They were not boys with whom I maintained lasting contact.

My first *Gemore-melamed* at age 8 was a tall and broad man called Mordecai Abba. There is one thing of which I am certain: he is without question not in *gan eydn*! If I had the slightest suspicion that he had managed to sneak his way in, I would immediately send a petition to the *beys-din shel mayle* [the Heavenly Court] along with no shortage of student signatures to have him "deported" and sent under guard to *sheol takhtis*, to the most fiery depths of the netherworld. He was a monster and a brute!

He barely maintained domestic peace with his wife, who was a calm and quiet person. He would curse her and insult her in the worst possible way. She hardly ever answered back. The worst curses that I have ever heard in my life came from this *rebbe*. Mordecai Abba was always angry and violent, and all of the children were deathly afraid of him. We were about 15 students seated on two benches at a long table, and we studied the first chapter of the Talmud, tractate *Bava Metzia*. Mordecai Abba sat at the head of the table clad in only his *talis-kotn*. In one hand he held a long ruler, and he would use it to guide and cane his "holy flock," usually boys of wealthy parents, because he had a reputation in town as a good teacher. Mordecai Abba lived on an upper floor and no one was permitted to leave all day. There was no courtyard for playing.

Every quarter or half hour, he would select a different boy and seat him at his left hand (the ruler never left his paw). That poor boy! Aside from whacking students with his ruler, Mordecai Abba had a habit of pinching. And because one cannot pinch from a distance, he would unleash all of his wrath and fury upon the boy currently seated at his left. On more than one occasion, the boy would let out such big gasping sobs that it was difficult to quiet him down. During a "pogrom" like this, the Rebbetzin would try to rescue the victim. She would run and wrench the boy from his grasp. She would calm down the "victim" with caramels and other sweets she kept to sell. The Rebbetzin would implore the "pinched" boy and give him lots of free caramels and candies until he calmed down and returned to the table. "Ratting on the *kheyder*" was absolutely forbidden in all *khadorim*, and all the boys would have shunned the informant and not want to play with him. The parents, especially the mothers, did not know what kind of abuse this Mordecai Abba inflicted on their often terrified children.

I also endured quite a lot with him. It made very little difference to him whether a boy actually knew or didn't know the piece of Gemara. The slightest gesture that he did not like was enough to be treated to the ruler or pinches so hard our eyes watered. I spent a whole summer as well as half a winter in his tutelage. Once, although I immediately apologized for whatever it was that I had done, he gave me a pinch that was so painful that I almost fainted. The good Rebbetzin had to put a lot of effort and sweets into me to calm me down, and I had to swear to her on my *tsitses*, and in front of two school-friend "witnesses" that I would not tell anyone about what happened at *kheyder*.

I would certainly have kept my "oath" and not told on the *kheyder*. However, it just so happened that the same evening Sosia, our servant-girl, who was with us for several years and actually got married in our house, was undressing me and changing me before putting me to bed. I argued with her and did not want to undress. My heart told me that no good would come of it. She was, however, much stronger than I was and dragged the clothes off me by force. She let out such a loud screech that my mother just about came running in from the bedroom. Sashia had spotted a black and blue mark on my knee and she had been so shocked that she had let out a shriek.

At first I had not wanted to reveal the truth about the *kheyder*. I claimed that I fell on the stairs and banged up my knees. However, I finally confessed the whole secret to Sosia, and told to her what had happened in *kheyder*, and that it was not the first time that I had been pinched like that by the *rebbe*. Sosia took me in her arms and applied cold compresses until the swelling and black and blue bruising had begun to subside. The next day I did not go back to *kheyder*. My father sent for Mordecai Abba and he soon came, trembling and afraid.

My father was furious with him—I had never seen my father so angry—and he told the *melamed* that he intended to bring him in front of the *din-toyre* so that the court would punish him for pinching and hitting small defenseless children. My father then realized that if he continued, all of the other fathers would withdraw their children and he would deprive him of a livelihood, which he did not want. My father therefore paid him the school fee for the entire period of study and I never saw his face again.

16

GEMARA MELAMDIM

As far as my other *Gemara melamdim* were concerned, very few other boys could claim that they shared my experience: my *Gemara melamdim* were a father with his two sons. First, I studied with the father, then with his younger son, and finally, until my father's death, with the older son.

Not far from the city of Rayshe in Galicia, there is a small *shtetl* called Sokolov. There is a popular expression in Galicia about someone who mixes into matters that are not his business: he is a "*Sokolover eydes* [Witness]." The meaning can be inferred. In this major metropolis there lived a man by the name of Mendel Weiner. He had two sons: Yehoshua and Moshe. All three possessed some learning, in particular the latter Reb Moshe, who became a *dayan* at the Lemberg *beys din* at the end of his days.

All three, the father with his two sons, were matchmakers. But they were no ordinary matchmakers that deal with small, poor matches. They dealt with the sort of matches that one might call "international matches." They arranged marches for very wealthy people with partners who were other international matchmakers, in different countries, across all of Galicia, Poland, Russia, Hungary, and other provinces and lands. Because of their business dealings they settled in Lemberg. Their families remained in Sokolov, but the matchmakers supported them in Lemberg and spent time with their wives during holidays.

It was simply more appropriate to the "business" to write letters to *mekhu-tonim* from a big city like Lemberg, the capital city of Galicia, than from a *shtetl* in the sticks like Sokolov. A Lemberg matchmaker was an important personage. He and his proposed matches were to be respected by any *mekhutn*, even someone who was very wealthy or of distinguished lineage. Who would want to even consider a match that was proposed by some matchmaker in Sokolov?

Because these three personages did not have much to do in the way of work, save the writing of several postcards a day to the *makhatonim* or to their partners, the other "international matchmakers," they decided to become *Gemara melamdim* and to instruct children as a unit. They did not find this difficult. Because of their matches, they had access to many affluent homes. Each one got several students, every one of whom paid 50–60 gulden in tuition per study period, which added up to about 600 gulden a year. This provided enough money for them in Lemberg, as well as their families in the small *shtetl* of Sokolov. For despite everything, these "*velt-shadkhonim*" were not wealthy themselves.

At first, I studied with the father, Reb Mendel, together with about five other boys. The *kheyder* was in a little *shul* in the courtyard of Reb Shloyme Hissen's house. The *shul* was called the Spodki Shulekhl because years ago, when all Jews used to wear "*spodiks,*" the Kirzheners, who manufactured these *spodiks,* lived there The *shul* was located in a dark, dirty and narrow courtyard. The sun never reached it, and it was cold and dark. Spending entire winter days there was simply agony. However, who concerned themselves with such trifles in those days? I had a friend there, Mordecai Polturak. His parents actually lived in the same building as the *shul* but at the front, facing the "broad street." They were always busy with a big flour business, also located in the same building, and we children could often be found in their rooms and played there, thereby avoiding the cold, dark little *shul*.

Reb Mendel only taught us during one study period. In the summer, my *rebbe* became his son, Reb Yehoshua. About five or six boys studied with him in the walled *sukkah* on the roof of our house. I did little in the way of learning with either father or this son. Firstly, they were almost always busy and preoccupied with their matches. In addition to this, although they had really sharp minds, both had limited ability when it came to elucidating the subject. They quickly "said their part" regarding the bit of Gemara with its commentary, and then had no idea what to do with nine and ten year old children who have to be taught slowly and with more explanation. I beg both of them their forgiveness here, but I don't know: it is possible that they were, in fact, great Jewish scholars. However, they were far from possessing pedagogical wisdom; they had no clue what that was. They had absolutely no idea how to teach us, and the result was that although by listening I, or the other students, could repeat what were taught all week pretty well, not a single one of us had any deeper knowledge or real understanding of the Gemara. This was the case even though some of us had really good heads on our shoulders.

The bit of understanding of Talmud that I did manage to develop in my youth is thanks to Reb Mendele's older son, Reb Moshe Wiener. Although he was more of an "international matchmaker" and thus had to engage in a much wider correspondence than the other two, he still always had time to devote himself to his students. Above all, he was much more adept at explaining the bit of Gemara to a boy. It was no longer just a matter of rote study; rather, the mind and logic played a part, too. He was also more savvy when it came to everyday matters than his father and brother, two shabby and unkempt small-town Jews. He was much more fastidious regarding his clothing and environment. With him we did not study in a cold little *shul* or *sukkah*. Instead, he rented a large and comfortable room and conducted his *kheyder* there. I studied a whole two years with Reb Moshe Weiner, until my Bar Mitzvah. I have him to thank for my bit of familiarity with the Gemara.

On the "broad street" there was a big tavern where well-to-do Jews, especially merchants from surrounding *shtetlekh,* would gather and drink mead. This tavern also had a restaurant, which was run by a fine man by the name of Reb

Abish Traktirer. Reb Abish, with his wife, were busy all day in the restaurant, and their apartment was always left unlocked. This "restaurateur" had one son with a very sharp mind and a great appetite for learning. Reb Abish thus arranged with the *melamed* to give him use of one of the rooms in his apartment for the whole day and part of the evening for use as a *kheyder*, in exchange for his teaching the son together with the rest of us. This boy, who soon became my friend, was called Samuel Gutman. Later, he served as Head Rabbi and preacher at the Lemberg "Temple" for progressive Jews. He also had a reputation as a very good speaker and Jewish scholar.

I also had one other friend at that time. This was a boy from the nearby *shtetl* of Yanov, close to Lemberg. He was called Yankele Richter. His grandfather, Reb Berl Richter, was a very wealthy man and the proprietor of a beer and mead brewery. Yankele was very talented in painting. He later studied with the renowned painter, Jan Mateiko, in Krakow, and became a very well-known painter.

I learned how to write Yiddish and Polish from separate teachers. At that time in Lemberg, there were two great "artists" for this purpose: Poltaver and Waschitz. They were major competitors, and each one claimed that he knew more Yiddish scripts than the other. Every few weeks, each would hang up a large framed piece of paper with more scripts. This continued until Waschitz finally "beat" my teacher, Poltaver, when his frame contained 22 different Jewish scripts. We wrote with goose quills, for script cannot be produced as finely with steel pens. The teacher also taught us how to trim a goose quill, which is in itself a major feat. For this reason, every boy had to have a "quill knife" with a very sharp blade.

17
MY TWO GIRLFRIENDS

I not only had fine and respectable male friends, though not a great many, in my youth. Two lovely and charming girls, girlfriends that I had when I was 11 or 12 years old, also spring to mind. I have nothing to be ashamed about regarding them, God forbid, and am overcome by genuinely warm feelings as I write these lines.

The most important and wealthiest man in Lemberg was at that time Reb Yerakhmiel Halevy Ish Horovitz, whose estate was estimated at about two million gulden. There was not another Jew as rich as him in all of Lemberg.

Aside from his affluence, he was also of very distinguished lineage: a grandson of the world-renowned ShaLa"H [Isaiah ben Abraham Ha-Levi Horovitz] and himself the son of a great *rebbe*, and a generous benefactor to boot. Just the small donations distributed by his wife amounted to over 100 gulden a week. For more important matters, people appealed to him directly and he always gave with an open hand.

Reb Yerakhmiel would often sit and devote himself to the Torah. In order that he not be lonely while studying, he fulfilled the clever piece of advice from our sages: "Buy yourself a teacher and make yourself a friend." He invited Lemberg's *Rosh Beys Din* [head of the rabbinical court], Rabbi Uri Wolf Salat, a revered great Torah scholar and a man who was very knowledgeable about everyday affairs. He would pay 20 gulden a week, a huge sum in those times, about 60 years ago, and every evening, right after prayers, they would sit down together to study and spend several hours in that fashion. The Rosh Beys Din and Reb Yerakhmiel would sit in the farthest back room, and one had to pass through four half-lit rooms in order to get from the front room to them.

My father was very friendly with Reb Yerakhmiel, as he was with all of the wealthy men of Lemberg. Since Reb Yerakhmiel had an annual subscription to the Vienna newspaper, *Die Neue Freie Presse* and would read it during the day, my father would get it from him in the evening. Every night, right after evening prayers, I would go to Reb Yerakhmiel's house to get the paper. The newspaper was always lying in Reb Yerakhmiel's study on the cashbox, and I would take it quietly so as not to disturb the two scholars. Each time, there was also a "*firer*" (a copper coin with a value of four kreuzer). Reb Yerakhmiel left this for me as a "delivery fee."

When I had the newspaper and my "*firer*," I returned to the front room, where my abovementioned two girlfriends were awaiting me. The front room was very large, and there were several tables. The hostess, an older, genteel woman who minded the large house, was seated by the door. She also distributed the smaller donations. Feigele Horovitz, the lady of the house, would sit at another table with her daughters. There was no son. And at the third table sat two 11 year old girls, and it was at their table that I sat down when I came for the newspaper.

One of the two girls was a granddaughter of Reb Yerakhmiel's through his deceased daughter, the wife of her cousin, Shmelke Horovitz. He later became a millionaire and a resident of the City of Brody and its surrounding vast forests and estates. He was, incidentally, ennobled with the title of "*von*" by the Emperor, and was the head of the Kehillah of Lemberg for years. The second girl, Mariamshte, was a daughter of Reb Yerakhmiel's grandson, the renowned man of wealth and distinguished lineage, Reb Shmelke Rokeah.

The former girl went on to marry the respected lawyer, Nathan Lowenstein of Lemberg, and son of the Lemberg "Temple" preacher, Reb Yisachar Dov Lowenstein. The young Lowenstein was already altogether a "Pollak" and

45

an assimilationist. He then became Imperial Council Representative of the Drohobitch district, and a lot of Jewish blood was shed because of his election. He was also ennobled by Emperor Franz Joseph and received, like his father-in-law, the title "*von.*" The latter girl married a very *frum* man: Dr. Meir Munk from Altona, a cousin of the world-renowned rabbi, Azriel Hildesheimer, Rabbi in Berlin and founder and director of the Rabbinical Seminary there.

The two girls would usually play cards, "*Konteshne*" for small coins. In the beginning, I, poor boy, did not know the game. We never saw a card in my father's house and there was just no one to play with. However, these two girls earned themselves major "*mitsve*" points and taught me the game until I played better than they did. Because I always had four *kreuzer*, I played with them. If I lost it as well as my own money, as almost always happened to me initially, they laughed at me but I never left with any damage: the Lady of the House or one of her daughters at the next table always reimbursed me for my losses so that I often still left with a profit.

No one at my house knew about this. Naturally, I was embarrassed to tell them at home; how was it that a boy like me, who had studied a *blat Gemara* with commentary and who had perused *loshn-koydesh* books, was playing with girls, and with cards to boot? This continued for over a year and a half, until my father got sick and then died, and I no longer had a reason to come to this affluent house.

From that time on, I only saw the two girls from afar, when I was in Lemberg some 15 years later at the funeral of one of their aunts, a daughter of Reb Yerakhmiel. Both were married women and wore black veils over their faces, so I could not see their features at all. If these two ladies are still alive, and if they are still able to read some Yiddish, and if they have the opportunity to see these lines, I send them a hearty greeting. I believe that these words will likewise awaken in them a warm memory of those happy, carefree and peaceful childhood years.

18

HASKALAH

At the age of eight, when I understood very little Hebrew, I liked to pore over books. At our house, there were three old-fashioned cabinets and all three were stuffed with books. Among them were quite a few Haskalah-*sforim*, as well as Hebrew poems, and flowery rhetoric by the earlier Hebrew poets, including

[Naftali Hertz] Wiesel, Shalom Hakohen, [Meir Ha-Levi] Letteris, and others. These particular books greatly attracted me. I pulled them all out from among the bigger volumes and placed them on two separate shelves. I considered myself to be their owner and no one had the nerve to take one of them without my knowledge.

The first book that I actually read was Reb Nahman Bratslaver's *Sippurei Mayses*. I found the first edition of this collection among our books: the format was large, almost like *Mishnayes*, and the text was *loshn-koydesh* on top, and Yiddish underneath. The stories were so simple, captivating, and simple to read; I could not tear myself away from them until I had read through all of them. My father sat at a big table in the "Long Room" with one or more writers, and the whole table was littered with papers and documents. In order not to disturb them at their work, I had my own little table with a tallow lamp. There I liked to sit and peruse my little *sforim*. After Reb Nakhman's *Mayses*, I read other Hassidic storybooks or easy Haskalah books, for example, *Ha-Podeh U-Matsil*, *Ben Melekh*, and such.

When I got a little older and was capable of accessing other, more difficult Haskalah *sforim*, I began to make friends with boys my age, and together we would discuss the books that we had already read or lent each other. Sometimes we would also trade books. Virtually every evening, some 15–20 of us boys would gather from all corners of the city *"Far der shul"* ("in front of the synagogue," a well-known street in the Jewish district). Almost everyone had a different Haskalah *seyfer*, displayed it to his friends, spoke about it, and shared his understanding. We also read the *Hamagid*, *Halevanon*, *Hakol*, and even *Haivri*, and knew the names of the writers and all about their private affairs.

Above everything, we would talk a lot and wonder at the young people of Lemberg who had thrust themselves into the wide world several years earlier, and studied abroad. Among them was Simon Bernfeld (I did not know him personally), who was already a regular contributor to *Hamagid* at age 16, and was the "editorial assistant" in Luck. He was our ideal, and we all aspired to reach those heights.

When the weather did not permit it, we would meet in the Anshei Mamod Synagogue not far away. Between *Mincha* and *Maariv*, we would engage in our Haskalah chats and book exchange. The *"haskole berze* [Haskalah Exchange] *far der shul"* wound up becoming so famous across town that every boy who had any affinity at all for things Maskilic tried to be present as often as possible. I only remember two of these Haskalah buddies (aside from the abovementioned Yehuda Leib Landau): Yekhiel Klein, whose later fate I do not know, and Yehoshua Geyer, who later became a renowned book dealer in Budapest.

Even respectable young people, already married homeowners touched by Haskalah or themselves authors of these types of books, were not shy to come out *"Far der shul"* in the evenings. They mingled with the boys, contributed a few comments, or examined the books that we had with us. Quite a few scholars emerged from *"Far der shul"* who made names for themselves in various fields. Prominent among them were some men who were studying to become rabbis and others wishing to become Hebrew poets and authors.

We would also read German books, but not novels; only the classics. Our favourites were [Friedrich] Schiller and [Gotthold Ephraim] Lessing. Virtually every one of us had read *Die Räuber, Wilhelm Tell, Kabale und Liebe,* as well as Lessing's *Nathan der Weise, Die Juden, Emilia Galotti,* and others. We thought little of [Johann Wolfgang von] Goethe. Firstly, he was too difficult for us (some did tackle *Faust,* or just claimed to; they understood little, if anything). Secondly, my friends said that he was not much of a friend to the Jews. Nevertheless, I read his *Dichtung und Warheit,* and even tried to read his *Wahlverwandtschaften* and *Werthers Leiden,* but I soon had to give it up.

Thus many of the older boys among us took up Schiller's and Heine's poems, and knew quite a few of them by heart. Almost none of us knew Polish, the language of the country, or even Ruthenian. Nobody showed even the slightest inclination to learn them. Only a few who attended state-run elementary schools understood these languages.

Our spirits were focused on ideals and we had no interest in practical life.

19
REB VOVTSHI'S KLOYZ

I cannot leave my birthplace of Lemberg without describing one of the places where I spent a large portion of my childhood, and with which my accumulated memories of that time are inextricably linked: Reb Vovtshi's Kloyz.

Overall, the Lemberg of my time was a *frum,* one might even say Hassidic, city. There were many "Germans," enlightened people, and even *apikorsim* and public Sabbath-violators, but they had nothing to do with our family. For some reason, I seldom even went to visit my mother's family and their children. They also very rarely came to see us. I did not even know them all in person. My father was particular about our house being truly Jewish/Hassidic, and my mother's family—aside from my uncle, Reb Zalman Leib, a great Jewish scholar and publisher of many *sforim*—were very far from it. There were several small Hassidic *kloyzn:* the Sadigora, the Stepiner, the "Khadoshim" Kloyz, as well as others whose names I don't recall.

48

Reb Vovtshi, whose *kloyz* carried his name, was an affluent Lemberger. He was an exalted Jew, a strong proponent of Hassidism, and the most important of the revered students of the world-renowned Hassidic *rebbe*, Rabbi Uri Strelisker, or "*Der Saraf*," [the Seraph].

The synagogue was located in the big building called the Sikstuska Shul (although it was located on a side street called Shaynokha). Reb Vovtshi's Kloyz was housed along with the *shul* and a *beys-medresh* and several smaller synagogues where different *khevres* gathered to pray. Years earlier, several wealthy men had purchased a piece of real estate in the synagogue yard and built the Kloyz. They had transferred their *minyan*, which carried Reb Vovtshi's name, to the new location.

I did not know Reb Vovtshi (he died many years before I was born); I only knew his two sons and brother-in-law. Reb Vovtshi's older son was Reb Avele Shaynblum, the Rabbi of the *shtetl* of Shtsherets, not far from Lemberg. He was also a practioner of Hassidism and had a little Hassidic following, mostly from Lemberg and the surrounding *shtetlekh*. The second son, Reb Shmuel Shaynblum, was a very wealthy man (an in-law and a *mekhutn* of the famous wealthy family, the Wexlers of Komárno). He was an accomplished Jewish scholar and a *maskil* to boot. He devoted himself to research and investigation and published several *sforim* of earlier *gaonim* with his own annotations and footnotes. His business was in old *sforim* and manuscripts. He would thus often travel to Italy to purchase books and then sell them to major libraries. People said that he was proficient in several languages. However, he was pompous and pretty full of himself: Not everyone had the privilege to have Reb Shmuel Shaynblum utter a word to him. Reb Vovtshi's brother-in-law was Reb Mordecai son of Z. P. Rappoport (the father of the previously mentioned Talner Hassid, Reb Shimon Son of Z. P. Rappoport, who lived in our house), an old man, a *kohen*, and therefore irascible.

Almost all of the Jewish scholars and wealthy men who lived on and around aristocratic Sikstuska Street prayed in Reb Vovtshi's Kloyz. They included: the Horovitzes; the Chajeses (a son of Rabbi Zvi Hirsch Chajes, and the renowned world-class *gaon* and *mekhutn* of the Horovitzes); Reb Israel Nathanson (an uncle of the Rabbi of Lemberg, Rabbi Joseph Shaul Ha-Levi Nathanson); Reb Shmuel Shaynblum and his Russian son-in-law, a very wealthy young man named Reb Noah Paperna, with his son, Saul; Reb Yitzhak Aaron Ittinga (the later Rabbi of Lemberg) and his son and sons-in-law; Reb Nahum Burshtin (the later President of the Machzikei Hadas) with his children; the wealthy Popov clan; Reb Yosele Kaufman with his sons, Reb Nachman and Vove, and other dignified people. "*Katshalabes*" [bunglers] and "*Fliaskedriges*" [unsavoury people] had no access to his Kloyz as they did to other synagogues. The exception was on weekdays, when they would come during prayers to collect alms.

Three morning services usually took place. My father and several other "lofty" Jews would always pray with the third *minyan*. Every day there had to

49

be "*Tikkun* [refreshments]": a full quart of brandy and two to three pieces of honeycake for twelve to fifteen people, all so that they could make a "*Lekhaim!*" The Kloyz was always full for *Mincha-Maariv*. Everyone considered it his most sacred duty never, God forbid, to miss a single evening's prayers. People did not leave right after prayers; they spent an hour or more at the Kloyz. The fastidious Reb Mordecai Son of Z. P. would immediately sit down with some twenty *balebatim* and they would study *mishnayes* with commentary. On Thursdays, he would read *khumesh* with Rashi. Meanwhile, the scholars gathered in another corner and held learned discussions. Reb Yitzhak Aaron Ittinga and Reb Nahum Burshtin were the discussion leaders, and almost everyone contributed ideas.

Friday nights, after Kabbalas Shabbos, they spent an extended period of time at the Kloyz. This was customary especially during the winter, when the days were short. According to Kabbalah, the hour between six and seven in the evening is ruled by the planet Saturn, which causes a very bad and inauspicious fortune. The Hassidim and Kabbalists were therefore fastidious about not making Kiddush during that hour: they did so either before six or after seven. This is why they stayed on in the Kloyz to discuss the Torah.

Reb Vovtshi's Kloyz (part was called the Sikstuska Kloyz) was renowned across Lemberg, and all of the city's wandering beggars knew that they would find the best Shabbes accommodations there. A great many guests would thus present themselves on Friday nights (sometimes 70–80) and each *balebos* would take one or two guests home for the entire duration of Shabbes. One small-town Jew, Reb Leybush, was our constant guest over a period of several years, and aside from him there were also at least one or two other Jews at our Shabbes table.

The *shaleshudesn* in Reb Vovtshi's Kloyz were really impressive. We lived not far from the Kloyz. My father would come home right after Mincha, wash in preparation to eat, and taking with him the requisite ritual amount of challah bread, return to the *kloyz* and spend time with everybody. For *shaleshudes*, everyone would usually drink mead. It always ended up that some *balebos* "was required to provide the liquor" and a soon a "big *zaddik*" or at least a "small *zaddik*" of mead would appear (a "big *zaddik*" was a bottle that held 90 glasses of mead, and a "small *zaddik*" only held 60). People would comment on the Torah, sing *zmires*, and each *zmire* had its regular singer. Reb Shumel Shayn-blum, Reb Vovtshi's son, had a nice, pleasant voice. And because he was a *maskil*, he sang the *zmires* that had been composed by the great old Hebrew poets, Rabbi Abraham Ibn Ezra and Dunash ben Labrat, i.e. "*Ki eshmera shabbos*" and "*Dror yikra*."

To mark Reb Vovtshi's Yahrzeit, which falls several days before Rosh Hashanah, a great celebration would be held with invited *balebatim* who had known him well and had thought highly of him. To mark the Yahrzeit, the "Bnei Binyomin" Society (in Reb Vovtshi's name) also held a *siyum* for all of Shas, whereby almost every *balebos* would commit to a tractate that he would study throughout the entire year, and then mark its conclusion on that day. My father, although he was always a busy man, would actually study two tractates each year, one from *Seder Nezikin* [Order of damages], and the second either from *Zevachim* [Tractate on animal sacrifices] or *Chulin* [Tractate on slaughtering].

An annual custom that lasted for many years involved a celebration of the eight days of Chanukah for all of the *balebatim*. Every evening was hosted by a different *balebos* and there was a lavish feast. As I mentioned above, my father would mark the Yahrzeit of his eldest son (by his first wife). The Yahrzeit fell on the last day of Chanukah (*Zot Chanukah*) and on that day we held an enormous party for seventy or eighty people. As soon as the guests had washed and sampled a bit of liquor and a piece of fish or herring, the *dreidl* playing began. Each *balebos* would put in a "*firer*" (a copper coin with a value of four kreuzer) and give the *dreidl* a spin. On each side of the four sides of the *dreidl* was a letter: N, G, H, Sh. (*Nes Godol Hoyo Sham* [A great miracle happened there].) There were certain rules and laws that governed the game, and by the time all of the *balebatim* had had their turns, there was enough money in the plate to send away for some mead.

The *balebatim* of the Kloyz shared a great unity and love. They considered themselves to be members of one family, even the wealthiest among them. If someone among them experienced joy or pain, almost all of them would get involved, even if that person were poorer than them. There were several well-off *balebatim* in the Kloyz who earned their entire income from the wealthier members of the group. They acted as brokers for the wealthy men's businesses or received generous long-term loans to enable them to engage in trade and support themselves in an honourable manner. Their status was due to their association with the Kloyz,

I loved the Kloyz with all of my heart, and always felt at home there; after all, I was there twice a day over several years for prayers. Even when I got older, this Kloyz did not lose its spell over me. When I had to present myself for "*Asentirung*" [military conscription] and had traveled from Tarnow to Lemberg ten days earlier in order to "busy myself" and get geared up, I attended the Kloyz every day for Mincha and Maariv. The Kloyz folks were thrilled to see me and everyone, even the wealthiest and most learned ones, wished me all the best and expressed their approval that I had "grown up." Even in later years, whenever I found myself in Lemberg for business, I always went to the Kloyz and met up with our good, old friends who were still alive. I would always take a couple of them to the mead bar and listen to their stories of earlier, happier times over a class of liquor.

Oh, if only I could somehow get back to Reb Vovtshi's Kloyz even once more in my life! There may still be a "remnant" of the old *balebatim* and I could refresh my memories of my best and final childhood years with them.

20
IN TARNOW

I left Lemberg as a boy but I arrived in Tarnow as a *bokher*. My brother Yehoshua had left Lemberg several moths earlier to settle in Tarnow, where he lived with his wife's family of Hassidic and wealthy Jews: the Lazers, the Aberdams, and the Wexlers. Yehoshua had written us endless letters urging me to settle in Tarnow with him. However, in each letter he wrote me a long harangue in *loshn-koydesh* where he offered loving and friendly words telling me that it was high time for me to abandon my childish games and grow up. The main thing was that I should not disgrace him if I were to come to Tarnow. I was still a child at the time, a boy of about 14, and both my brother and mother wanted to make a grown up out of me.

In truth, I was quite a prankster and really enjoyed hanging around with my friends and talking Haskalah. I had to go wherever there was some kind of a parade or spectacle in town. But my brother and mother did not want to hear about what "attracted" me so much, and they demanded of me, the scamp, that I become a man. They began to consider practical possibilities for me, and this entailed a wealthy *shidekh* and a wedding in the near future. In Tarnow, which was a much smaller city than Lemberg and in a more *frum* and Hassidic milieu, they would be able to realize their plan much more easily.

I left Lemberg in a short top hat but I arrived in Tarnow in a satin, Hassidic cap.

We arrived in Tarnow two weeks before Purim, in the year 1881. I was 14 and a quarter years old at the time, but they wanted me to act with "poise," like a *bokher* ready for a *shidekh*.

21
THE TARNOW KLOYZ

The Tarnow Kloyz had a reputation across all of Galicia and the voice of the Torah was heard there twenty-four hours a day. This Kloyz was not a Yeshivah where a Rabbi studied with students; here everyone studied individually, or at most in groups of two or three. But everyone in town—which consisted of a large community of over 15,000 Jews including many scholars—who had any aptitude for study had a connection to this Kloyz. It was a symbol and a stronghold of Hassidism, in particular of Sanzer Hassidim. Virtually all of the *frum* Jews of Tarnow were adherents of the Sanzer Rebbe, and of his children and grandchildren after his passing. Tarnow Orthodoxy had its stronghold in the Kloyz, and every community matter, no matter how great or small, prompted questions as to what the Kloyz's stance would be on the issue.

As in every city in Galicia, there were many poor people in the Kloyz. However, there were also a fair number of wealthy men. These wealthy men were in complete charge there. Besides the enlightened and "German" families, they were also the leaders and tone-setters of Jewish Tarnow. There were two particularly large, prominent, and well-connected families: the Schiffs and the Lazers.

When I first met Reb Yosl Schiff, he was already an old man. He headed the largest iron business in all of Tarnow together with his sons and sons-in-law. They had exclusive representation of a number of big international and national factories and iron foundries. When Tarnow and the surrounding towns needed anything to do with iron, they had to come to the Schiffs. This old Reb Yosl Schiff was no longer involved in the business, and devoted himself instead to Hassidic and community matters. Although he was never a great Jewish scholar, everyone in town showed him a lot of respect and reckoned with his opinions. He was the oldest and most important Sanzer Hassid in Tarnow. There were, incidentally, no men of great wealth in this particular extended family of sons and sons-in-law. Like all Tarnow merchants, they were perpetually dependant on promissory notes and loans until after the death of the old man, when they bankrupted the business to the tune of 200,000 gulden and were left destitute. Only one son-in-law, Reb Yosef Shmuel Erlich, who later left for London, was highly successful. He earned himself a good reputation among local Jews as a charitable and hospitable man.

The second truly wealthy and highly influential family in Tarnow was the Lazer family. Old Reb Wolf Lazer was a son of the renowned Rabbi of Strizov, Rebbe Menachem Mendel Lazer. This Rebbe was the author of two important *sforim*, both titled *Sova Simakhoys*, the former on the Torah according to Hassidism, and the second on the Tractates of *Kiddushin* and *Kesuvos*. The son, Reb Wolf, was no great Jewish scholar, and was at the same time an idler and bench-warmer. Luckily for him, God blessed him with an *eyshes khayel* for a wife as well as several very capable daughters who headed the largest cloth and silk business in all of Tarnow. All of the neighbouring Polish *pritsim* and local Christian inhabitants were regular customers there, and refused to deal with anyone but the "*Bobovska*" (she came from the nearby town of Bobov). She amassed a fortune, married off all of her children (all of her daughters became very wealthy), and gave large donations, while her husband sat in Sanz with the *Rebbe* or in the Kloyz in Tarnow to practice Hassidism.

53

Two of his sons-in-law were extremely wealthy: Reb Zechariah Mendel Aberdam and Reb Moshe Wexler. Both had major contract and exchange businesses. One of Reb Wolf Lazer's sons, Reb Dovid, was my brother Yehoshua's father-in-law. He was a partner in the office with his brother-in-law, Reb Moshe Wexler. Incidentally, he died as a young man of less than forty soon after my brother's wedding, and his widow later married the Baranover Rebbe, Reb Israel Horovitz, a son of the Rebbe, Reb Eliezer of Dzikov, who was himself a son of the great Ropshitzer Rebbe, Reb Naftali.

These two families, with their sons and sons-in-law and a whole line of grandchildren, constituted the leadership of the Hassidic Kloyz in Tarnow, and I became closely connected to them by marriage.

I fell into the Kloyz milieu soon after our arrival in Tarnow. Our reception was enthusiastic. As a boy, there was initially little fuss about me. However, my mother, as an important woman of wealth and from Lemberg to boot, was visited by all of the women from my sister-in-law's rich family, and was also invited to reciprocate and visit them. My mother was a sickly woman who stayed at home, but for the sake of appearances she undertook a visit to all of the women who had come to see her, one time only. My mother and especially my sister-in-law were of the opinion that it is always good to maintain friendly relations with a wealthy family.

22

KLOYZ-BOYS

As soon as I arrived in Tarnow, my brother Yehoshua took me to the Kloyz and presented me to his wife's family. Everyone was friendly to me. However, because they were all much older than me, I had no interest in their company and thus had very little to do with them socially. Among their children were several boys my age, but they were all simple ignoramuses and there was nothing to talk about with any of them. Since there were at the time only a couple of weeks to go before Passover and it was not worth sending me to a Gemara *malamed*, I spent all of my time at home except when I went to the Kloyz to pray twice a day.

In the Kloyz there were quite a few boys of my age and social standing, and I tried to start a conversation with some of them to "test the waters" about Haskalah and *loshn-koydesh* books. They had no idea what I was talking about and had not even heard that such books existed. That had never heard of

Letteris, whose *Yonah Homiah* was celebrated and praised by all *maskilim* at that time, nor of [Micha Yosef] Levenson—father and son—and [Abraham] Mapu. They had never heard of them and never glimpsed their books. Among these boys were a couple who displayed some aptitude for learning and studied with a Gemara *melamed*, or alone in the Kloyz. But most of them were neither here nor there, and knew nothing, but possessed long, curly *peyes*. I realized that that there was no one for me to relate to. On top of this, I was afraid of acquiring a "bad reputation" for devoting myself to heretical books, so I soon withdrew and did not seek to befriend them any further during the entire time that I was in Tarnow.

I had one solitary friend and he has remained dear and a kindred spirit all the years of my life. This was a boy who was a little older than me who approached me as soon as he spotted me, and our friendship has not been interrupted since that time. This is my friend Yehudah Leybush Koretz. He was the only one I could talk to about Haskalah books, and I became his *rebbe* and taught him a little *dikduk, loshn-koydesh* writing, and also lent him the books that I had brought from Lemberg. He later became a Hebrew writer and one of the earliest and most important members of the Hovevei Zion in Galicia. He published several interesting pamphlets on the subject. After his wedding, he lived in Ropshits (a few miles from Tarnow, his birthplace) and headed a big delicatessen business in Hürth and was quite an affluent man. Now, in his old age, he lives with his three daughters and sons-in-laws in the Tel Mond Colony in Eretz Yisroel. Another daughter and her husband live in the town of Ozone Park, near New York. He often writes me "love letters" and remembers the pleasant years of our youth with fondness.

23

REB NAFTOLI REB PESAKH'S

Because I could not hang around idle all day, and because this did not befit an upper class boy of marriageable age, soon after Passover my brother Yehoshua sent me to the greatest and most important Gemara-*melamed* in Tarnow: Reb Naftoli Reb Pesakh's, the chief *dayan* of the city.

Usually, Reb Naftoli (his family name was Goldberg) charged each student 100 gulden per term. However, because I was an orphan with a reputation as a young man with a good head on his shoulders, Reb Naftoli agreed to take me on for only 70 gulden. Six or seven boys were studying together with him. We were no great geniuses any of us, and so we studied (or had to be in the Rabbi's house) for many hours a day. Soon after Passover, we began to study *poskim*, *Choshen Mishpat*, and the *halakhot* of *To'en ve-Nit'an* [plaintiff and defendant].

We sat down to study before 6:00 AM. However, we wanted to avoid interrupting the sleep of the Rabbi's household, especially the young Rebbetzin. She, incidentally, was his second or perhaps even his third wife. She was quite an attractive young woman, but only on one side of her face because on her other cheek was a very ugly birthmark: a mouse with legs and even fur. In order not to wake them, we studied mornings in "Dvoyve Menkis' Shul," which was directly across from the Rabbi's apartment. After 8:00 AM, we went to the nearby Kloyz for morning prayers and were back at 10:00 AM to study Gemara until about 2:00 PM. In the winter, we studied another two hours in the evenings. As far as I know, none of Reb Naftoli's students grew up to be great Jewish scholars.

Although this rabbi was a remarkable scholar, author of a great *seyfer* titled *Beys Levi* on Tractate *Gittin* [Divorce], and a *pilpulist*, he lacked the qualities and skills required of a *melamed*. In addition to this, he was the most important *dayan* in town, and his house, which was in the centre of the Jewish quarter, was always full of people. They came with the kinds of legal queries, *gets*, and *shayles* about whether their kitchenware was kosher that we students could almost have ruled on ourselves. This all took place during the time that we were seated over our Gemaras in the middle of our lessons.

The *gets* and especially the *khalitzas* took up a lot of time. These things are not arranged as quickly as one might think. First, the parties attack each other and fight, and they never come alone: they always bring a couple of family members and close friends. When they reach the point of the *get* and the *beys-din* sits down with the scribe, then begins the hair-splitting and disputes about the names and nicknames of the persons involved in the *get*, and other matters of this kind. This kind of *get* often took an entire day or more. On these occasions, we did not study. Instead, we stayed at the Rabbi's house and observed everything that happened.

On days that involved a *khalitza*, things took a lot longer. The laws and customs around *khalitzas*, which take place pretty rarely, are difficult, intricate; not every Rabbi or *dayan*, especially in small towns, knows how to handle them. My Rabbi, however, was a consummate professional in this particular area. All *khalitzas* that took place during his time in Tarnow and the surrounding towns were handled by him. In year and a half that I studied with him, there were four *khalitzas* in all and we students acquired quite a solid knowledge of the process.

This is how they were conducted: First the Rabbi, or the *dayan*, had to systematically instruct and clarify the entire *parshe* (in *Parsha Ki Tetse* [Deut. 25:5–10]) that deals with *yibbum* and *khalitza* for the two parties—the husband's brother and his brother's widow. Thus, the Rabbi would sit down for an evening with them both and, like a *khumesh melamed*, teach and elucidate all ten verse of the *parshe*. This was a very arduous, laborious task. Imagine a simple Jew, often a real ignoramus, and an even more foolish, ignorant and harried woman both having to be taught all ten verses of the *khumesh* thoroughly. Then, both have to be able to recite several verses in actual correct *loshn-koydesh* in front of the *beys-din* during the *khalitza* ceremony. When this kind of Jew has to pronounce the Biblical words: "*Lo khofatsti lekakhto*" [I do not want to marry her]," they have to emerge from his mouth cleanly, clearly and grammatically: "*lo kho-fats-ti lekakh-to*," not too quickly and not too slowly.

These difficulties were magnified when the widow then had to appear before the *beys-din* and recite from memory this entire long verse: "*Me-eyn yabo-mi leho-kim shem be-yisro-el loy o-vo ya-bmi* [My husband's brother refuses to raise up his brother's name in Israel and will not perform the duty of a brother's brother to me]." It was pitiful to behold the poor widow struggle painfully through this particular verse. The Rabbi's wife would often assist the widow with memorizing it.

And the *khalitza* shoe used during the ceremony! This was a shoe owned by the community that was so large and wide that it fit any foot. The shoe had such long straps that when it was put on the man and fastened in some random manner, the wretched woman simply had to undo it with her left hand in front of the *beys-din*. The Rabbi, with the help of the Rebbetzin, had to instruct the widow in this tough job until she was competent. We, the students, were involved: we observed, kept ourselves busy, and offered support. We did not study.

Reb Naftoli was always preoccupied and in a bad mood, and had a terrible temper. However, he lacked a target for his frequent rages. He was afraid of his young wife: she once left him for several weeks with their young child and it was awful. There was no one to take care of him and the children from his first wife and he begged them to come back to him. He could not be too aggressive with his students: we were all children of wealthy families and two of us were engaged to be married, and sported golden watches and chains. When he got mad at them, he was careful not to direct his anger at any one in particular but rather expressed it to us as a group. He honoured us with common nicknames: dimwit, ignoramus, hooligan, and other such titles. When he got really angry, he would let out his rage on the chair upon which he sat. He would suddenly stand up, grab the chair by the back, hold it tightly with both hands and start whacking the floor with it, and dance around the room. This would go on for several minutes until he had calmed down a little. Then he exhaled loudly, sat back down on the chair, and reopened the Gemara to continue teaching us.

24
SHIDUKHIM

Jewish economic life in Galicia was always uncertain. People who had done well for years and lived an upper-class existence suddenly became paupers due to unforeseen circumstances that they could not control or alter. This sort of thing was a daily occurrence common in big cities as well as smaller towns and even in the villages. A feeling of constant uncertainty led Galician Jewish parents of boys or girls aged 14 or 15 to feel a heavy burden on their shoulders. This feeling was accompanied by an urge to get rid of this burden as soon as possible through marriage, and wipe their hands of the matter. Among *frum* Jews, their religious worldview also played a part. This entailed marrying off young children to avoid moral lassitude, or strange and sinful thoughts, God forbid.

A young man like me—an orphan without a father and without a guide and mentor—was naturally a candidate for a speedy marriage. My mother, my brother Yehoshua and my sister-in-law had been concerning themselves with this matter since my arrival in Tarnow at the age of 14 and three months of age. I left my childhood behind and carried myself like a full-fledged *bokher*.

There were six *bokhrim* between 14 and 16 years of age at Reb Naftoli Reb Pesakh's, all of us upper class children and all of us in the process of *shidukhim*. It goes without saying that parents never spoke to their children about their proposed matches or about their prospects. Nonetheless, every boy sensed and understood what was in store for them: a word or a short conversation between the parents gave things away, or an older brother or sister "took pity" on them and let them know what was going on, or gave them a hint. There were also braggarts among the boys who secretly told their friends about matches that were being discussed with some wealthy man. These were usually lies because the matches they mentioned were much higher than the boys' actual social status.

A week rarely went by where one man, or two or three at once, did not turn up at our Rabbi's while we were sitting and studying. This was a *shadkhen*, an in-law, or both together wanting to have a look at the "investment" before anything more concrete happened. These men almost never spoke with us boys. Rather they consulted discreetly with the Rabbi, who was some kind of a partner in the match, and then went on their way. We all sat red-faced and swayed over our Gemaras. We did not know for certain which of us was in question. Our young blood boiled and seethed and we would have given up God-knows-what to know for certain which of us was in question. When the Rabbi left us alone or after our studies, we soon started to talk and one of us would tease someone that *he* was the one under discussion.

The *shadkhonim* soon set their sights on me. I was a tall, good-looking boy, from a renowned family of good pedigree, closely related to the most genteel families in Tarnow and with a dowry of a whole 1,000 gulden. These matchmakers saw a gem in me and talked all kinds of "*shmaltz*" to my mother. I also had a reputation as a boy with an aptitude for study (my reputation far exceeded my actual abilities) from the Big City as I came from Lemberg, and also as a bit of a *maskil* with nice handwriting to boot. How could this package not be snapped up?

As soon as I arrived to Tarnow and began to study with the Rabbi, I was presented with several matches from Tarnow proper. From a short conversation that I overheard between my mother and my sister-in-law, I discovered that they wanted to marry me off to [the daughter of a] wealthy tenant farmer from a village, or even to an actual owner of an estate. They saw a lot more opportunities for me there than in an urban match. I was very happy about this. First of all, I had read a lot about the beauty and comforts of village life in my Haskalah books (Mapu, Rabbi Moshe Chaim Luzzatto, Letteris, A. D. M. Ha-Cohen Levenson and many others). Secondly, I had never felt the slightest inclination to become a merchant. The trade and shady dealings that my mind conjured up had always been distasteful to me.

Once, a match from Tarnow was negotiated with a wealthy man who was a big egg-vendor. I knew nothing about this. I was even examined and I had no clue what was going on. My friend Yehudah Leibush Koretz told me that his former Rabbi, Reb Yudele Orshitzer, the *magid* in the city's *beys-medresh*, had heard that I was a *maskil* and that he had wanted to see me. My friend promised me that we would go and see Reb Yudele, and I did not suspect anything and agreed. We arranged to go on Friday afternoon. As I had suspected, Reb Yudele knew in advance that we were coming to see him. Thus, aside from him, a man of about 40 years of age was also there. I did not know him and did not pay much attention to him. Reb Yudele greeted us very amicably and soon engaged me in a conversation about various things. Then he asked with whom I was studying, as well as what. I responded and could see that he was pleased with my answers. Then he went to his bookcase and took out a big, thick *seyfer*. This was the renowed *Akeydes Yitskhok* (also known as the *Akeyde*), a commentary on the Torah based on careful research that the old *maskilim* and *maggidim* were always quibbling about. He asked whether I had ever read or looked at this book. Although I responded that I had not, he asked me to look at today's portion and recite the bit of interpretation that he indicated with his finger. The three of them left me alone with the *Akeyde*. It did not take very long until I was done. I recited the bit of text and he was very pleased. After he had offered us some fruit, we went home.

A few days later, I learned the big secret from my friend: this visit had been about a match for me. The man who was there with us was actually the girl's father and he had requested that Reb Yudele arrange my examination in front of him. Reb Yudele had warned Leibush not to tell me about this under threat of severe punishment. However, he could not keep the information hidden for long and soon revealed the big secret to me. After having seen and heard me, the egg merchant approved the match in principle. He sent his matchmakers to our house on several occasions. However, nothing came of it because my brother Yehoshua found out that the proposal was "exaggerated." When I found out about this later, I was really pleased. I was not at all keen on being an egg merchant.

Several other matches were proposed for me, this time with wealthy villagers. These were, however, unrefined upstarts of a very low social status, and my mother said that it would bring shame to my father's grave to have this kind of in-laws.

25
I Become a *Khosn* [Groom]

In Radomishla [Radomysl Wielki] ("*Groys* [Greater] Radomishla," near Tarnow, not to be confused with "*Kleyn* [Smaller] Radomishla," another *shtetl* near Rozvadov) there was a *shadkhen*, Reb Mendel Reb Berishes Geltzahler. He was, incidentally, the grandfather of the well-known poet and journalist, Reuben Iceland. This Reb Mendel would often travel to Tarnow and frequent the home of my rabbi, Reb Naftoli. When he first laid eyes on me, he was very taken with me and he decided that he had to make me a bridegroom at all costs. It did not take long for him to get his way.

It was an accepted custom for all matchmakers to lie. The nature of their "vocation" required of them to exaggerate and to tell the in-laws, who were always seeking the best possible prospects, things that stretched the truth and were patently false. I don't know if this Reb Mendel was an exception to this rule, but in the two or three matches that he proposed for me, he generally stuck pretty close to the truth as much as he could.

In the above-mentioned *shtetl* of Radomishla there lived an older, well-respected *balebos* by the name of Reb Yudl Shtiglitz, with sons and sons-in-laws. They were called "The Shtiglitzes" as a unit. He was not particularly wealthy or learned, but a very genteel and refined *balebos*. He traded in lumber, and his wife Nekhome, a great *eyshes khayel*, ran a tavern, which alone made them a good living. On top of this, they also traded with the "burghers," the urban gentiles who would travel to fairs across Galicia and buy up pigs. They would lend them money and earn good interest.

Their eldest son was Reb Mordecai Shtiglitz. He owned a big estate in the village of Zgursk [Zgurski], half a mile from Radomishla. Because Zgursk would play a considerable role in my life, I am going to write a little more about this village.

The village of Zgursk, along with several neighbouring villages and many forests, once belonged to the renowned Polish count, Osolinski. Because he was childless he left his large estate, in the form of cash and deeds for the property, for the public good. The renowned Osolinski Library in Lemberg was founded with these funds. He made his lands, with a special concession from the government, into a *fide commis*. This meant that they could never be sold or leased; they had to be administered by the families that he had specified in his will. As far as I know, these consisted of three families of Polish nobles: Broniovski, Bayer, and the royal Lubomirski family.

The lands and the forests, several thousand acres in total, were first to be given in trust to the Broniovski family for as long as there were male heirs. If the males died off, everything would be transferred to the Bayer family, and then finally to the Lubomirski family. The Osolinski Library was to receive just 350 gulden a year from the total estate.

The first Broniovski to take over the estate after Count Osolinski's death was a frugal person. He administered everything in good order like a true *balesbos*. When he died years later, he left his only son, Anton (Antek) over half a million gulden of capital in addition to the estate. This son was the exact opposite of his father: a big-time spendthrift and a major drinker. To top it all off, he was also something of a scatterbrain and given over to sensuality, like so many of the debauched Polish *pritsim*. Soon after his father's death, Antek left for Paris and other places, and began to live the high life. His holdings were administered by strangers. Before several years had passed, nothing was left of Antek's half a million gulden. The fortune had been squandered and vanished much more easily than it had been amassed. Antek did not alter his lifestyle, although it became a little less lavish; he now began to live off of the Osolinski estates, in particular the big old-growth forests. This enterprise, however, could not be sustained: the Polish administrators on the estates stole what they could, and it reached the point that there was nothing left to send Antek in Paris. There was not even enough money for the comparatively small sum of 350 gulden for the Osolinski Library. With no other choice remaining, Antek returned from Paris and settled in one of the estates in the village of Pshibish and became a *balebos*. However, he did not know how to manage the estates and forests, and he soon decided to lease the estates, one after the other, to Jews.

Didn't the *fide commis* expressly prohibit the lease of the estates? Well, there existed smart and shrewd lawyers who were able to find a solution. They simply analyzed the *fide commis* until they determined that that the estates could indeed be leased, for a single year. The contract simply had to be renewed every year. By the time they had reached this point, there were already Jews waiting to lease the estates. The contract was, in fact, only for a single year, but the *porets* had to be paid for a number of years upfront. There was a secret agreement with various safeguards in place that stipulated that the contract extended over a period of 12 years. Antek was, however, already the last male in the Broniovski line, and next in line after his death was the Bayer family, poor Polish nobility that had long been anticipating his demise. This placed all of the funds that the Jews paid in advance in jeopardy, the danger being that the Jews would have to leave the estates immediately after Antek's death. Of course, under these circumstances everything was at risk of being lost, and the estates had to be leased extremely cheaply. There were a very few who were initially interested. Only two Jews took a chance, gave the *porets* 15,000 gulden, and leased two estates.

Meanwhile Broniovski did *not* die. He also did not travel to Paris any more. Rather, he lived it up in Pshibish, and the two Jews became rich in the meantime. They were brothers-in-law of Reb Mordecai Dovid Shtiglitz, who was just then in the process of relinquishing one of his holdings with 25,000 gulden in capital and very good credit to boot. *Porets* Broniovski still "presided" over one estate, Zgursk, the best and the largest estate that he owned: over 1,000 acres of fertile land. He also became fed up with this estate and leased it to Shtiglitz in exchange for the entire 25,000 gulden. Shtiglitz made a very good, though risky, deal. The livestock and equipment as well as the grain included with the estate yielded a tidy profit. He also had to pay virtually no tribute for the next seven years. He earned back his 25,000 gulden in the first two years. Provided that Broniovski did not die, he was well on his way to becoming a very wealthy man with the biggest estate in the whole region. It was with this Reb Mordecai Dovid Shtiglitz, the possessor of the estate, that the matchmaker, Reb Mendel Berishes, proposed a match for me.

This match appealed to my mother and brother. My sister-in-law went to look at the bride and came back enchanted and enthusiastic about my great prospects. A week later, old Reb Yudel Shtiglitz and his *eyshes khayel*, Nekhome, came to visit us in Tarnow. They also brought along a fellow townsman of theirs, Reb Zelig Neuman, also known as "*Royter* (Red) Zelig." He had been a Gemara *melamed* in his youth, and was at the time a moneylender, and a very wealthy man. Reb Zelig examined me on a fair amount of Gemara and Tosephos as well as *Choshen Mishpat*, and the *halakhot* of *Toen ve-Nitan*. And for the "grand finale," he gave me a theme and had me compose a letter in *loshn-koydesh* right there on the spot. I passed the test with flying colours and did everything to their full satisfaction. Afterwards he said to the matchmaker, Reb Mendel, that if the Shtiglitzes did not hurry up and arrange the match, he would take me as bridegroom for his only daughter.

About two weeks later, we all arrived at the nearby train station in Tshorno. The entire Shtiglitz family was present. My retinue included several wealthy men, Reb Zechariah Mendel Aberdam and Reb Moshe Wexler. There I had the good fortune to become a groom, and upon my return I was wearing a big golden watch with a thick chain. Old Reb Yudel gave me a Serbian lottery ticket, and everyone wished me good luck in winning the big prize by the time of the wedding.

This was during the winter, around Chanukah-time. Seven months later, in Tammuz of 1882, when I was 16 years old minus four months, I got married. My mother and brother breathed easier. They had removed the heavy yoke from their heads and had brought me to a proper conclusion.

26
MY WEDDING

My wedding was celebrated with great pomp and circumstance. It was famous across the entire region and people were still recounting its marvels years later. My father-in-law, Reb Mordecai Dovid Shtiglitz, was a person who liked to do things in style and to show himself as a major proprietor. With two large estates under his charge, Zgursk and Yozefov, on top of which God had helped him unite with such genteel and esteemed families, he had cause to host lavish and extravagant festivities on this day.

Three entire feasts were prepared in honour of the wedding. The first dinner was the "*orime moltsayt* [Poor people's meal]." Over 100 poor Jews and beggars gathered with their wives and children. They came from quite a few miles away. A huge feast was prepared for them, a real wedding with *klezmorim* and *badkhonim*, except that the groom was not present. The guests ate and drank and partied the whole night until early the next morning. Upon their departure, everyone was given two big buns with roasted meat plus 20 kreuzer in cash. This bunch ate and drank so much all night that many were dead drunk and lay for hours in the garden or the surrounding fields.

The second feast was the "*pritsishe [porets's]*." Including the *Kaiserweg* [Imperial Road], Radomishla was only a half-mile from the Zgursk manor. In the town of Zgursk, there was a district courthouse and a tax office as well as financial offices and gendarmes. The Shtiglitz family got along well with these people. First, old Reb Yudel Shtiglitz had been functioning as assistant mayor for years. The elected mayor was a wealthy pig merchant who traveled for business and was rarely at home. Reb Yudel thus ran the city. He could speak Polish well but could not read or write, so the secretary would read all the letters and documents that arrived in the municipality to him, and Reb Yudel would make his Yiddish notes on the letters and other legal documents and then take care of them. In addition, all of the government officials were regular customers and frequenters of the "Pania Shtiglitzova's" tavern. With a feast and coaches sent for them, all of these people came with some of their neighbours from the surrounding estates, and they stayed and partied at the fantastic feast.

The third and main feast was on the day of the wedding. There were over 200 people present. These were all wealthy people and *balebatim* from Rado-mishla. There were also the local *sheyne yidn*, and notably all of the relatives from the mother-in-law's side, amounting to about 40–50 people in all.

There was a nasty situation between two in-laws due to a family dispute. Reb Mordecai Dovid Shtiglitz had a brother-in-law, Yoske Chaim, also a wealthy leaser of land, in the nearby village of Pshibish. These two brothers-in-law were embroiled in a feud at the time. So, when Yoske found out that Mordecai Dovid had chosen the day for his daughter's wedding, he chose the same day for his daughter's wedding out of spite. The whole family intervened and appealed to Yoske to postpone the wedding to another week, but he was a man who was tough as nails and nothing could be done to convince him. So the unfortunate family had to tear itself apart and dance at two weddings on the same night.

My father-in-law sent four carriages with the best "Zugov" horses to Tarnow to bring me to the wedding. I was escorted by Rabbi Naftoli Reb Pesakh's and three young men who were my friends, as well as several wealthy men from Tarnow from my sister-in-law's family. When we finally arrived in Radomishla in the middle of the day, all of the carriages were driven around the town's marketplace three times to a great cracking of whips while the whole *shtetl* crowded to watch and admire us.

27
AFTER THE WEDDING

A new and completely unknown world opened up for me when I arrived and stayed in the village. The wedding hoopla had passed. My mother, who stayed with me for another week, returned to Tarnow. And I, the young man of 16, remained alone with my wife for three years of *kest* with my mother- and father-in-law.

Initially I did not really know my bride; we had only seen each other and talked very little during the engagement ceremony, and then not even exchanged a letter. However, as soon as we got to know each other better after the wedding, we became as intimate and loving as if we had known one another for many years. This heartfelt love has continued to this day, thank God, for over fifty years and will remain until the end of our lives.

When I got married, my father-in-law, Reb Mordecai Dovid Shtiglitz, was a man of barely forty years of age. He had eight children. My wife, Rokhl-Leye, was his second daughter. His older daughter, Eydl, had gotten married two years earlier to a fine young man, Berl Lev from Shendishov. My mother-in-law's family was quite sizable, spread out, and rich to boot. All of them made their livings by managing lands and leasing estates of various sizes.

My mother-in-law's father, Reb Yisroel Lind, whom I never met, had been a tenant innkeeper in the village of Rida near Radomishla. That was during the time when there were no trains yet in Galicia and all of the oxen that were sold at the big fairs of Olmütz, Brünn and Vienna were herded over certain pre-specified routes. Yisroel Rider's inn was on the highway that thousands of oxen traversed each week. As a result, this inn was the oxen stop and resting place. They were fed hay, purchased from the innkeeper, and were given water. The oxen trade was huge at the time and was completely in Jewish hands. Many people were employed in the trade. Aside from the non-Jews who drove the oxen, Jews accompanied the transports, and functioned as trustees, cashiers, and bookkeepers. Everyone traveled in fine carriages, especially the merchants who would often follow along in order to sell the oxen at the fairs. All of these people who would pass through Rida and stop there, or spend the night in the inn, spent a lot of money. Yisroel the innkeeper spent many years at the inn and became rich.

When trains were later introduced to Galicia and oxen were no longer driven but transported by train, all of this prosperity dried up at once. It thus no longer paid for the innkeeper to remain in the village. Since he already had a lot of money, he leased large estates for himself, his children, sons and sons-in-laws (about 10 in total). They were all adept in looking after their lands and were very successful. Almost none of his children and grandchildren lived in town; rather they lived in the villages and leased—and later purchased—estates. There was a period during my time when his children and grandchildren held a total of twenty-two estates of various sizes simultaneously, all of them close to Radomishla. Incidentally, during my time, Reb Yisroel was known as Yisroel Kelkiover. He was no longer known by the name of the village of Rida, but by his biggest estate, Kelkiov, that he had held for years and then passed on to this youngest son, Moshe Lind, who lived as opulently as a real noble. If one of Reb Yisroel Kelkiover's sons or sons-in-law was marrying off a child, a piece of land to lease was soon arranged for him.

My father-in-law, who was considered a very wealthy man at the time, did the same thing. When he settled in Zgursk on Broniovski's large estate, he still held a small estate from before, Konietz at Pshezlov, near Radomishla. This was a small estate but had very fertile soil that earned a lot of money every year. His first son-in-law, Berl Lev, a city boy, knew nothing about estate matters. Like me, he understood almost no Polish. But his young wife, Eydl, was a very skillful housewife and a highly efficient person, and it was to her that her father handed over the management of the Konietz property. However, she remained there only one year. The contract expired and her father leased a much bigger estate for her, Yozefov, which consisted of about 450 acres of good earth. He invested over 20,000 gulden of capital in it.

Reb Mordecai Dovid Shtiglitz was a very good and trustworthy father and always went above and beyond his capabilities for his children. However, he never expressed his love for anyone. He was a very strict and rigid character and everyone, even those closest to him, trembled before him and made sure that they did not spend a single extraneous moment in his presence. He also enjoyed receiving respect and was very proud. Everything he expressed had to be implemented immediately.

28

VILLAGE WORK

When I arrived in the village, it was summer and harvest-time. This was a major enterprise with thousands of acres of land plus many head of cattle. There were about 40 sturdy workhorses and the same number of work-oxen, about 70–80 milk cows, as well as many young: about 200 animals in total. There were about 20 male and about 10 female peasants who were all contracted for the full year, along with room and board in the gentile kitchen located in the manor yard. Things were cooking: it had been a very good year. A lot of grain and grass had grown, and hundreds of cutters and other workers were engaged in harvesting it from the fields, bringing it into the barns, or laying down big bales.

As I stated earlier, my father-in-law had eight children at the time. Of these the eldest daughter, Eydl, was already living on her own estate, Yozefov, a mile away from Zgursk. All of the children aside from the two littlest ones were busy all day supervising the workers in the fields and in the barns, and all of them were extremely adept.

The first days after my wedding (during the *Shivas yemei hamishte* [the Seven Days of Celebration]), my young wife was home and did not take part in the harvest. My mother stayed with us a week after the wedding. However, as soon as my mother returned home, my wife ceased to be a bride and joined everyone in the daily toil. She did not go into the fields or barns to supervise, probably on account of me. But she had her hands full in the manor yard proper, in the kosher and gentile kitchens, and was kept busy from morning until evening. My father-in-law's holdings as well as the family were unfamiliar with the concept of idly hanging around doing nothing.

The prime example of unflagging industry was my mother-in-law. I was repeatedly amazed at how this skinny and small-boned woman found the energy to work so much. At 4:00 AM (much earlier in the summertime), she was already on her feet. She woke up the gentile cook to light the fire and set up the big pots of cooked food for the farmhands and the maids. Then she went with these women to milk the cows, and when all of the many cows had been milked, she supervised the transport of the milk into town to her relative, Yosele Riglitzer, who was her regular buyer. As soon as she had taken a little coffee, which she called "*Brove*," and had something to eat, she drove with the workers into the fields to the various tasks, and she would spend the entire day there until after sunset. Then she did the evening milking of the cows. She simply could not sit idle. If there was nothing to do, she found some kind of work. In the winter, for example, when each day the grain was threshed by machine or by hand (with *tsepes* [handheld threshers]). She had a lot to do on Sundays dealing with the many sacks that had torn during the course of the week. Aside from all of this, she was also mother to 10 or 11 children (three died in childhood), and having and raising that many little children must also have required a lot of time, effort and exertion.

The manor yard was always bustling like a country fair. My wife had to supervise everything and keep everyone happy as much as possible. The Zgursk manor yard lay right next to the *Kaiserweg* (Imperial Road), half a mile from Radomishla and a mile and a half from Melitz.

* * *

This was truly the main road, and itinerant paupers were constantly wandering through. A day rarely passed that 10–15 poor Jews did not appear in the manor yard. These vagrants would often wander in whole families: man and wife, several small children, and sometimes even infants at the breast. Every poor person that came to the manor yard received in a generous portion of hot food, and a big piece of bread for the road, along with two kreuzer in alms. They were just not allowed to spend the night in the manor yard; their ranks included a lot of undesirable people and thieves. They were sent away to the nearby inn, or if space was short, to the "*Hekdesh* [Poorhouse]" in Radomishla.

67

My mother-in-law was a very charitable woman. Quite a few poor Jews in Radomishla and Rzokhow received regular support from her. She sent them cheese, butter, grain, and other food, as well as cash. There were also several *sheyne yidlekh* in Radomishla: Reb Yisroel Poylisher, Reb Shmuel Yosel, and two or three others, whom she often sent entire sacks of grain so that they would have flour to bake bread. On *Erev Peysekh* (Passover Eve), several landholders from the Kelkiov family would send entire wagons of potatoes for the poor. For the "secret poor," they sent sacks home. There was also no shortage of *sheyne yidlekh* descendents of Hassidic *rebbes*, and regular recipients [of community charity for their upkeep]. Some of them had their own horses and wagons and were often on the road. They also received their allotments in the Zgursk manor yard: a *renish* (a gulden) and sometimes more. They also got hay for their horses. My wife supervised all of this, and it kept her busy from the early morning until late in the evening. Initially I was left to my own devices, and not assigned any work, so I sat in the manor yard and perused the books that I had brought from Tarnow, and wrote letters to my family and friends.

29
I Get "Shot"

In the first two or three weeks after my wedding, I did nothing: I spent time in the garden and ate a lot of fruit. Right by the gates of the manor yard in Zgursk lay a fine, sprawling garden full of different fruit trees. During the time that *Porets* Broniovski had administered the place, he had a special, trained "*ogrodnik* (gardener)," along with two or three helpers who were constantly at work tending each tree individually and almost pulling the flowers by their heads to grow faster and more beautifully. My father-in-law naturally did not think much of this kind of nonsense and he did not keep a gardener. My mother-in-law set aside a corner in the garden for the very young calves. The only flowers that grew there any more were wildflowers, but fruit trees produce fruit without the help of a gardener, and I was constantly drawn to them. Until my wedding, I had never been in a fruit garden, and it opened a new, glorious and wondrous world for me: take and eat as much as your heart desires! I took and ate my fill.

I was slender, wiry, small-boned and tall, and thus easily able to learn how to climb the highest trees. I sat for hours in the branches of the cherry trees, sour-cherry trees, pear trees, and apple trees. I did not care if the fruits were ripe enough or not. I sat in the trees and shook the branches with a long stick, broke a lot of them, and greatly enjoyed the beautiful and tasty fruits. Soon after my wedding I neglected the Gemara and seldom opened it, although I did still peruse my *loshn-koydesh* books. Every second day, I wrote a letter to my mother: I had been forced to give my word. However, as soon as it was nice outside, I sat in the trees and ate fruit. My stomach and digestive system must have been pretty tough; if not, there is no way that I would have been able to pack away that much fruit. My father-in-law and his household observed all of this and did not bother me. They just laughed and told me that I would eat so much fruit that I would eventually not even be able to look at it. At the time, I was far from it.

On one occasion, my father-in-law played a joke on me that could have caused me great injury. As usual, I was sitting among the thick, tall branches and eating fruit. My father-in-law, who was at home, noticed this. Because he was in a good mood, he had the urge to scare me a little. So he took the loaded gun that always hung over his bed and took a shot through the window. The loud bang threw me to the ground virtually unharmed. However, when I spotted my father-in-law standing at the window and holding his sides laughing, I almost burst into tears of agitation and chagrin. My wife soon came running to me in the garden and was barely able to calm me down. I "protested" and wanted to return home to my mother immediately. My wife was not in a position to reprimand her father, but when my mother-in-law returned from the field that night, my wife gave her a whole sob story that I wanted to leave her and return home. My mother-in-law marched over to her *"kol-boynik"* ["scoundrel"] (this was what she called him when she was angry) to settle things: why was he bothering the "child" for nothing? He did not answer her much and would not stop laughing.

I did not talk to him for whole week until we gradually made up. My mother-in-law liked me a lot. She repeatedly told her children and relatives that I was more important to her than her very own estate. This was at a time when two of her brothers already owned their own vast estates. You can well imagine that I did not go home. I also did not mention the whole incident in my letters home to my mother. A few days later my mother-in-law handed me 10 gulden, without my even asking:

"Here you go. Your father-in-law is giving you this to buy some of those books that you like to read so much." I sent the money to Aaron Faust, the book vender in Krakow, and I soon forgot the whole incident. I also rarely climbed the trees after that point. When the fruits were ripe, they fell on their own. The season for those wonderful grapes and red gooseberries was also approaching: they grow on low shrubs and one can simply bend down and eat them. If I did feel the desire to climb a tree, I was careful to do it when my father-in-law was not at home, especially on Thursdays when he would drive to the local market days in Radomishla or Melitz. Then I was the boss and sole-ruler over the big garden and did whatever my heart desired.

30
I GET "BOUND"

I got married during *Rosh khoydesh* Tammuz and a few weeks later it was time for the harvest. The holdings in Zgusk, as I have already said, were vast and consisted of about 1,000 acres of very good soil. On top of this, it was a very successful year; my mother-in-law said that I brought them luck. A vast quantity of grain grew along with various grasses and clovers. Great numbers of workers toiled hard in the fields, often several hundred each day. The usual workers from the surrounding villages did not suffice; others had to be drawn from among the mountain peasants. These were poor peasants from the mountains around Tarnow and the Sanz region. Wagons were sent for them and they came along with their wives and children to spend the entire summer. They did not cut the grains with the usual sickles but used scythes instead. They charged a lot more than the local peasants: two gulden per day for a husband and wife. They also had to receive provisions to cook for themselves. It paid off, however, because they were good, quick workers. The main jobs, however, were carried out by the regular local male and female peasants. My mother-in-law had her own cadre of female peasants whom she would not exchange for anything. She would often oblige them with a few extra kreuzer and an extra shot of liquor.

The Zgursk fields all lay on only one side of the manor yard. They did not lie in the direction of Radomishla, but rather extended a considerable way the other way, almost to Wadovitz. Each separate field was over 100 square acres, and was cultivated with only one kind of grain, rye, wheat, barley, or oats. When the grain growing on one of these fields was ready to be harvested, several hundred cutters or choppers were needed.

The regular wages for these workers differed widely and depended on the time of the year and the nature of the work. In the winter, when there was nothing to do but the daily threshing of grain, the wages for an adult male amounted to 16 ½ kreuzer per day. This amounted to half a "*Tsvantsiker* [20]," a currency no longer in existence but that was still used by farmers for their calculations. A good-sized adult woman received 15 kreuzer, while the smaller ones received 12. However, in the spring, the wages rose suddenly and peaked during the harvest, when even the women were paid 60 kreuzer a day. These high wages attracted large numbers of farmers from very far away. There were also those who came daily on foot—in rare cases they were sent for with wagons—a mile in total both ways, if a certain manor paid five or ten kreuzer more than their local manor. During the height of the season or during the potato harvest, the cutters also received liquor twice a day. These day labourers were usually very

70

lazy and sought to pass the day with as little work as possible. They thus had to be supervised and not let out of sight the entire day.

My mother-in-law, together with the help of her children and several hired Jewish and gentile overseers, were constantly encouraging the workers with endless shouting:

"*Zhni! Zhni! Zhni!*" (Cut! Cut! Cut!)

In order to speed up the work and better supervise the workers, she divided them into several sections, with 40–50 people in each place. The pace of the work depended on the *"pshdovnik"* [team leader], the first cutter, who set the pace for everyone else. If the work was being done by a speedy cutter, the other worker had no choice but to keep up and not fall behind too much.

Each manor had its top and most experienced workers,—usually big, diligent peasant women—who were employed as *"pshdovnikes."* They received a few extra kreuzers every day, and were aristocrats in their own circles. Even during slow times when there was not much too do in the manor and a lot of other workers were sent home, work was always found for these *"pshdovnikes."*

* * *

Once, as wheat was being cut in a far-off field, my wife invited me to accompany her because she wanted to bring a bit of dinner to her mother who had been out since early that morning. It was about 11:00 AM when we got to the field. The whole field was full of people: there were over 200 cutters there at the time. My mother-in-law was at the head of the first workers, all of whom were half-naked and barefoot. My wife handed her the pot of food and my mother-in-law stepped aside. My wife took her place and began to shout:

"*Zhni! Zhni! Zhni!*"

I stood next to her in my long *bekeshe,* and satin cap. I was not yet wearing short coats as there was fear in the village that my mother would find out and complain that I had been turned into a "German." So I stood there and chatted with my wife.

All of a sudden, before I had the chance to look around, one of the peasant women, the *"pshdovnike,"* herself, came running to me, and bound me tightly in a piece of rope woven out of cut wheat. I stood there, in my long black cloak, bound with a straw *"povrosla* [trap]." At first I had no idea what was going on. But my wife and all of the workers began to shriek with laughter and they explained to me that this was an old peasant custom: when a guest comes to visit the field, he is immediately bound and must be ransomed. Before this, the *"povrosla"* cannot be removed. My wife redeemed me from these peasant hands with a whole gulden and in honour of her *"novi zhents"* ["new son-in-law"], my mother-in-law ordered that all of the workers be given liquor on top of the drink they had already received with breakfast, and more in the evening at their *"pod-vietshorek"* [supper].

Over the next week or two, wherever I went to observe the various village duties, I was constantly being "bound" and I had to pay ransom money, although not a full gulden like the first time. In the end, I got away with 20 or 30 kreuzer.

31
RIDING A HORSE

As soon as I arrived in the village, I had the burning desire to ride a horse. Actually, I had had this desire even longer, ever since becoming a bridegroom. As soon as he proposed the match, Reb Mendel Reb Berishes the *shadkhen* felt it necessary to point this out as a benefit. I don't even know what my mother, brother, and sister-in-law thought of this, but I was thrilled about it and looked forward to finally having this wish fulfilled. In truth, I was still really afraid of horses at the time. Whenever I had seen a horse in Lemberg or Tarnow, I had always moved out of its way; when a horse lifted its tail or kicked with its hind leg, I simply fled. However, I understood that this was a silly fear, and that if I ever had the opportunity, I would be able to handle a horse as well as anyone else. My friends at Reb Naftoli Reb Pesakh's and the other Kloyz-*bokhrim* were jealous of me for having such a bucolic existence and always being able to ride around on a horse like a real *porets*, or being able to drive around in my own carriage: things that they would never get to do.

A few days after my wedding, as soon as my mother had left (she would certainly not have let me anywhere near a horse out of fear that it would kick me), I began to hang around horses. I avoided the horses standing in their stalls or working in the field and opted for those that were harnessed to the heavy *britzkas* [carriage] and driven around.

My father-in-law, unlike his brothers-in-law, liked to live opulently and he always drove around on a rig as fancy as the greatest *porets* in the area. He was called the "Baron" as a joke. He had a pair of fancy horses that alone cost him the enormous sum of 600 gulden and were valued at even more. One of them was a gelding and the other was a stallion. My first acquaintance with horses was with these two animals. When I first laid eyes on them, I was instantly drawn to them, and my greatest wish at that time was to have the privilege of riding them, or at least to be their coachman.

I gradually become accustomed to these horses. At first I gave them lumps of sugar, although I was still afraid that the horses would bite me. Despite their high price and speed, these two horses were friendly creatures: they never bit me and permitted my increasingly bold strokes. I would pet them on their manes and they did not protest.

* * *

My wife had a brother who was just about two years younger than me: he was about 16 at this time, and his name was Mikhl. Mikhl was a good-natured and very trustworthy guy. He took a liking to me at our first meeting and we remained friends until he died. He was the most refined and educated of my father-in-law's sons; my father-in-law had invested a lot of money on him. He paid for him to study with a *melamed* in Radomishla, and later in Tarnow: the reputation of this teacher, Yudl Hayman, spanned the entire area. Mikhl was eager to learn *loshn-koydesh* as well as a little German. There was no one to teach him these subjects in Radomishla, although later on, a religion teacher by the name of Blumenkrantz, would offer private lessons. I started to teach Mikhl. He did not have much of a head for learning, but he was really motivated and struggled through [Friedrich] Schiller's *Kabale und Liebe*, with me having to explain every sentence. So I became Mikhl's language instructor and he became mine: in horseback riding.

Although there were 40–50 horses in the Zgursk Manor, none was suited to riding. Any horse can be ridden, but there is a difference between riding and *riding*. The arrangement with the horses was as follows: Every team of four horses (*a fornalke*) had its own attendant who ploughed or rode them. He oversaw them, fed them, and made sure that they remained in top shape. These horses were a reflection of the attendant and he crowed if they looked good. It was impossible to take a horse away from one of these farmhands for the purpose of riding. The horses worked day-in and day-out and rested on Sundays, and there was no way he was going to lend one out for riding. This left only the two "special" horses, the finest and the nicest in the manor, for riding. They never worked harnessed up; they were driven around, and only my father-in-law would occasionally ride one of them to a distant field. Mikhl and I set our sights on these two horses.

Their attendant was a young and handsome peasant called Yendrek. He rode the "special" horses and was their groom. Yendrek was a perpetual *"pan potshebovski"* [big spender] and always needed money. Although he received his tips whenever he drove someone somewhere, he was always "short." He had several girlfriends whom he bought gifts every time he was in Tarnow. We bribed Yendrek; that is, not I, who could barely communicate with him, but Mikhl. He would often give him 10, 20, or more kreuzer to give us his horses for riding.

It was no big deal to learn.

I had long since traded my long cloak for a short jacket. For the winter, my father-in-law had a very fine coat made for me, lined with black fur, along with a fancy lambskin hat to match, and my cloak was left hanging in the closet. I only wore it when I drove into town or when some respected Jews or a *sheyner yid* came to the manor, and my father-in-law introduced his new and "virtuous" son-in-law.

These two horses—the gelding as well as the stallion—were big and wide, but very comfortable and good-natured. They almost never struggled when they were being ridden. They simply did not feel the light load of both Mikhl and myself.

So, we had our horses for riding; what we lacked was opportunity. My father-in-law could not bear the thought of someone touching "his" horses; if he found out, he would give Yendrek savage beatings. However, our money was more powerful. Yendrek happily accepted the tips and often turned a blind eye when we were with the horses.

Initially, when I was not proficient yet, I learned how to ride when the horses were taken to be watered. The Zgursk Manor was located on a hill and at the foot flowed a small but clean stream. The attendants would lead their horses there to drink or to wash them off. That is where I would ride the two "special horses," sometimes alone and other times with Mikhl. This would have been less of a sin in the eyes of my father-in-law, had he ever witnessed it.

I soon learned all there was to know about riding and was able to sit properly on a horse. I later became such a good rider that we would take the horses out for a ride at night, after both my father-in-law and Yendrek were in bed. We rode without saddles and even without reins; we used only the long chain that ties the horse to the cart, thrown over its snout, and the horses responded to the lightest pull on the chain. Especially by night with the frost crackling underfoot, we would get on the horses and have a "go" for half or even a whole mile, just behind Melitz, or we would hop over to our brother-in-law, Berel's, in Yozefov.

But our riding did not always go smoothly.

Once, when I was riding away from the water and crossing the bridge that leads to the stall, the horse suddenly slipped and I found myself with my leg pinned under the big, heavy horse. I could not get up. I had to be carried into the manor yard and laid on my bed. The leg soon became so swollen that my boot could not be removed and it had to be cut off with a knife. I had to spend several days in bed until the swelling went down. My father-in-law did not get angry with me; he simply said with a smile:

"Good for you! I have my revenge. Don't ride horses!" But he did not stay cheerful about it forever. Once, Mikhl and I were riding behind Melitz and because we were in hurry to get home, we did not mind the horses and drove them "at top speed." The heavy and large-boned horses were soon covered with sweat. The next day Yendrek overslept and failed to brush the horses in time to hide the evidence of their nighttime sweat. On that very day, my father got up early and entered the horse-stall. When he saw the horses, in their sorry state with their entire "*shertsh*" [hair] glued to their bodies, he became enraged. After he had given Yendrek a good beating, he marched into my bedroom and shouted angrily:

"Yoshe, since you have married my daughter, you can consider yourself my partner. But you are not a partner with the 'special' horses!"

He also caught us committing this serious sin on another occasion. He did not see me so he didn't say anything, but he met Mikhl in the manor yard and wanted to catch him to give him a beating. Mihkl spun around and rode several times around the well until he finally headed out onto the *Kaiser-shtroz* [Imperial Highway]. My father-in-law chased him but saw that he would not be able to catch him. So he grabbed a handful of small stones that were lying in the dirt on the road and threw them after him. Afterwards, all of us, including my father-in-law, laughed our heads off about it.

It was easier to petition my mother-in-law to let us ride on the precious horses. The Zgursk fields bordered the Polish fields of Wadovitz. There was a wide strip of earth between the two fields several cubits in size that was a no-man's land, and was only used as an access road between the fields. No one was allowed to graze livestock on this road, or "Border," as it was called. Because a lot of grass grew on this road, the farmers were not vigilant and their animals did end up grazing there. My mother-in-law would not stand for this because the Polish shepherds did a lot of damage to our fields. So she would send her supervisors, her "*karbovnikes*," to chase the animals away or seize them so that the owner had to come into the manor yard and ask for them back.

When my father-in-law was away and Mikhl and I wanted to do a little horseback riding, we easily appealed to our mother-in-law: we convinced her that we would ride to the border and have a look at what was going on. She was always willing, and asked us to seize ("arrest") any trespassing animal.

This is what once happened to me: Mikhl was not home and I rode to the border alone. I found several stray animals there, and because the shepherd was a young boy of six or seven (I would have been afraid of anyone bigger), I decided to "confiscate" at least one sheep and bring it to our manor yard to show off my "heroism." I got off the horse, left it standing in the middle of the field, and went running to catch a sheep. I did not succeed because the shepherd gave one whistle and, because they were already "weary," they came running to him from all sides. With no other choice, I returned to the horse to ride home and to recount to my mother-in-law the tremendous deed that I had almost accomplished. But as soon as I got to the horse and was about to grab it by the bridle, the horse got a fright and began to run whinnying madly, and it fled, with the saddle and bridle dragging on the ground, back to the manor yard. I was left standing in the middle of the field, at least half a mile from the manor yard. I had no other choice but to get home on foot. However, when the horse returned directly into the stall and the peasants saw that I was not there, they immediately told my mother-in-law. Everyone was sure that I had been thrown off the horse and who knew what could have happened to me.

I had a sister-in-law, a girl of about eight years of age, who could not pronounce some words very clearly, so she called:

"Good thing that the *saddidle* (saddle) was not lost!"

This is how I learned to ride, and I got to know as much about it as a born villager. Later, when I became a *balebos* with my own holdings, especially on the Shtsustiner Meadows, I would spend entire days on horseback, like a real officer.

32
I Become a Merchant

When I got married, I possessed a dowry of over 4,500 gulden. I had my own 1,000 gulden as my inheritance from my father, *zikhroyno livrokho,* and the rest was my wife's. *Porets* Broniovski, whose estates were held by my father- and brothers-in-law, lived in close proximity to my father-in-law, and would often come and visit him.

Soon after my wedding he came by, and sitting outside in his carriage, told my father-in-law that he wanted to meet his "*novi zhents*" [new son-in-law]. When I was called over and presented to him, he greeted me and congratulated me, in German. He understood all too well that someone like me could barely speak any Polish at all. He also sent my wife 25 gulden as a wedding gift. This particular *porets* knew that I had several thousand gulden of dowry money and greatly desired it. Unfortunately, he had nothing to offer for the money: all of his estates were already leased out to other Jews for periods of many years, and the best and thickest forests had already been stripped by Jews from Melitz, leaving nothing left to sell.

However, once during the winter several months after my wedding while I was still in *kest* in Zgursk, the *Porets's* debts caught up with him, and he desperately needed at least a couple of hundred gulden. He sent for my father-in-law, whom he called "*Panye Baron* [Mister Baron]" in jest, and asked after me: did I have some kind of occupation? My father-in-law responded that I was still too young for business and still had two or three years ahead of me before I undertook anything.

The *Porets* proposed the following plan to him: he would sell me several hundred fathoms of wood in the nearby Piontkovitz Forest, half a mile from Melitz and a mile and a half from Radomshila. He did not even have the fathoms yet and the Melitz *Bezirkshauptmanschaft* [district] had strictly forbidden him to harvest any trees because the forest was still young and the old trees had been cut down. But a Polish *porets* has no regard for such prohibitions, especially when he desperately needs money. He presented the plan to my father-in-law: he would go into the forest with some peasants and cut down trees as long as he was allowed, and the governor of the province would not find out and interfere. Later, the trees would be stacked in fathoms that I could collect for my money. Meanwhile he would need at least 500 gulden. They soon agreed on a price: three gulden per fathom and I had to cover all expenses relating to the tree cutting and the stacking of the fathoms.

I soon traveled to Tarnow and withdrew five hundred gulden from my executor, Reb Moshe Wexler, deposited them with *Porets* Broniovski, and lucky me became a lumber merchant. My mother and brother were very pleased, and it made them especially happy to see that I was showing such an affinity for trade. A week later the *karbovnikes* were dispatched from the manor yard to the nearby towns to call for peasants to appear the next day to cut down trees in the Piontkovitz Forest. They would be paid 80 kreuzer for their labour. The following day, Monday, there were about 200 peasants with their axes cutting trees, but only those that were at least 10–12 inches around.

I, together with my father-in-law, drove into the forest. There was, however, nothing for us to do: the peasants were given several glasses of liquor throughout the day and they were cutting down trees. It was just plain dangerous to be in the forest: so many trees were being cut down. The process of cutting took two-and-a-half days. On the third day, they came from the office of the governor of Melitz along with several gendarmes and all of the peasants were chased out of the forest. However, enough trees had been cut down to make several hundred fathoms. Now the work of stacking the fathoms began. Usually one of these fathoms is two meters high and two meters wide. About 20 centimeters are added to the height because the fathoms settle into the ground and lose their true size. However, because we were the bosses in the forest and were stacking the fathoms ourselves, we devised the following plan: We made the "*yazmes*" (the measure by which one stacks the wood) a few centimeters bigger and wider. In this way, each fathom came out much larger and was worth at least a full gulden more.

We hired a Jew not far from the forest to help me supervise the forest-workers, and I drove down every day to see how things were progressing. We also had several piles of branches that had fallen from the trees, and we began to sell these for a gulden a pile. Every day the forest was full of peasants who came with their wagons for these piles.

I was not a lumber merchant for long. I found the whole business tedious. My father-in-law and wife did not care for it much; they figured that it was beneath my dignity to devote myself to this sort of work.

We soon found a taker. Another young man from Radomishla, also on *kest*, bought everything from me and gave me a couple of hundred gulden in profit, and my career as a lumber merchant came to a close. Still, the two to three months that I spent in the forest were extremely valuable for me. I began to circulate among people and slowly picked up enough Polish to be able to talk to anyone. This was a very necessary introduction to becoming a villager and future leaseholder.

33
YOZEFOV

I spent the best ten years of my life in the village of Yozefov. I will therefore write a little more expansively on the subject.

The village and estate of Yozefov were located about a mile from Zgursk (and a mile and a quarter from the *shtetl* of Shtsutsin [Szczucin]). It consisted of about 450 acres of land for plowing and planting grain, and about 150 acres of pasture below that, where hay and grasses grew on their own. The whole estate was located in a low-lying region between streams and was difficult to cultivate, but at the same time extremely well suited to wheat. The owner of all of this was a "German" Jew by the name of Wilhelm Damask who lived in Krakow and administered the estate at his own expense. We will see what kind of person this Herr Damask was later. He was a very peculiar type of old *maskil* and a pain in the neck to boot.

Yozefov had a reputation as a fine estate: it was not far from Budzin, where Uncle Shimen Sandhaus, a brother-in-law of my father-in-law's, had his holdings. This uncle was thus very familiar with it. When my father-in-law needed a holding for his daughter Eydl and her husband Berl Lev, Uncle Shimen got to work and acted as broker for this particular estate. The deal was sealed. The price was 4,000 gulden for one year. Although the price was not too high, the conditions were, as it would later become apparent, unfavourable. This had a major impact on the business as a whole.

The accepted custom when an estate was taken over, usually in the summer, was for the fields to be already cultivated and sown with all kinds of summer and winter grain. This meant that the lessee would find a ready income. When the lease ended, he had to return it ploughed and sown in preparation for his successor. This meant that not too much capital had to be poured into a holding—several thousand gulden at most—and one was ready for business.

This is not how my father-in-law arranged matters in Yozefov. The owner, Herr Damask, was a very underhanded person and he "pulled a fast one on him." My father-in-law took possession in the spring, when the winter grains had long been sown, but the spring work had not even been started yet. He paid Damask in "hard cash" for the entire winter's work and undertook the cultivation of the estate for the summer himself. Thus, with God's help, when the contract ended 12 years later, he would have to return the whole state uncultivated for his successor to begin from scratch, at his own expense. This was the only estate in the entire region that was leased under these conditions. My father-in-law figured that in 12 years, when the already elderly Damask had passed away and the estate was left uncultivated, he would be able to purchase it for a song.

Meanwhile, he had to pay for everything upfront and this amounted to a small fortune. Damask also sold him his livestock and equipment and so my father-in-law invested a sum of over 12,000 gulden in this not overly large estate. In addition, the contract was faulty and included several very unfavourable points. My father-in-law had not paid attention when the contract had been drawn up, but later everything turned out for the worst. Herr Damask, a pettifogger and big-time swindler, understood how to write a contract like this one. Hidden behind obfuscating words and omitted phrases lay conditions that seemed really innocuous in theory, but posed great difficulties to the leaseholder in practice.

There were several buildings, barns, stables, and granaries as well as other structures, but all in a very poor and neglected condition. Instead of seeing to it that everything be put into working condition at the owner's expense, my father-in-law had authorized a point on the contract that stated that Damask was only responsible for restoring the buildings if they were *completely* ruined. Initially, my father-in-law did not understand what that entailed, but when the issue came up, Damask stuck by the term *complete ruination*; to him this meant that a building was collapsing all at once, or was destroyed by fire or wind. Those buildings kept us busy during the entire 12-year period that we held Yozefov. There had to be constant repairs or the buildings would have been unusable. These cost hundreds of gulden a year. Moreover, the soil was shallow and the ditches were in terrible shape. We often had to spend hundreds of gulden a year to keep the fields from being covered in water so that they could be ploughed and sown. My father-in-law was savvy in his dealings with *Porets* Broniovski, but this Herr Damask was much more clever and cunning than him and swindled him soundly. No matter how good a year it was, we in Yozefov had expenses that other landholders never had, and they ate up our entire profit.

Another man would not have lasted three to four years in Yozefov. My father-in-law, however, had a very profitable business in Zgursk and had money he could afford to lose. He took possession of the estate in March and my brother-in-law, Berl Lev, moved in. He was not born lucky, as my mother-in-law used to put it. His young wife, Eydl, who was very clever and a consummate businesswoman,

79

soon took ill and was unable to recover. She paid this no mind and always worked herself to the bone. On top of this, she already had two small children at the time. She was a very intelligent woman and she understood early on that her father had been duped leasing Yozefov. But because her father was a strict person and no one dared to tell him anything that contradicted him, she opted to keep quiet and worked way above and beyond what her strength permitted.

The upshot was that she had to be treated by doctors. A year and a half after my wedding, she was so sick that she had to leave the village and travel to the city for treatment: she had already been diagnosed with a heart defect at that time. In the middle of winter, she left for her in-laws' in Shendishov, and she never returned. She died there after several months of illness and left behind a husband with two tiny children.

When Eydl left Yozefov, we were told that the whole thing would take a few weeks and my wife went there, together with me, to deal with the business. When Eydl died, we stayed in Yozefov permanently and took over the holding.

My father-in-law never kept accounts when it came to his children; his attitude was always "what is mine is yours and yours is mine." He never nickeled and dimed. When Berl Lev took over Yozefov, his name was not on the contract; only my father-in-law's was. He did not calculate how much money he had invested in the holding. Instead, he gave him back the few thousand gulden of dowry and cleared his account. When Berl left, accounts were not settled with him; he stayed in the family. He married a younger sister of Eydl's, and when he settled in town in Radomishla, my father-in-law handed him his entire dowry, despite the fact that several thousand gulden had been lost in Yozefov.

Several months after Eydl's death, my father-in-law came to see us in Yozefov and very casually said to me and my wife:

"Yoshe! Drive to Tarnow this week and bring back your entire dowry. You are staying in Yozefov." This was the entire discussion. We did not figure out how much the enterprise was worth at the time and what my cut would be, or even more broadly, whether we were amenable to the proposal. He did not even consider it worth asking about these things. He had decided and everyone had to submit to his will.

I spent just about ten years in Yozefov. During the entire period, I kept the "books" where I recorded the expenses and profits. If there was money, my father-in-law took it, and if there were expenses, he covered them. No accounts were kept between us indicating what was mine, or his, or even what constituted a loss and what constituted a profit. He wasn't really interested in knowing.

When the contract ended, and we did not have to plough and sow the fields, thousands of gulden of surplus were simply left lying around. My father-in-law did not settle accounts with me, even then. He returned my entire dowry and I opened a business in my own name. In addition, I took as much livestock and equipment out of Yozefov as I needed for my own new holdings. This did not concern or bother my in-laws at all. They helped in all sorts of ways from Zgursk. My father-in-law liked to be strict but generous, like a true Polish noble: his word was the holiest law, but one could live comfortably off him.

* * *

There, in Yozefov, I became my own boss, a holder of a great estate with many fields and cattle. I wanted to introduce a few reforms to the estate because I was subscribing to two German agricultural newspapers, and I itched to introduce some innovations. My father-in-law, however, did not even want to hear about it, and everything stayed the way he wanted. Nevertheless, hindrances aside, I often managed to introduce something novel to the business, and when it went smoothly and worked, even my father-in-law smiled and had to admit that I was right.

On one occasion, I introduced an innovation that brought the estate several thousand gulden over the course of time, and also helped several other leaseholders in our area get on their feet.

The fields in the area were sown with clover. This is a kind of productive seed that is very good for the livestock. The clover is not planted in a separate field and requires no preparation; in the spring, when the field has already been sown with another grain, it is sown over again with the small clover seeds. When the grain is harvested from the fields, the young clover begins to grow in nicely and you have a very good pasture for the horses. In its young state clover is, incidentally, very harmful to oxen and cows; they immediately get bloated with gas and soon drop dead on the spot. The following year, nothing remains but clover. It grows so densely and robustly that you can harvest three or four large wagonfulls per acre, sometimes twice per summer. This is the best food for all cattle, including in dried form for oxen and cows. Farmers make great efforts to buy it, and one can earn 50–60 gulden per acre. There were some leaseholders that were kept on their feet by this clover. If they had several dozen acres of clover to sell, a large proportion of their expenses was covered. However, for the purpose of selling, this clover only lasted a single year. The second year it grew sparsely and was not worth bothering with. The fields had to be ploughed and sown with other grains.

When I began to study the German agricultural journals in Yozefov, I read about a new type of grass that was being imported from America. This grass is called "Timothy." The advantage to this grass is that it is sown together with clover and it only really starts to grow a year after the clover. In other words, when the clover begins to lose its growth and potency, the Timothy grass is as good and maybe even better. When I read this in my journals, it appealed to me greatly, and without much delay, I imported five kilos of Timothy seeds from Vienna. I sowed it together with the clover and did not tell anyone. I was simply afraid that if it did not work out, the other leaseholders and especially my father-in-law would laugh at me.

I could barely wait for the two years to pass. The Timothy started to grow to its full bulk. It covered all of the acre's plots, but much better than the clover, which often had a terrible enemy: a weed called "*Vilob*" that wrapped itself around the clover and did not let it grow properly. The Timothy seed was very expensive: it easily cost as much as the clover, which often reached a cost of 50–60 or more gulden per sack. One year, therefore, I decided to let the entire field covered with the Timothy mature for seeds. I was lucky again: the Timothy turned out well and grew tall, almost as high as rye. We cut it pretty high and in such a way that the "*Shtshirne* [grindings]," the remaining stalks together with the underbrush consisting of a lot of clover and other grasses, could be sold as hay for cutting as well. I sold a whole 40 acres of "*Shtshirne*" at the high price of 14 gulden per acre, and the buyer, who sold it individually to the farmers, earned himself several hundred gulden. There was also quite a lot of seed: over a hundred sacks. They fetched over 30 gulden per 100 kilos. We thus enjoyed a very profitable year in Yozefov and earned ourselves several thousand gulden.

Starting then, the whole area began to trade in Timothy. My father-in-law sowed over 100 acres with this valuable grass seed and other leaseholders did the same. This got many of them back on their feet.

34
Velvele Damask

Velvele, or Herr Wilhelm Damask, was a very peculiar type of Jew, without equal in the entire area. This is why I think that it is worth immortalizing him.

He was born in the city of Dobrov, about two miles from Tarnow. He stemmed from a family of wealth and good pedigree. In his youth he had a reputation as a great Jewish scholar and very *frum* to boot. He then "went astray" and began to assume the role of a *maskil*. After the death of his *frum* grandfather, he began to dress "German-style." He then left the *shtetl* altogether and settled in Krakow.

He was a rich man and possessed many inheritances from his and his wife's families. He thus opened a banking house in Krakow, played the stock market and made a fortune. At the time, he owned three estates and several large houses in Krakow. However, when the big Vienna stock market crash of 1873 hit, Damask took a heavy loss. He ceased to be a banker and lost the houses. He was left with only two estates: Yozefov, and a small estate near Nowy Targ (Neumark), near Neu Sandetz.

At the time that he leased Yozefov to my father-in-law, he was living in Krakow and was administering the estate himself. When I met him, he was already a man in his sixties, but still filled with life and enterprise. He was a very secular person and did not think much of *yiddishkayt*. He did a lot of things "to spite God." Naturally he did not want to speak Yiddish, and he only knew Polish passably. Consequently, he spoke only German and read German books and newspapers. When he got to know me, he livened up. He told me that he had nothing to talk about with anyone in the entire region:

"*Alle sind doch dummköpfe und farstehen garnichts* [All of these people are idiots and understand nothing]!" He always liked to talk about the earlier *maskilim* and writers, many of whom he knew personally, and considered himself their disciple. He remembered a lot of Gemara by heart and liked to show it off.

One Shabbes, he accompanied me into the field. It was harvest time. He pulled up a couple of stalks, tore out the kernels by hand and threw them back onto the field, as if he were sowing them. Then he began to talk to me how many of the 39 forbidden acts [on the Sabbath] he had just committed. I gave him my opinion. He showed a great deal of expertise and remembered all 39 acts by heart.

He did not think much of so-called "morals." He had been a major skirt-chaser in his youth. He had been in business in Yozefov for a good many years; his wife had never been there. So, he had two peasant women, sisters, with whom he lived openly as husband and wife. They had several of his children, who he never acknowledged although they bore great similarity to him and even kept their heads stooped, just like him. He never cared for them. They grew up to be farmers and peasant women, just like everyone else in the village; they would go to work like all of the other *shikses*.

A while after Damask's death, one of his legitimate sons, an accountant in a Krakow bank, came to visit us and see what was doing on the estate. I drove with him over the fields and showed him everything. We came to a bit of field that was closed off with wooden bars so that the cattle would not damage the pasture. When one of the shepherds spotted us driving around, he ran over to the gate and opened it for us. The young Damask took a whole silver half-gulden out of his pocket and handed it to him. When he noticed how I was looking at him as if to say that it was too much, he said to me with a smile:

"Yeah, you never know. Maybe he is my brother!"

The elder Damask liked to show off to me that he had been a big *apikoyres,* even when he had still been in Dobrov. He recounted to me:

"Once, for *Kol Nidrei*, I was reciting the "*Shir Hayichud* [prayer]" in *shul*. But when I got home, I smoked a good cigar." He always had something to say against Jews. He did not like a single Jewish thing. But he himself was not free of them.

He was a tremendous swindler and cunning person! We have already seen how he cheated my father-in-law with the contract. However, even when someone was doing business with him, he always searched for a way to cheat and defraud him. The whole region would recount stories about him, and honourable merchants did not want to do business with him.

A Radomishla grain-dealer told me about business deal that he had had with this Herr Damask. He purchased 200 sacks of wheat at a specified rate and got a note about the sale from him stating that the wheat was to be ready on certain date. Meanwhile, the price of grain rose a lot and the merchant looked forward to collecting his wheat on the specified day. He drove to Yozafov the day before and asked Herr Damask whether the wheat was ready and when he should come by with wagons to pick it up.

"Your crop is long since ready and you can take it with you on your wagon today!" The merchant looked at him astonished as if to say: how is it possible to fit 200 sacks of wheat onto a single wagon? He asked him what he meant.

"Who told you that you would be receiving 200 sacks of wheat?" Damask played dumb. "I will give you three sacks of wheat and you can take that with you easily!" To make a long story short: the merchant saw that he had been tricked, and drove to a lawyer in Tarnow. There he was shown that he had no basis for complaint against the seller because the note stated that he was being sold *up to 200 sacks of wheat*. In other words, Damask had the option of giving him *up to* 200 sacks of wheat and the merchant had to accept it. However, the note did not specify how much Damask had to give him.

When Damask leased the Yozefov estate to my father-in-law, Shimen Sandhaus, my father-in-law's brother-in-law, was the broker and middleman between them. Damask left Yozefov with a lot more money than if he had acted on his own behalf, with over 20,000 gulden that my father-in-law had paid him at once in cash. Shimen Sandhaus, the broker, had counted on receiving a big cut: 1,000 or at least 500 gulden. He really needed the money at that time; he was always in need. When he spoke with Herr Damask about how much he would receive for his extensive and valuable efforts, Damask would reassure him down and smack him on the back:

"Leave it up to me, *Herr* Sandhaus! You will receive a very nice and valuable gift from me!" When the transaction was wrapped up, Shimen Sandhaus received a couple of silver candleholders, worth about thirty gulden, for his effort and work. It goes without saying that Sandhaus did not want to accept the candlesticks and took Damask to court. The upshot of the story was that he had to pay about 100 gulden in court fees. Damask swore that they had never discussed money: they had been neighbours for years and Sandhaus had just intended for his own brother-in-law to make his fortune by taking over the estate. He maintained that a pair of candlesticks was enough, more than enough, of a gift. Because Shimen Sandhaus was really down and out, and did not have the money to pay the court fees, my father-in-law had to do it. This fine Herr Damask did not want to part with a single kreuzer.

A small house with three little rooms was located in the Yozefov manor yard. Damask used to live there when he came to the estate. When he leased it to my father-in-law, he stipulated in the contract that this little house was not to be used by anyone; it had to be reserved for his exclusive use if he ever came to visit. Meanwhile, he installed a lover of his, a *shikse* named The Ignazova in the house. He arranged that she be able to reside there as well as keep three cows in our stall and pasture them on our fields. We were also obliged to give her straw and hay for the cows. My father-in-law was so blinded by the great fortune that awaited him in Yozefov that he also gave in on this point. What did it matter if there were three cows in the manor yard?

However, this soon turned out to be a major troublemaker. The Ignazova was a very nasty and proud woman. She imagined herself as a real *balesboste* like before Damask's times, and she began to display great ill will when it came to her cows from the onset. Nowhere they were put and nothing that they were given to eat suited her, and she was constantly picking fights.

My father-in-law, however, was not the type of person to be led by the nose by this kind of woman. When his daughter, Eydl, told him about the trouble she had with The Ignazova, it did not take him long to act. He soon came to Yozefov and sharply told The Ignazova to leave the premises, together with her three cows. When she did not obey fast enough, he started to assault her but good, and chased her away from the manor yard together with her three cows. He wrote a stern letter to Damask stating that he did not want that *shikse* as a *baleboste* in the manor yard, and if Damask wanted, he could take him to court.

The "German" understood that it was not worth going to court for this woman, and he opted to keep quiet. However, every time that he would come to Yozefov, The Ignazova was with him and he made up for the damage that she endured in having to leave the manor yard and lose her post as *baleboste*. She acknowledged defeat and then became very servile: she would come to Eydl and then to my wife and do sewing for them.

Wilhelm Damask was the only "German" and *apikoyres* in our region. There was never another one, and there was no one aside from me with the ability and desire to peruse *loshn-koydesh* books, or even a German or Polish book. Even the women and girls, with very few exceptions, did not think much of these things.

35

RADOMISHLA

Radomishla, located some three miles from Tarnow and two miles from the Tshorno train station, was a very pleasant *shtetl* completely different from the surrounding towns in many ways. In the nearby *shtetlekh* of Shtsutsin, Pshetslav, Rzokhow and several others, the local Jews maintained lifestyles that did not differ much from the town gentiles. Any Jew of means owned his own cow or cows along with some sort of horse that he either owned or rented, which provided most of his livelihood. Every morning, Jewish *balebostes* in these towns would herd their cows onto the common pastures and not would hesitate to be the ones to feed and water them two or three times a day, or even to milk them themselves. Behind his house, almost every Jew had his own garden where he grew potatoes and various vegetables. He was the one who worked this little garden together with his wife and children to eke out whatever the family needed to survive.

Things were very different in Radomishla. Radomishla Jews acted like big-city Jews, even during my time. Almost no Jew in Radomishla owned a cow or garden. They were always engaged in trade and made a much better living than the Jews in the surrounding towns. Radomishla was also the only town for miles that had a large number of fabulously rich Jews.

This is not to say that there were no poor people in Radomishla; there were more than enough. There is, after all, a verse in the Torah that plainly states: "For the poor shall never cease" (Deuteronomy 15:11). However, in Radomishla these indigents were also not as destitute as elsewhere.

Radomishla had several families that were filthy rich and ran major businesses. A number traded in timber across all of Galicia. There were also several cattle dealers who spent thousands of gulden per week buying up animals and then transported them for sale to Krakow or Vienna. The Jews in Radomishla were also heavily involved in commerce, specifically lending money for interest. The Aberdams, Rappoports, Schlossers and the others were substantial moneylenders who charged high interest, and their fortunes increased from year to year. In Radomishla, there were many town-gentiles (*myestshanes*) who were on the road all over Galicia and at the fairs buying up hogs for sale abroad. These gentiles traded using Jewish money and paid high interest. These *myestshanes* included the Yarases and Kostokovitches, who owned their own large estates while also traveling the countryside buying up hogs and paying the Jews high interest.

Several Radomishla Jews also owned their own estates and forests. Mordkhele Gorlitzer (with whom I later held the Oshitz Farm) was one of the wealthiest men in the area. Together with his brother-in-law, he inherited the great Yashtsombke estate from his very ill father: 600 acres plus 1,500 acres of estates and ancient, thick forests. He later split the property with his brother-in-law and took the forest, whose value rose steadily each year and was valued at about 250,000 gulden.

The Gutwirth family owned two estates close to the city: Greater Diltsch and Smaller Diltsch. Both contained several hundred acres of prime fields as well as several hundred acres of forests. Although these woods were not worth as much as the Yashtsombke Forest, they still amounted to 100,000 gulden. On top of this, the Gutwirths also possessed their urban *propinatsye* (the exclusive rights to sell alcoholic beverages). They leased out this privilege for eight to ten thousand gulden a year. Later, when the government took over all *propinatsyes* and paid the owners large sums of money, these particular Jews became even more affluent.

Aside from all of the above, Radomishla boasted several Jewish villagers from the surrounding area who were also filthy rich. No one, including they themselves, had any clue how much money they had. I am not going to detail all of the rich Jews of Radomishla; I do think, however, that it would not be an exaggeration to observe that together they were worth about two million gulden, and this was an enormous sum of money fifty years ago. These wealthy people included different types: genteel folk along with rats, and the good-hearted alongside tightfisted individuals who did not want to part with their money.

There was in Radomishla a Jewish woman who had remained an old maid for years and years and then married a man she barely managed to divorce. This "old lady" was stuffed to the gills with cash, at least half a million gulden. She was not interested in doing anyone any favours and was reluctant to lend even the wealthiest of gentlemen several thousand gulden. To make a long story short, when she took ill, several rich men took pity on her and took her in. They then wrote up a false will and seized her entire fortune. Although she did have several poor relatives, she had never been willing to support them, and the wealthy men who seized her fortune later, out of fear, threw them some kind of bone.

Quite a few other families lived off the affluent people, and were employed by them as clerks, foresters, and trustees in their many business dealings. Overall, Radomishla was quite a respectable trading center. Everyone had some sort of occupation and earned a decent living.

Even the city's three judges were not paupers as is the case elsewhere; they could not, after all, live on *toyre ve-avoyde* (Torah and good works) alone. The eldest of the judges, Reb Refoyl Hersh, was a *velt-shadkhen* [wide-ranging matchmaker] and often traveled for his matches. Yantshe the Judge was a "part-timer" who was occasionally seen helping out his wife at her "*shrogn*" (little table) of farmers' products in the market when things got busy. He helped her trade with the male and female peasants, especially on Thursdays during the weekly fair. The youngest of the judges, Borekh Fuks (or "Fuksl," as he was called), was a big scholar and highly knowledgeable in contemporary, worldly affairs. He was quite wealthy and a major egg merchant. Thursdays at the fair, he along with his helpers collected hundreds of *shok* (a *shok* is 60) of eggs, sorted them, and packed them into boxes for shipment abroad. When a servant girl or *baleboste* had some kind of *shayle* about whether a chicken or her pots and pans were kosher, she never went to the Rabbi to ask; she would run to Fuksl standing in the middle of the marketplace amongst his boxes of eggs. All he had to do was glance at the chicken or briefly listen to the *shayle* in order to pronounce his "verdict": *kosher* or *treyf*.

Radomishla was a city packed with Hassidism, but not the kind of unkempt bunglers that hung around the Belzer area. Any *balebos* was expected to make pilgrimage to a *rebbe*, or he was not considered a full human being. People generally were followers of the Ropshitzer dynasty. Many traveled to the *rebbes* in surrounding *shtetlekh*: Zhabna, Dembitz, Melitz, or Dzikov. There were also those among the wealthy, including my brother-in-law, Berl Lev, who traveled as far as Tshortkov or Husiatyn, which were quite a long journey from Radomishla. However, people said that these Hassidim were not as keen to see their *rebbes* as they were to drive through Lemberg on their way and live it up.

Some *rebbes* also took the initiative to come to Radomishla on their own steam, and each of these *rebbes* left with several hundred gulden at least. Radomishla Jews were generous and spent money easily. There was a time when the Plantsher Rebbe, son of the Rozvadover Rebbe and a grandson of the great Roptshitser, resided in Radomishla with his entire entourage, and held "court" (so to speak), and the city and surrounding villages supported him with great pomp and circumstance.

Radomishla of yore was such pleasant town!

36
A FALLEN *"TAKEF"*

At some point in your life, you might witnessed the fall of a man, but you have never seen a downfall as terrible as that of the *"Takef"* of Radomishla, Reb Avraham Moyshe Kleinman.

I have been away from Galicia for 30-odd years and am thus not that well informed about the internal conditions of its Jewish communities. However, from what I can ascertain as an avid reader of its Jewish newspapers, there are no more *"takifim"* there. Since the War, circumstances in the *shtetlekh* have worsened a great deal, and the institution of the *"takifim"* had already been on the decline in the years leading up to it. However, fifty or more years ago, there was not a single *shtetl* in Galicia that did not have its own *"Takef"* as leader. His word was law and everyone had to obey, or else.

I knew several of these *"takifim"* in the *shtetlekh* around Radomishla: there was Reb Lipe Sanitorye in Dobrov; Alter Kampf in Shtsutsin; Yisroel Binshtok in Pshetslav; Khayim Klein in Melitz; Dovid Binshtok in Zabno; and most important of all, Reb Avraham Moyshe Kleinman in Radomishla. Because I knew Avraham Moyshe Kleinman much better than the other *"Takifim"* and because his fall was much greater, I will focus on him.

After I got married, I soon had the opportunity to become acquainted with the *"Takef,"* Reb Avraham Moyshe Kleinman. He was a man of about sixty, tall and sturdy, with a very nice white beard. He was very snappily and neatly dressed and he was a pleasure to look at. His whole appearance demanded respect and reverence. He was an in-law of ours: his son, Mendel, was a son-in-law of my grandfather-in-law, Reb Yudl Shtiglitz, i.e., Mendel was my father-in-law's brother-in-law and my wife's uncle. When I got to know him, he had already fallen quite far from his previous glory, but he was still enough of a *"Takef"* that his word was a force to be reckoned with.

At one time, he had been the only community head in the city, as appointed by the chief officer of the Melitz government, and one of the city's seven *"radnikes"* (councilmen). He was the person in change of birth certificates; that is, he had to be consulted in every case of a birth or death. He held the government's *haupt-trafik* which entailed a monopoly on tobacco, cigars, and other items relating to snuff and smoking. All of the innkeepers in the region had to come and "answer to him," that is, purchase all of these items. In addition, he ran the government's lottery, where all of the people played their lucky numbers.

All of this was, however, insignificant compared to other areas where the *"Takef"* was a major VIP: first, in the Zasov (Zassow) courts, as Radomishla did not have its own courts or tax-bureau at that time, and these were located in Zasov, half a mile from town; second, at the tax-bureau, and third and most important of all, at the *starosta* (local government official) in Melitz. He could do major favours anywhere, as well as the reverse. If someone—that is to say, a Jew from town or from the surrounding villages—was called for conscription to the army, Kleinman was indispensable. He was the only broker and advisor to the commission and he could free whomever he wanted from military duty. As can be gathered from all of his various and many occupations, he was the true leader of the city and had power over everyone's welfare and even over human freedom. However, despite all of this, he was no "fleecer" like the other *"Takifim."* He was not constantly squeezing the last cent out of his "subjects." He earned more than enough from all of his other businesses. His position was just a matter of honour and he wanted his every word to be transformed into reality.

I do not know exactly when his fall began as it happened several years before my wedding. However, at the heart of the matter was a virulent town feud about the Rabbi. The *"Takef"* was constantly persecuting the Rabbi. However, the wealthy men of the town sided with the Rabbi, and some of them were his close associates. The *Takef*'s downfall came at the hands of the Gutvirt Family.

In his youth, the elder Avraham Mordecai Gutvirt had been a Gemara *malamed.* However, he came into a large fortune, I don't know how. He had two estates with a large forest right next to town, and held the city's *propinatsye* (exclusive rights) for gold mining. This Avraham Mordecai Gutvirt was a most peculiar person with a very strong spirit, the kind of person one just doesn't see anymore. He was a great scholar as well as a shrewd merchant, cultivated but not very compassionate. He also really liked to be shown respect, but the old "*Takef*," Reb Avraham Moyshe Kleinman, would not let him hold his head up. Gutvirt also had his heart set on some sort of municipal post—not for money because he certainly had enough—but Avraham Moyshe stood on his guard to ensure that all of his ambitions were thwarted.

I remember Reb Avraham Mordecai, the "Melamed Baron," in his old age when he was already half paralyzed. Despite this, he refused to give up his old right to lead the "Musaf" prayers at the town's Beys-medresh during the high holydays. He was brought on a pushcart, and prayed seated in front of the lectern. Despite his paralysis, however, he had a very strong, powerful voice, a real "lion's roar": when he gave a cry during the Kedusha or the Avodah sections of the service, the walls simply shook.

He has several sons, one of whom, Nokhtshe, was a simpleton and later became a full-fledged idiot. Three of his sons were very industrious and quarrelsome people. None of them were scholars like their father, but they were capable businessmen, and around them and their gold-mining enterprise, they gathered a whole clique of people whose sole purpose was an ongoing crusade against the "*Takef*" to slowly but surely tear him down from his high status. This feud lasted for years and cost both sides thousands of gulden.

The tragic end was that the Gutvirts emerged victorious and Reb Avraham Moyshe Kleinman, the "*Takef*," began to lose one position after another. Both sides employed denunciation tactics and threw money at civil servants. Kleinman's rivals began to monitor him whenever possible, and when one seeks, one finds: it came out that he had committed treason against the government. First, his two biggest and most important business ventures were torn out of his hands: the tobacco and the lottery, which brought him enormous earnings. Both were handed over to a wealthy young man who automatically joined the ranks of Kleinman's opponents.

Every spring, at the onset of the "*asentirung*" (review), Kleinman's opponents would hire sly little urchins to follow him everywhere and not allow him to meet with his "Lords." Due to these practices and reports, more than one of these accomplices found himself forced to serve in the military as a soldier when Avraham Moyshe Kleinman sought an easy way of getting rid of him. It goes without saying that the "*Takef*" was constantly trying to defend himself, and the city's feud grew and grew.

During this time, the Austrian government decided to take over all *propi-natsyes* across the country, but first, it had to purchase the rights from their holders. The basic calculation used in buying out these rights was "14 percent": the government paid 14 times the annual profits claimed by the previous owners over the last few years when their taxes were filed. Thus, the scrupulous owners, who had not tried to swindle the government and had claimed their actual income, became very affluent; they received a huge, unanticipated lump sum. There were others—especially Polish *pritsim* who knew what the government was planning behind the scenes—who had claimed their incomes from the *propinatsyes* to be much higher than they actually were for the previous few years. They struck gold and became wealthy nobles. However, those who had claimed low income from their *propinatsyes* received very little and this caused them tremendous aggravation that they could do nothing about. This latter group included the Gutvirts. The father was no longer living at that time, and all of the businesses were run by the three brothers: Rafael, Leizer and Zalmen. However, being the shrewd people that they were, they managed to submit falsified documents and contracts that entitled them to much more money than they were actually owed.

Their old enemy, Avraham Moyshe Kleinman, was, however, also hard at work. He caught wind of their intentions and passed on the information to the appropriate officials. This brought new court cases and sentences, with the end result of several years' prison time for all three Gutvirts. However, they bought their way out and came out on top: they received whatever they wanted for their *propinatsyes*, and emerged even wealthier than before. Now the Gutvirts went after the "*Takef*" with increased acrimony. Through denunciations and other malicious deeds, they took away his final source of livelihood: the tobacco business. On top of this, he had to serve time for several cases of forgery that were found in his books. It goes without saying that as a felon he could no longer serve as community head. He lost all of his influence and found himself destitute. He had wasted his entire fortune on court cases against his enemies and on his own defense. He became so poor that there was there was not enough bread on the table at home.

In addition, one terrible misfortune after another befell him. He had a daughter named Reyzl who was a very pretty, intelligent girl with no equal among all of Radomishla's wealthiest families. His intention had been to get the biggest possible *shidekh* for her. While her father was serving his sentence, she did everything possible for him. She was constantly busy with all of the civil servants to plead for mercy on behalf of her father, who was being persecuted for nothing by his many enemies. Everyone knew that the reason he received such a short sentence—a few months rather than the minimum of the three years people expected—was thanks only to her. She also did all sorts of things to make his life easier for him when he was in jail.

When he had finally served his sentence and returned home, Reyzl was ecstatic. She was so overwhelmed with joy at the return of her father, whom she idolized, that she lost her mind and remained that way until the end of her life. Despite interventions by doctors and hospitals, no one was able to help her, and she became a quiet madwoman. She did not bother anyone except when she entered into fits of wild rage: then she would run to the Gutvirts' and knock out their windows while cursing violently. Reyzl's father led her around—this was after her mother's death—like a small child, and when she was overcome by fury, she would beat him viciously. It was tragic to watch him walk around battered and swollen.

By this time, he had become so impoverished that he had to appeal for outside assistance. At first, he went about honourably, and when he would come to me or someone else, he would still speak with his former dignity: "Lend me a tener or a fiver." However, little by little, he became a run-of-the-mill vagabond who had to content himself with what he was given: a gulden or two. In his prime, he had been a Dzikov Hassid, and it was in this court that he stayed during the period of his terrible decline. The Dzikov Rebbe, Reb Yehoshua Horovitz, would often provide him with income.

He died several years after his fall in Dzikov, during Rosh Hashana, the sad end of one of the last *"Takifim,"* completely destroyed by a city dispute. Thus is the dark power of a Jewish civil war.

37
AT THE REBBE'S IN DEMBITZ

In a previous chapter, I wrote that when someone aspired to a reputation as a cultivated person, he *had* to travel to a Rebbe. However, the Radomishla Jews were no fanatic Hassidim or "elevated" Jews. One traveled to the Rebbe to satisfy the outer world more than out of an inner drive to achieve spiritual perfection.

"Royter (Red) Zelig" (my "examiner") was a scholar of some repute and a very insightful man, but not much of a Hassid. He once said the following to me:

"Have you ever seen the way in which *pritsim* go on '*polovanye* (the hunt)'? They gather 15–20 people together and go to shoot animals. This kind of *polovanye* sets them back hundreds of gulden, on top of which the participants often get so tired from the running around that they actually shoot few, if any, animals. This begs the question: what is the point of this whole production when a quarter of the cost of one of these hunts would buy them many hares, deer, and other animals without the effort and trouble? In truth, the animals are hardly the point. The main thing is running around in the woods, the thrill of the chase accompanied by feasting and all washed down with a little something to drink. This going to see a Rebbe," said Reb Zelig with a smile, is a sort of Jewish '*polovanye*. You travel, hustle and run around. You push and grab *shirayim*. You have fun from the excitement all the while enjoying a tasty meal and a good glass or beer or wine. And above all, you can forget the wife and children and other worries and problems from home for several days. This is the reality that drives Hassidism today!"

Anyone who has had the opportunity to observe the daily affairs of Galician *shtetlekh* knows that Reb Zelig was not wide of the mark.

* * *

Rosh Hashana fell about two months after my wedding, and I wanted to be a Hassid and travel, at least to Belz. However, nothing came of it: during the "*Shana Rishona*," that is, the first year after the wedding, one does not travel anywhere; instead, one stays at home and fulfills the Biblical ordinance: "He shall be free for his house for one year, and shall cheer the wife he has taken" (Deut. 24: 5). I had no choice but to travel to Radomishla with my father-in-law and spend a fine Rosh Hashana and Yom Kippur there.

In the middle of the winter, the Dembitzer Rebbe, Reb Alter Horovitz, came to Radomishla and spent an entire week as the guest of my grandfather-in-law, Reb Yudl Shtiglitz. Reb Yudl was one of his most important followers, and had also been in the habit of traveling to see his father, Reb Reuven Horovitz, a grandson of the old Ropshitzer. Naturally, on the first day that he arrived, I was there to "welcome" him. I also spent *Shabbes* there in Radomishla and took part in his *tish*. Before he left for home, I came to see him again and presented him with a "*kvitl*" and a "*pidyon*" of a whole 5 gulden. I didn't have anything to write in the *kvitl*: I was no merchant or vendor, and I had no children. I therefore wrote my name and the name of my spouse and the following words: "For success and physical health." He took the *pidyon* and placed it in his pocket, and then proceeded to reread the *kvitl* several times, despite its brevity. He then and then said to me:

"You need a *kvitl*?!"

Initially I did not understand the meaning behind his words. However, when I later recounted it to my grandfather-in-law, he smiled, amused, and clarified: since I was a young man living on *kest* without any children yet, he had nothing to wish me for the time being. I, however, interpreted his words completely differently: he knew very well that I was a *maskil* "of little faith," so what was I doing fooling around with a *kvitl*?

I visited him several times after that first meeting and considered him a very intelligent man. I would often come to consult with him about my business affairs and always obliged him with generous donations. However, I never gave him another *kvitl* and he was smart enough not to request one of me. Any other man would certainly have insisted.

* * *

When the next Rosh Hashana rolled around after the "*Shana Rishona*" had passed, I was overcome by the same urge to visit a Rebbe. I was very keen on going to Belz, where I was well-known, in order to show myself in my expensive

93

shtreiml and fine *talis* with its broad silver collar. However, my plan was foiled yet again. I was dependent on the wills of others. My wife would not allow me to undertake a long journey of some 30 miles by train, and it would have cost me about 100 gulden to travel in proper style. Above all, my grandfather-in-law wanted me to become familiar with the Dembitzer Rebbe and join his followers. I got a little upset, to no avail: I traveled to Dembitz.

On the eve of Rosh Hashana, my father-in-law gave me 25 gulden to cover expenses so that I could go in style. He had even wanted to send me off to Dembitz with his dear "Zugov" horses, but I declined. I preferred to ride in a simple wagon together with other Hassidim where it was livelier and more festive. The total distance from Radomishla to Dembitz is about two and a half miles, and the whole trip takes about three hours. It also requires crossing the Vistula River, which flows behind Dembitz, by boat.

My grandfather-in-law's son-in-law, Reb Mendel Kleinman (son of the "*Takef,*" Reb Avraham Moyshe Kleinman) was part of the inner circle of the Dembitzer Rebbe. He took me under his wing and promised my grandfather-in-law that he would make sure that I behaved in a manner befitting the son of a wealthy family. However, his supervision of me was limited. I already knew from Belz how to behave appropriately: purchase a nice *aliyah*, provide wine at every "*tish,*" offer a decent "*pidyon,*" and finally provide a parting tip for the *gaboim*, the old Rebbetzin as well as for the Rebbe's brother-in-law, Reb Tsalel. Pretty soon nothing was left of my 25 gulden, and I actually had to borrow ten gulden from Mendel Kleinman after the holiday.

Still, I enjoyed a great spiritual delight during the entire duration of Rosh Hashana. I took special pleasure in the Ropshitzer *nigunim*, which I had never heard before. The *bal-mussaf* was an amazing man. He was an elderly man of about eighty by the name of Reb Leybush Zinger, and he was a pearl merchant. But he had a thin voice just like a canary, and when he chanted the "*Malkhuyot, Zikhronot and Shofarot*" prayers, it sounded like a bird singing. He also had several assistants including his son-in-law named Reb Zolki Kanorek who was also a very fine musician as well as a great scholar. He later became the government-appointed official Rabbi in Tarnow and after that, a rabbi in New York.

Still, this turned out to be the only Rosh Hashana that I would spend in Dembitz. Later, when I was independent and no one could tell me where to go, I would sometimes sneak off to Belz. I spent one Rosh Hashana in Shinievo with Reb Yehezkel Halberstam, son of the world-renowned Sanzer Rabbi. After that, I didn't go anywhere; I had had my fill of Hasidism.

* * *

The Dembitzer Rabbi, Reb Alter Horovitz, was a truly fine human being and a considerable connoisseur of secular matters. He was as knowledgeable in various business matters as the most experienced merchant, and some of his devotees would review their business affairs with him in exacting detail. My own father-in-law was not much of a Hassid and occasionally traveled to Belz or Shinievo to make an appearance. He and the Dembitzer Rabbi went way back to their childhood years, and because they were constantly goofing around and roughhousing, his heart would not allow him to call him by the title of "Rabbi" or to give him a *kvitl*. Nevertheless, he thought very highly of the Dembitzer Rabbi and offered him extensive financial support. He would even send him hay and oats for his horses all the way from Zgursk, a distance of over three miles from Dembitz. Every time my father-in-law had some business to wrap up, he always conferred with the Dembitzer Rabbi, whom he considered a loyal childhood-friend. When my father-in-law left Zgursk in search of another estate, the Dembitzer Rabbi was deeply involved in the process and proposed several potential estates for him to lease.

In addition to being well-versed in secular matters, Reb Alter was also a major expert in horses. His followers included a Radomishla horse merchant named Hershl who traded on a large scale; he would send horses by the carload (with fourteen horses per car) to Prussia. With no train station in Radomishla and the village of Tshorno lacking the necessary amenities, Hershl had his headquarters in Dembitz. He and his assistant traveled to the fairs in many *shtetlekh*, brought the traded horses to Dembitz, and then sent them to Prussia by train.

Hershel's custom was to present a *kvitl* to the Dembitzer Rabbi before each shipment of horses to Prussia in order to receive his blessing on the merchandise. He always gave the Rabbi as many gulden as there were horses in the shipment, often forty or more per week. However, the Dembitzer Rabbi never stopped at just a blessing for his devotee; he demanded that for each shipment, the horses be brought by his house prior to boarding the train for sale so that he could observe them first. On several occasions, I had the opportunity to be present for the parading of Hershl's horses in front of the Dembitzer Rabbi. Reb Alter would stand outside on the porch of his house right on the Kaiserweg that leads to the *shtetl* of Pilno. There would be some forty horses with their attendants in the large open area in front of the house. Each horse was paraded separately and the Rabbi would ask Hershl how much it had cost. The Rabbi held a stick in his hand and examined each horse closely, with his sharp eye and considerable expertise.

"Hershl," he would often blurt out, "Tell me, what is that on his right foot?" Hershl, who had not noticed this before, had to admit that the Rabbi was right: the horse had a small growth on its foot that had to be bandaged.

Sometimes, when he really liked a horse, the Rabbi would ask one of the attendants to get on the horse and gallop by a few times so that he could see "how it rides." He had a solid understanding of the pricing for horses and on more than one occasion, he said to Hershl:

"Wow, did they take you in! You aren't going to get much for this Sorrel!"

When the Dembitzer Rabbi passed away at the age of fifty, Hershl the horse merchant, found himself without a *rebbe*. Because the Plontsher Rabbi, who was a relative of the Dembitzer Rabbi, was living in Radomishla at the time, he was urged to become his Hassid and give him the gulden that he used to contribute for each horse. He allowed himself to be talked into it: after all, what is the difference? A *rebbe* is a *rebbe*. The first time he went to see the Plontsher Rabbi, he presented him a *kvitl* with a *pidyon* with the request that the rabbi pray for his success because he was transporting 42 horses to Prussia. The Plontsher Rabbi tried to make an impression and show that he understood about secular matters as well as the Dembitzer Rabbi. He thus asked Hershl:

"Please tell me: how much do threescore horses cost?" This was the first and last time that the simple but honest horse dealer went to him.

"This is not a *rebbe*!" he said with a heavy sigh. "No Dembitzer Rabbi."

The Dembtizer Rabbi, Reb Alter, did not have any children, and he was also not a big consumer. His post as Rabbi of Dembitz and the *rabistvo* (governmental rabbinical post) brought in a pretty penny each week and he always had cash on hand. He would lend money to his Hassidim at low interest, or became an investor in their business endeavors and become a sort of partner. His close associate, Mendel Kleinman, a big lumber merchant, constantly owed him several thousand gulden. When he was forced into bankruptcy in the feud with the Gutvirts, the Dembitzer Rabbi was out several thousand gulden that he never saw again. Nonetheless, Mendel remained his Hassid and the Rabbi would help him out with cash.

The Dembitzer Rabbi was an intelligent, decent and genteel man. There aren't many like him. May his soul be bound in the bond of life!

38

A STRIKE IN THE ZGURSK MANOR

The big Zgursk estate where my father-in-law resided was a small kingdom in itself. Aside from the large number of laborers that would come every morning to do various jobs in the field and manor, there were always servants hired on an annual basis, about forty *parobkes* [farmhands], *shikses*, herdsmen of large and small beasts, and a blacksmith. All of these people were unmarried and received room and board in the manor. There isn't much to say about their "living quarters": everyone found a place to sleep in one of three stables atop hay and straw and that was it. No pillows or sleepwear were provided, and a "*dere*"— the blanket used to cover horses—served as a cover; it was warm in the stalls in the winter. However, feeding a gang of young people with healthy appetites three times a day was not so simple. The Zgursk manor had a very big kitchen with long tables and benches where the *parobkes* and *shikses* sat. Every *parobek* had his own box in the stall where he kept his personal belongings as well as two big loaves of black bread that he received every Sunday to eat outside of mealtimes.

The gentile kitchen had its own cook and an assistant, and my wife or one of my other sisters-in-law supervised so that everything ran as smoothly as possible. Above all, they did not skimp on the lard, which was purchased by the tub to be added to the food and keep the servants happy. My father-in-law maintained that young people must eat a lot in order to have the strength to work.

The central command in the manor was held by its two generals: my father- and mother-in-law. However, they were two very different characters: She was a very good person, affable and yielding, while he was strict, proud and a tough *porits*. He was also a very good person overall, and if you caught him at a "good time," you could get him to do anything you wanted. However, in general, he possessed a cold and strict demeanor, and everyone in the manor avoided him when they did not have to deal with him directly; instead, they sought out someone else, notably my mother-in-law. The same held true in the case of the servants and laborers. She would handle matters constructively by handing out an extra bit of food or a drink of whiskey; he, on the other hand, would make use of his pride and firm character.

It was the harvest season the year after my wedding. A lot of grain had already been harvested, and stood in heaps in the fields. These had to be brought into the barns as fast as possible or be turned into "*stoygen*" (piles). Every horse or ox and wagon was occupied with bringing in the bundles of hay. The custom was that everyone headed out to the fields right after sunrise, and only two to three hours later, around eight o'clock, was food served. Ordinarily, when there was no great urgency to the work, and the *parobeks* were not in a huge rush, it was no big deal if they lingered over their meals, during dinner or especially at lunch. Things were completely different during the height of the harvest season: every minute was valuable, especially when it threatened to rain and wet the hay. Then the workers were barely allowed to eat up before they were chased back out to work.

One time, my mother-in-law was busy in the field with the cutters, and my father-in-law was at home, making sure that the laborers didn't have too much fun during their meals. He entered the gentile kitchen and came upon a group of *parobkes* and several *shikses* who had finished eating and were just sitting around, chatting. Some were fighting with the cook because that day's meal had not been smothered in enough lard.

"*Do vozov! Do roboti!* (To the wagons! To work!)," yelled my father-in-law loudly. When the young men did not jump up and run out of the kitchen, instead continuing to sit with their wooden spoons scratching their empty clay bowls, my perpetually agitated and excitable father-in-law got even angrier and began to beat some of the boys with his paddle. He hit blindly left and right, striking heads, backs, and wherever he could. The screams and calls for help brought us all into the kitchen—myself, my wife, and several other people, Jews and Christians—to witness the terrible massacre that he was committing on these *parobkes*. Meanwhile, one of them screamed loudly,

"*Khloptsi! Nyema vas* (Boys, where are you?)" This was a call not to let the beating go on, and to hit the slaughterer back. But it did not come to this. The cook, a giant of a woman and all of the others that were there, would not allow it: we chased the few boys out of the kitchen, calmed my father-in-law down a little and brought him to his quarters.

However, the boys stayed in the yard. Soon a few other *parobkes* joined the mob. They conferred with each other and decided not to return to the field for the bundles of hay. My wife and the other children pleaded with them not to do this, but the *parobkes* were too upset and stubborn to listen. With my father-in-law nowhere to be seen in the yard, they managed to find some laborers from the outside who knew how to drive four horses or oxen in a wagon filled with bales of hay, and the work continued.

Meanwhile, lunchtime came and the boys, who were used to eating at fixed mealtimes, were hungry again. Now they found themselves in a quandary. They did not want to go into the kitchen to eat; they were, after all, the ones who had opted not to work. There was no food to buy and nowhere to buy it. The twenty-odd *parobkes* (the girls had not stopped working) deliberated and went to Radomishla to the "*Stara-pani*" (the old mistress, my grandmother-in-law) to tell her about the injustice they had encountered in the Zgursk court.

My grandmother-in-law, Nekhome, was a very clever lady and a great business-woman. When the *parobkes* wanted to present their case to her, she first asked them whether they had had lunch as it was around three o'clock. When the boys responded that they had not, she immediately sent away for several loaves of bread, butter and herring and ordered the *parobkes* to sit at the tables in her tavern and eat their fill. She also placed several bottles of light wine in front of them so that they could also drink as much as they wanted.

"Now, children," she said to them when they had finished eating and drinking, "go home in good health. You know my son: he is not a bad *porits*, just a little excitable. Hurry up," she added with a kind smile, "since you have left your '*khodobes*' (cattle) in foreign hands and they won't know how to handle them. Go home, and I will soon follow and have a talk with my son." After she had given each man 10 kreuzer for tobacco or cigarettes, she sent them back to the Zgursk manor.

To make a long story short, the young and carefree boys soon forgot the injustice, and found themselves longing for their animals, whom they had not seen all day. That evening, "Bobe Nekhome" drove into the yard. She saw to it that all of the "strikers" received a good dinner along with a glass of whiskey. This incident was soon forgotten by everyone involved. The *parobkes* were certainly not interested in discussing it. I do not know whether my grandmother-in-law actually talked with her son and scolded him, but it is most likely that she did. I say this because several months later, an old building was fixed up and given the name of "*Pieklo*" (Hell). For New Year's, all of the unmarried *parobkes* were exempted from having to stay in the building, and in their stead, only the married help was housed in there.

Every year, they were given nine sacks of various grains, numerous garden plots to use for growing potatoes and vegetables, and everyone was allowed to keep one of his own cows. On top of this, they received 20 gulden in cash as annual salary. A married *parobek,* with a wife and often several children, was generally more willing to work and more submissive than the unmarried men, some of whom had wanderlust and could not stay in one place for long.

39
JEWS AND PEASANTS

I cannot speak with accuracy about other areas in Galicia because I am not well enough acquainted with them. However, I can say this with confidence about the stretch from Rayshe (Rzeszow), Tarnow to Krakow, which is about 25 miles in total: the peasant has long acknowledged the "hegemony" of the Jew, and openly admitted it. During the period between the 1880s and the War, this part of Galicia was a true paradise for Jews in some respects. They had it better there than ever before, and certainly than they ever would again; I have my doubts that these times will ever return.

Anti-Jewish persecution was unknown during this period. When several thousand peasants would gather at the weekly fairs, the Jews never feared attack or abuse of any sort. On the rare occasions that some of the gentiles got drunk and did starting beating the Jews or breaking dishes in a tavern, they faced nasty consequences. Instead of actually getting to hit a Jew, they were beaten to a pulp, and then arrested and sentenced to several days in prison. They also had to pay for any damages that they caused. Even in the villages, where very few Jews lived, they were as secure as in the cities and *shtetlekh*. It never even occurred to anyone to be afraid that a peasant might harm them or was hanging around with the intent of taking his life.

The Jews and the farmers lived in a state of perpetual friendship and helped each other out in the same way as Christian neighbors. If a gentile needed to borrow some money or was short on food before the *"pshednovek"* (new grain harvest), he always received help from the Jew, be it in a town, a village, or especially on the Jewish estates. The Jewish estate-holders were always happy to give a peasant grain during this time because they always needed labor and the gentiles worked off their debts. This provided the Jews a service that was much more valuable than cash.

If a Jew fought, or even exchanged blows, with a peasant, as is wont to happen among people who know each other well, the Jew almost always came out the winner. If a peasant insulted a Jew, the latter soon prepared a *"Skarga dela abrazo honoro"* (a complaint for an insult to one's honour). Even for an anti-Jewish curse, a gentile had to spend three days, or 48 hours at the least, in jail, as well as cover the court costs. Although the Polish peasants were not very fastidious when it came to private property, especially when it came to the Jews, big thefts and burglaries were rare; the gendarmes and the courts were very stringent in this respect. Robberies and surprise attacks never happened at all. The whole area was safe and there was nothing to be afraid of. I personally was often seen walking around with several thousand gulden cash in my pocket. I also liked to ride my carriage without a coachman during all hours of the day and night across fields and forests. It never occurred to me to be afraid during those many years; although the peasants from all of the surrounding villages knew that I was carrying a lot of money, nothing bad ever happened to me.

When a peasant spotted a Jewish estate-holder driving on the road, he would doff his cap to greet him. There were, however, those among the village-gentiles who did not like Jews much and were not keen to doff their caps. Still, they were afraid that a Polish *porits,* civil servant or well-known estate-holder might drive by, which would require doffing one's cap. So they came up with a solution so smart that it could only have come from a peasant: when they spotted a wagon coming from afar, they placed their hands on their caps. If it was someone that they had to greet, the hand was ready and they quickly yanked their caps off of their heads. If it was an ordinary Jew, they used the hand to scratch their heads and the cap stayed on. *Kokhmes-yovn* (gentile wisdom)!

Not a single peasant, and certainly not a *parobek*, would have dared to enter a Jewish estate, even the kitchen, without removing his cap and standing bareheaded. If he forgot, a strict *porits* like my father-in-law would give him a good beating and toss him out. A more lenient estate-holder would shout,

"Zhdim tshapke! Nye yestesh v'kartshmye!" (Take off your cap! You're not in a tavern!)

Often, under specific circumstances, most often when they had received something like a drink of whiskey, some peasants would kiss the hands of the estate-holder or his wife, and bow deeply. This was especially true of the *parobkes* and the *shikses*.

The kids also knew that they had to be polite to a Jew and show him respect; insulting him was out of the question. I was once on my way to the fair in Shtsutsin, and rode past the large and wealthy village of Sluptse. It was early in the morning and several 10–12 year-old boys were on their way to school. As I passed them, they tossed a few small stones at me, the way children are wont to do, none of which hit me. Still, this upset me a lot, and I ordered my driver to head directly over to the school. There I sharply addressed the teacher, a young Polish man: Did he instruct his pupils in morality and good manners that do not allow for people to pass by peacefully? I also threatened to take the matter to his supervisor in Dombrova. The poor teacher was alarmed, apologized profusely and promised me that he would punish the boys when they arrived. If I wanted to, I was welcome to stay and witness the punishment that they would receive; this sort of behavior would certainly not happen again in the future. I did not want to wait, said goodbye, and went on my way. The next day, I received a letter from him through a special messenger informing me that two of the guilty boys had been punished and had promised him that they would never commit such evil deeds again.

At that time, like now, I was not involved in politics. However, anyone paying attention would have noted the liberal tendencies in Galicia. The government was in cahoots with the Polish *porets*, who promoted the good treatment of the Jews in the country at the expense of the oppressed Polish peasant. There was another thing that was no secret to anybody, although people did not like to talk about it openly. Barely forty years had passed since the great peasant uprising, the "*Povstanie*," which had taken place in the area between Rzeszow and Krakow in 1846. A number of Polish *pritsim* and their families lost their lives under horrible circumstances at the hands of enraged peasants. Many *pritsim* and peasants who had taken part in this "*Povstanie*" were still alive during my time. The government, and especially the *pritsim*, had not overcome their anger at the peasants and would not let them hold their heads up. The winner in all of this was the Jew, in particular the village-Jew, who came into constant contact with the peasant. If there was a trial involving a Jew and a peasant—and it was never about major dealings and usually just had to do with borrowed funds or grain— the Jew was almost always the winner and the peasant had to pay significant court costs that usually exceeded the original sum under dispute.

During my time, a new district judge named Hauser (not a Jew but a geniune Pole) came to Radomishla. He was tall and broad-shouldered with a long, grey beard. He was very harsh and everyone was afraid of him. Initially, he was reputed to be an anti-Semite, and the peasants had great hopes for him. However, with time he altered these views while remaining harsh towards the peasants. Peasants were addressed either in the informal, *thou*, or formal, *you*, whereas a Jew of any age was always addressed as "Sir" (*pan*), even by this strict judge.

I was not involved in very much litigation with the peasants: we lived peacefully together and generally got along. However, I once brought two peasants before the law, and the trial took place with Judge Hauser presiding. He did not know me at all and I won the case. This is the story: The Yozefov Estate, where I lived, constantly suffered from a shortage of workers, and there was always more work than there were bodies to do it. Once, during a dry year, the peasants had very little grain and many of them were experiencing a food shortage by the time the harvest came around. Several gentiles came to me to ask for wheat or rye, to be paid off in labor. I agreed and distributed about 25 sacks of grain, and each man took one, two or three sacks according to the size of his family. I did not inflate the price; I charged them the same cost as in town. However, as soon as they got their hands on the grain, they vanished. Although I sent word that the debt could wait and that I would pay them in cash, they still opted to work for anyone but me.

The whole summer went by and very few of the men worked off their debts. They did not even present themselves to me that winter, when they had little else to do. This greatly upset me and my wife and we decided to take them to court. Because I was reluctant to go to court with 10–12 peasants, I settled on two. I selected the worst of the lot, the two who thought they were "clever." I wanted to see how Judge Hauser would rule.

During the trial, Judge Hauser asked one of the peasants what he had to say about my accusations, and he innocently responded that instead of actual grain, he had only received "*stokles*" (chaff) from me. As soon as he had finished uttering these words, the judge leapt up from his chair and shouted angrily,

"How is that when you were hungry and took the food, it was grain, but when it comes time to pay, it suddenly becomes '*stokles*'?" He did not even look at the frightened peasant after this point; he only asked me how much I was owed. I begged the Judge's indulgence: I was not a merchant and had given each farmer several sacks of grain to be repaid in the form of labour, and now they were laughing at me. There had not even been any talk of money.

"Bring them all to me and I will teach them respect," was the Judge's reply. I said that I would rely on him to determine the costs. He soon calculated the full sum that I was owed, plus about five gulden in expenses. He did not bother much with the second peasant, who stood before him trembling and afraid to open his mouth. He immediately pleaded "guilty" and the Judge calculated the same penalties for him. During the course of the week, all of the guilty peasants presented themselves to me and begged me not to take them to court; from here on in, they would be good and God-fearing and pay off their debts in labor. This they did.

The unrestricted hegemony that village Jews, that is to say, estate-holders, had over the peasants was also apparent when it came to the female gender, both married and single women. There were various reasons behind this. The estate-holders, especially the younger ones, went around more nicely and richly dressed than the average peasant. They also had better and more genteel manners and this elevated them in the eyes of the young peasant women or *shikses*.

In a manor economy, there are always jobs that require a single female worker in a storehouse or other location. And leaving two young people alone never leads to any good. However, the young Jews had enough common sense not to get involved for too long with a single woman—like Damask did—and become an "item" with her. There were certainly enough cases of this sort of encounter: most everyone in the area knew, but no one talked about it or gave on that they knew. This was also true of the Catholic priests, the guardians of morality: every one of their believers had to go to confession several times a year, or once at the very least, and their female constituents certainly told them about their relations with Jews. Still, the priests never talked and did not denounce them to the church, as was their habit.

This was, however, only true concerning Jewish men in the villages. The city Jews had no opportunity for such behavior. And when it came to Jewish females in the villages, be it women or girls, they were really modest and no one ever had a bad word to say about them. On a moral and spiritual level, they stood much too far above the peasants to lower themselves for them. During all of my 17 or 18 years of living in villages, there were only two known cases of Jewish girls apostatizing and marrying gentile men. One of these was born to an 86 year-old leaseholder and a very young mother.

I will write more about the other Christians, including *pritsim*, gendarmes, and priests, the next chapter.

40
Pritsim, Gendarmes, and Priests

In our area, there were no rich *pritsim* like the Pototskis, Golokhovskis or other Polish magnates. The other *pritsim* were not very wealthy and had to rely on the Jews in some form. Almost all of them were very liberal people and displayed no resentment towards the Jews, although one cannot know what was in their hearts.

In my neighbourhood in the village of Sluptse, there lived a *porits* named Kishilevski. Our fields bordered on each other. Aside from both of us taking special care to ensure that our livestock did not sneak onto the other's fields and cause damage, we were very friendly, although from a distance. We never became friends and we really had nothing in common. Nevertheless, we got along well as neighbors, and if one of us was in need of assistance, the other was always ready to help. I was once very sick and no one had much hope for me. When Kishilevski found out about this, he sent his lackey on two separate occasions to inquire how I was doing. When I began to recuperate, his wife sent my wife a large piece of home-made bullion to give me with soup to help me regain my strength. Once during the winter, when all of the grain had been brought in from the fields, a fire broke out in Slupke and destroyed all of the grain and buildings. The *porits* was well insured and did not suffer big financial losses. He was, however, short on straw and hay for his cattle. The next day, I sent him my steward and offered to take in several of his animals for the winter, or loan him several wagons full of straw and hay. He refused the first offer; he claimed that he did not want to burden me too much. But he did borrow ten wagons of hay and straw, which he gratefully repaid the following year. I never heard of a case in the entire region of a *porits* who had negative relations with a Jew, or where he insulted a Jew or harmed him in any way.

In the same village of Slupke, there was another *porits* called Gavronski. He was one of those bona fide Polish troublemakers as well as a lunatic to boot. He was not much of a friend to the Jews and refused to trade with Jewish merchants. His grains, dairy products and other agricultural goods were always sent to a Polish bank in Lemberg that was associated with some *"spulka rolnitsha"* (agricultural union). He was a mean and harsh *porits*: aside from severely beating his servants, it was said that he also beat his own wife, a born countess and a quiet and calm woman.

At one point, the Polish bank and the *spulka* both suddenly went bankrupt and Gavronski was left with major debts. The misfortune left the *porits* so depressed that he put a bullet in his own head. With time, his widow took over the business with the help of relatives. However, she was unable to maintain it for long, and I heard from America, where I was living by that time, that two Jews had taken the estate off her hands under very favorable conditions. At the time that Gavronski had committed suicide, the Poles said to each other that if had traded with Jews, he never would have met this tragic end.

* * *

Among all of the "keepers of law and order" in European lands, the Austro-Hungarian gendarmes played an important role. They were considered very capable and it was largely thanks to them that calm and order prevailed in all of the provinces and that security of person and property was never disturbed.

The imperial gendarmes belonged to the military, but they were always under separate and special command and subject to a strict discipline that far exceeded that of the other soldiers. The gendarmes were thus in a much better position to maintain security and order than other soldiers. It was almost unheard of for a gendarme to be bribed to cause him neglect his duties or not arrest someone, or even for him to be accused of breaking one of the laws of the land.

There was a law that caused leaseholders a lot of anxiety and discomfort and the gendarmes had to uphold it. Every village had an "*oglandatsh*," a peasant who functioned as a sort of lower-rank civil-servant whose job it was to maintain a "*katastre* (public register)" where the number of each estate-holder's calves, cows and oxen were registered (the law did not apply to horses). At the age of just three months, every calf had to be registered in the "*katastre*," and at the age of 18 months, each animal had to be branded indicating the village to which it belonged. However, because the brand soon healed, the "*oglandatsh*" had to return every few months with his hot iron to redo the mark. If one wanted to sell an animal or even to bring it into another village, one needed a special pass. This gentile received a few kreuzer in a fixed tax for everything. The gendarmes had the duty to ensure that every animal was registered with the appropriate symbols, colors, and so on. This ceaselessly drove the estate-holder crazy, especially when he was subject to the constant strict vigilance of the gendarmes. If they chose, they could cause you enormous aggravation as well as monetary expenses.

Once, about three months after settling at Yozefov, I received a summons from the Tarnow district attorney to appear in court on a certain date. My wife and I did not know what to think. I had not committed any crime and could not imagine what the distract attorney could possibly want from me: who knows what kind of punishment was awaiting me? I had no choice but to present myself on the allotted day. It turned out that a gendarme had accused me of violating a certain paragraph of the legal code because a calf of mine was spotted without the correct symbol on him. I was not even asked if I had anything to say in my defense. A civil servant said a few words that I couldn't even understand, and then another civil servant announced my punishment: a fine of a single gulden! If the "*posev*" (summons) had stated the "crime" that I was being accused of, I would not have dragged myself so many miles and avoided the few gulden of unnecessary accompanying expenses. But this was the modus operandi of the Galician courts: they never took into account the interests of the citizens and just carried on in their old, ossified ways.

Since then, whenever I received a summons like this, I paid it no heed and did not travel the six miles all the way to Tarnow. Instead, I was "*konstomatsirt*," that is, sentenced in absentia and fined a whole gulden. If I paid the fine quickly, the Tarnow district attorney's office sent the "*Virok*" (sentence) to the district court of Radomishla, and they dispatched a "*Vozhni*" (court usher) to collect the gulden from me, two miles away. At that point, I also had to pay him the required tax of 17 kreuzer. On top of this, I offered him—he was, after all, a governmental official—a nip of whiskey. Sometimes my wife would also lay out some bread, butter and a glass of milk that the official consumed with great gusto and appreciation.

However, a gendarme is, in the end, just flesh and blood with desires. If the gendarmes needed something, they had no choice but to come to the village Jew, particularly to the estate-holder. The post of a gendarme was very difficult: he was almost constantly on the road, regardless of the weather. When others were asleep with a roof over their heads, the gendarme had to walk from village to village and be exposed to the elements: rain, snow and darkness, heat and cold.

The gendarme station in our region was in Radomishla and controlled a two-mile perimeter around the city. The Constable was a Jew called Hershl (or Hessel). Overall, there were very few Jews in the gendarmerie: Jews were never eager to join this particular difficult service for which one had to volunteer. The higher officers were also not exactly falling over themselves to have Jewish gendarmes. All of the gendarmes were experienced soldiers, train conductors, or sergeants and had to have some kind of education, at the least reading and writing. Without these qualifications, one could not become a gendarme. No one knew whether this Constable Hershl was an apostate or not. He used to talk with me a lot, but never about himself.

All of the gendarmes lived and ate together in one barracks except for the Constable, who lived alone. If one of them left on "*sluzshbe*" (duty), it was normally for a period of 24 to 30 hours. During this time, he had to be on his feet the entire time to stop in at every manor, inn and at every peasant's and "judge's" to find out any news, but he was not allowed to eat, drink or sleep anywhere. He had a piece of bread and sausage in his "*tornister*" (bag) to quell his hunger. These gendarmes were, however, young guys with healthy appetites and it was impossible for them to follow these requirements too strictly. There was no better place to assuage their hunger and thirst, and to catch a little sleep than at the Jewish estate-holder's.

To appeal to the peasants for these things was beneath the dignity of the gendarmes. First of all, the peasants' "*khates*" (little houses) were never as clean as what the gendarme was accustomed to: even though he himself was a peasant boy or a town gentile, a "*miestshan*" (townlet dweller), he had become accustomed to the military life of the gendarme. Secondly, it would have been degrading to befriend a peasant whom he might very well have to deal with harshly the next day. The same applied to the Jewish villagers or tenant farmers, although to a lesser extent. There were "too many eyes" at the inn and he often found himself in the company of drunks and other suspicious persons from whom he had to protect himself and his honor, and with whom he had to deal pretty harshly. He was thus left with no other option but to become a sort of household member at the Jewish estate-holder's, where he always found a ready table and a place to rest his head for a couple of hours. These visits certainly suited the estate-holder. After all, one could not bribe a gendarme, and no one dared to try. But once he had eaten and drunk, he could not be so crude as to cause an estate-holder too many difficulties, although there were some individuals who did just that.

On countless nights when it was snowing, or storming, I would get a knock at my window from a gendarme. I, or oftentimes my wife, had to get out of bed, let him in, offer him food and drink, brew hot tea, and chat with him for two or three hours until he left or lay down on the sofa to nap. The Chief Constable always kept his gendarmes under the strictest of discipline. In order to assure himself that they were really fulfilling their prescribed duty, he would send a controller or go out after them himself, despite the fact that he was slightly lame in one leg. Even in the worst weather, he would sometimes seek out, and inquire about the whereabouts of his gendarmes.

Once, a very funny story happened that could have resulted in a very tragic end for a gendarme. It was a winter night, and the weather outside was very raw and stormy. The night was young: it was about eight o'clock. Just then, a gendarme was sitting at our house, eating and drinking. His "*zhona*" (gendarmes always call their loaded rifles "*zhona*," or wife) was standing in the corner of the room. This was strictly forbidden: during his entire period of duty, a gendarme must wear his rifle on his shoulder or have it in his hand at all times. A gendarme without a rifle is no gendarme at all. While this gendarme, my wife and I sat and chatted, there came a sudden knock at the shutters.

"*Vakhtmishtsh!*" uttered the gendarme quietly, and turned as white as a ghost.

We soon grasped the implications of what was happening and understood that the entire future of this young man was at stake. However, my wife did not lose her wits. She quickly shoved the gendarme into an adjacent bedroom and gave him a wink indicating that he should crawl as is into my bed. She handed him his rifle in the bedroom and he hid it under the bed.

Meanwhile, I went to answer the door. Yes, it really was Constable Hershl. His first words, once he had come inside, were to ask whether the gendarme had been at our place that night. We answered him that he had been by about an hour before to inquire whether there was any news, and then promptly headed off to the nearby village of Budzin. As I was talking with him in the kitchen, my wife was busy tidying up the dining room table, set a place, and brought in fresh bread, butter and cheese as well as a bottle of whiskey for "Mr. Constable." Although Hershl was a tough disciplinarian with the other gendarmes, he was only human, and frozen and famished to boot. It was not hard to convince him to have a drink and wash down some bread and butter with hot tea. The best part was that "Mr. Constable" stood his own "*zhona*" in the same corner where the rifle of the gendarme had stood only moments earlier, the same gendarme he was now looking for who was lying in my bed next door, listening to everything that we were saying.

My wife and I noticed this, exchanged glances, and were barely able to keep from bursting into laughter. I also noted that this could go on forever: the Constable obviously had no intention of leaving and might very well want to lie down for a few hours on the sofa in the same room. What to do with the gendarme when the bedroom had no other exit but through the dining room where we were all sitting? Things looked really bad.

But I soon had a thought, and my wife cleverly picked up on it and immediately grasped my intention to get rid of the Constable. I began to talk about the bad weather and pitied myself for having to head over to my uncle Shimen's place in Budzin to talk over an important matter: Should I go or not? Perhaps put it off until the next day?

"Don't be lazy! If you have to go, then go!" My wife accused me of laziness: "By the time you get dressed tomorrow, your uncle will have already left for town and will tarry there until late in the evening!" So it was decided that I would go, and because I did not want to waken one of the workers, who were already asleep, I harnessed a couple of horses to the wagon and soon returned to the house. And if "Mr. Constable" so desired, he could ride with me to Budzin. He soon agreed and after we had both had a few drinks of whiskey, we found ourselves in the wagon on the way to Budzin. He was silent for a few minutes. Then he tapped me lightly on the shoulder and spoke to me for the first and last time in Yiddish:

"You are a clever young man, a real *gemore-kepl*. Do you think that I don't know that that boy is in your bedroom? You are only driving now in order to fool me and get me out of the house so that he has a chance to escape. I saw him through the window sitting at the table with his rifle in the corner. You were really clever and this most certainly would have caused a major scandal. I would have had to arrest him. I have to be really strict with the boys, especially because I am a Jew. My position requires it." By this time, we had arrived near Budzin. The Constable shook my hand and said a heartfelt goodbye. I did not bother stopping at my uncle Shimen's place. Instead I headed right home. The gendarme and his rifle were gone and my wife was really pleased that things had turned out so well.

A week later, the gendarme was at our place again. This simple and decent boy could not thank us enough for the favor we had done: we had saved his life, plain and simple. He also told us that he would not be staying in our area for much longer. He had already put in a request to be transferred to another post in a different part of the country.

"I have a feeling that the Constable knows that I was hidden here, and although he has not said a word about it, I can't look him in the eye."

* * *

By and by, my wife and I became "confidants" and "bigwigs" among all of the gendarmes. We were in their good graces and they tried to cause us as little trouble as possible.

One evening, a gendarme suddenly visited one of our stalls and he found the old cattle-hand holding his lantern in one hand and doing something to the animals with the other. A candle was burning in the lantern, one of the glass panes was missing in the wooden lantern. The gendarme brought the anxious man into the house and reviewed the rules and regulations with him. He wanted to know how long the glass pane had been missing from the lantern: was it a day or two, or a whole week? It seemed to me that this fine gendarme also wanted to get me involved me in the matter, and this was not the sort of infraction, like a calf, that one could get out of with a gulden at the Tarnow court; it was worth a whole 25 gulden, and if the judge was so inclined, it could include several days in jail.

When the gendarme had finished with the cattle-hand, he dismissed him and continued writing. After some time, when he had finished and was putting the paper into his bag, I requested to see what he had written. When handed me the piece of paper, I immediately ripped it up without even looking at him.

"*Tso pan zrobil* (What have you done, *porits*)?" He jumped up, clearly agitated. My wife was also shocked. You didn't start anything with a gentile, especially a gendarme; it was a bad idea. But I stood and laughed.

"You're my friend, and now you want to stir up so much trouble for me over a little piece of glass that just went missing this evening? I would never have expected this sort of thing from you."

The gendarme softened up. He smiled, gathered up all of the pieces of paper lying on the table, and burned them in the fire.

"Please buy a new lantern tomorrow, a tin one. If tomorrow's patrol is another gendarme or the Constable, they won't be so nice about it."

My wife and I were not only able to prevail upon the gendarmes or Constable on our own behalf, but all of the village Jews and some of the estate-holders in the area knew that if they ran into trouble, they could come to us and we would smooth things over. In fact, the biggest favor that we ever did was for my father-in-law.

The gendarmes, who had never had a great relationship with the few Polish *pritsim* in our area, also avoided the Zgursk manor and never wanted have a bite or drink there. They limited dealing with the Polish *pritsim* as much as possible because they were afraid of them. The *pritsim* were well connected and if a gendarme harassed them too much, they knew where to go and complain. The outcome was that this too-strict gendarme would suddenly vanish from the area: he was deported somewhere to the mountains far away in a remote region of the country.

However, the gendarmes were very afraid of my father-in-law. They knew full well that he couldn't do anything to them and that he lacked access to the upper echelons of their superior officers. And because he did not treat them like most of the Jewish estate-holders and give them free reign, they often subjected him to minor and major pranks. They also generally filed charges of "transgressions" to the court where no lawyers were permitted in one's defense and one had to pay through the nose whatever the judge ruled. When my father-in-law, and especially my mother-in-law, found out that my wife and I lived so peaceably with the gendarmes, they asked us to exert our influence to stop the harassment in the Zgursk Manor.

This was not so easy for us. Some of the gendarmes were sharp and bitter boys who complained that they did not like proud and unfriendly people. Still, we did not give up and enlisted the help of Bobe Nekhome, the "*Stari Pani Shtiglitsova*," who ran a wine bar. All of the gendarmes and watchmen were her clients and knew her well. She was eloquent and was a popular and very clever lady. With her help, we prevailed upon the gendarmes to come to the Zgursk Manor outside of their periods of duty, with the promise that they would be received as welcome guests. My father-in-law swallowed his pride and spent time with the gendarmes and they considered it a major honor to be received in such a friendly manner by the estate-holder of Zgursk. From that time on, the charges ceased completely and if the gendarmes occasionally spotted a "transgression," they pretended not to see it.

Often, when the circumstances permitted it, I would try to convince my father-in-law that friendliness and flexibility can accomplish more than pride and rigidity. He almost never responded to my lectures; he was a man of few words to begin with. He understood that I was right, but he continued on in his accustomed ways that he found difficult to change.

41
PRITSIM, GENDARMES, AND PRIESTS
(*continued*)

Let's not kid ourselves. Priests, especially Catholic priests, cannot ever really be friends of the Jews. If a priest is really knowledgeable in the basic tenets of his faith—there are major ignoramuses among them, too—he knows all too well that it is almost against his religion to love people of another faith. Quite a few Church laws and Papal Bulls remain from earlier, darker times of the Middle Ages that have not lost their power and effectiveness to the present day. Because both the government and economic circumstances work against them, these laws are not applied in practice as widely as before. Still, a priest can cause the Jews a lot of anxiety and unpleasantness if he so desires.

There is, for example, a Church law that dates back several hundred years that prohibits gentiles from occupying positions as servants in Jewish homes; it explicitly prohibits them from being wet nurses. When Jews began to get involved in agriculture and became big estate-holders and needed large numbers of workers, this rotten Church law lost its significance. Even if the peasants wanted to uphold this particular law, where would they find work, if not with the Jewish estate-holder? Nevertheless, if a priest desired, he took this law out of his old and rusty butter cask and held sermons in his church, sometimes going so far as to threaten that transgressors would be denied access to confession.

* * *

Luckily for the Jewish estate-holders, our region did not have these kinds of priests. There were no great friends of the Jews among them, but there were also no outspoken anti-Semites. They remained neutral, neither positive nor negative. However, I once become acquainted with a young priest and our "friendship" lasted for some time.

Every big village has its own church, a "*parafia*" (parish) that services the few surrounding villages. There were usually two priests. The older one, the "*probotsht*," lives on the "*plebania*" (church grounds) and has many fields and a large number of cattle at his disposal. The younger priest is an assistant, the vicar. This person is usually a recent graduate of the seminary and is doing his practicum with the senior priest. His upkeep is very small: he receives room and board from his boss. He does, however, have several enterprises going on the side that bring in quite a tidy sum during the course of the year.

One of these enterprises is the "*dzsheieshiontik*," the tithe. When the grain has been harvested from the fields, the vicar travels around to all of the villages in his *parafia* and the peasants have to give him a tenth of their grain. This was an old Church law that had been rescinded: in exchange, the priests received their *plebanias from* the Polish *pritsim*. However, the custom remained: every peasant gave the priest several sacks of his grain, according to his wealth and his level of religious observance.

The Yozefov Estate belonged to the Wadovitz parish. My arrival coincided with the arrival of a new vicar and he began making the rounds of "his" villages soon after the harvest. I was once standing in the yard of my estate when I spotted a big haycart, and seated next to the driver was a priest wearing a broad, black hat. I approached the wagon. As soon as the young man saw me, he seemed a little embarrassed and ordered the driver to turn the horses around and leave the yard. After all, what business did he have at a Jew's? But I immediately went over and greeted him,

"Now that Mr. Vicar has, even if by accident, entered my yard, he must do me the honor of coming inside." It did not take long to convince him. He had probably never set foot in a Jewish house before and wanted to see what it looked like, and he got down from the wagon and came inside. As was the custom, we first had a little drink of whiskey with something to eat and had a pleasant time. Meanwhile, my wife asked the peasant to drive to one of our storehouses and had him get out ten big bundles of wheat. When he returned and the priest saw the bundles of grain, he was initially reluctant to accept them. He did not know, or so he thought to himself, whether it was in accord with "*kostshelni zakon*" (church law) to accept the "tithe" from a "*nievierni*" (from a non-believer, that is, a Jew). However, I persuaded him and he allowed himself to be talked into taking the bundles of wheat.

From then on, we became friendly. He would invite me to visit him at his home for a glass of tea and a game of chess, and I was there on several occasions and had a good time. Several months later, mid-winter, came the season of the Christian holidays when all Catholics, big and small, have to confess to the priest. The young priest traveled across the villages to collect eggs, butter, honey, and vegetables from the peasants. He also visited me, but asked my wife not to give him anything because he was there not as a priest but as a friend. We never spoke about religious matters. He often liked to talk about the German classics: Schiller, Lessing, Heine and the others whose names he knew but had never read because such literature was considered heretical at the seminary. But this was precisely why he wanted to read them now. I owned several of these publications, acquired through the Reclams Universalbibliothek at 12 kreuzer a piece new and 5–6 kreuzer secondhand. I gave him some of these volumes as a gift and also loaned him a Polish-German dictionary. The unfortunate man struggled with these classics because he was no expert in the German language.

Our friendship was cut short because of an act of tactlessness on his part. Once, when I was at his house playing a game of chess and drinking tea, he suddenly asked me whether I had ever been inside a Catholic church. When I replied in the negative, he became very enthusiastic and began to describe the beauty of the Catholic church and the splendor found there; they were not as dry and simple as the Jewish synagogues. He proposed that we go immediately to the nearby church, and he would explain it all to me. When I declined and said that I did not have the time, he proposed a much better plan: every Sunday evening, he held his "*kazania*" (sermon); I could come and hear him speak and then he would show me the whole church. I hurriedly bade him farewell, and we did not see each other again. I did not go to see him, and he did not come and see me. I understood that it was high time to end our friendship. I certainly did not need it to be known that I was friends with a priest and that I was going to see him at church!

* * *

I never got to know the "*probotsht*" of the Wadovitz parish, the superior of "my" vicar. I never had any real dealings with him until I once brought him a gift: six big, live carp. The circumstances were as follows:

The four million Galician Poles who were followers of the Roman Catholic Church have about ten bishops in total. This means that every bishop has authority over about half a million people as well as a large number of priests and churches. At that time, a new bishop came to Tarnow, the bishopric. His name was Lobus, and I think that he had been bishop of Premishla before. He had a reputation as a liberal and something of a friend of the Jews because he would not permit his priests to convert Jewish girls who were still minors without their parents' permission, as was the practice in other parts of Galicia. It is an old custom that when a bishop takes over a new post, he spends some time traveling to all of the cities, towns, and important villages of his diocese to get to know the land and its people. When this Bishop Lobus assumed his seat in Tarnow, he did the same: he took a trip across the entire region.

He arrived in Radomishla right on the eve of Rosh Hashana (or maybe it was Yom Kippur). The city was filled with thousands of people who had come from the surrounding villages with their crosses and icons. At the entrance of the town market, a *"brama,"* or honourary gate, had been erected next to which all of the town's civil servants and VIPs stood, including the Jewish community leaders and other important Jews. The Bishop's greeting to the people was friendly but very brief. He soon drove off to the town priest's, whose guest he was during his entire stay in the region.

Several days later, the Jewish community leaders went to welcome him. They gathered in the home of my grandfather-in-law, Reb Yudl Shtiglitz, and because I just so happened to be there at the time, I also attended. The reception was very friendly. We were all invited to sit and the Bishop sat among us and carried on a conversation with us. He asked how many Jews there were in the city, what their occupations were, and their overall economic state. He also asked whether we had a *"dukhovni"* (a spiritual leader or rabbi), and when we answered in the affirmative but that the Rabbi was currently ill and bedridden, he expressed his sympathy and wished him a speedy recovery.

I had the ideal opportunity to make the observation that the higher priests were, in some respects, similar to our rabbis and Hassidic *rebbes*. The Bishop was a tall and sturdy man, about 50 years old and clean-shaven. He wore a satin skullcap on his head and his broad body was covered in a black satin fur-lined coat. He smoked a long pipe with a big mouthpiece that he kept in his mouth all the time. From a pocket in his satin cloak, a red kerchief protruded and on the table lay a big, thick silver watch (that was called a *"tsibele zeyger,"* an onion watch), just like I had seen among some Hassidic *rebbes*. He held a fine and large silver tobacco box into which he would often reach and bring a little snuff between his fingers to his nose. He would often lift his eyes to the heavens and heave a light sigh, *"al goles hashkhine* (for the Divine Presence's exile)." If you had not heard him speak Polish and not seen his clean-shaven face, you would surely have assumed that this was a rabbi or even a Hassidic *rebbe*.

About eight days later, I received a letter via a special messenger from my "friend," the Wadovitz Vicar (this was before our "friendship" was suspended) with a small request: his superior had the privilege of having the Bishop of Tarnow as his guest and was preparing a great feast for his invited guests; would I perhaps be willing to honor this feast with a little fish? We in Yozefov had always been the "capital" of fish. Aside from two rivers, the bigger Bren and the much smaller Ribnitsa that cut through our fields where we caught many fish, I also had my own private stream with many big carp in it. I was the only estate-holder in the area that owned a river with fish like this. I soon called on two of my laborers to get me six of the biggest carp out of the river. I had learned from my father-and-law as well as from my wife that if you do something, you should do it with open hands.

The six live carp weighed about eight kilograms a piece, or at least fifty kilograms in all. A barrel of water was placed on a wagon and the fish were thrown into it. The journey from Yozefov to the Wadovitz parish was not far—maybe three quarters of a mile—and I, together with my laborer and the messenger, soon arrived. The joy of the young vicar, when he saw me with the barrel of fish, was indescribable. He soon ran to his superior to tell him the good news. Meanwhile, several workers took the barrel off the wagon and brought it into the kitchen. When the Senior Priest saw the big carp thrashing like calves, he went right back into the house and returned with the Bishop. He proudly showed him the live fish that *Pan Dzsherdzavtsa* (Mr. Estate-holder) had brought. Within a moment, I realized that not only Jewish scholars have a sharp eye: As soon as the Bishop had taken a look at me, he said,

"If I am not mistaken, I saw you last week at the Radomishla *plebania*." There he had seen me in a long cloak, and here I was in a short coat.

"Yes," I replied with deep bow. "I have already had the great honor to greet His Eminence. I was there with my *teshtsh* (father-in-law)." He gave a slight nod with his head and headed back into the house.

Some forty years have passed since then, but every time that I remember this event, I am also forced to recall the question of the Vicar, who asked me several weeks later whether I had ever been inside a church and would I like to hear him preach. Who knows whether there was not some kind of connection between the young Vicar's question and the old Bishop? Maybe they chatted about me and said that it would be a great achievement to cause a nice soul like mine to enter "*takhas kanfey heshkhine* (under the wings of the Divine Presence)"?

* * *

I did not really know the Radomishla Priest. Like the other Jews in town, I had no dealings, neither positive nor negative, with this small, thin, but lively man. However, I was once present when this priest made a faux pas that caused his moral defeat, specifically at the hands of my father-in-law. I and the other Jews derived great pleasure from this.

The Radomishla marketplace was flanked by Jewish homes on three sides. The fourth and much shorter side bordered the priests' *plebania*, which is hidden by shrubs and trees. Adjacent to the priest's grounds were several houses, including my father-in-law's house. The grounds included several buildings around the house—a stable, a stall, and another small building—as well as several acres of fields: an entire farm in miniature.

Once summer Sunday afternoon, the "*yingl* (boy)" from Zgursk—one always had a Jewish assistant, a "*yingl*," aside from one's general manager—came with a wagon in order to transport a dozen wooden boards from the townhouse to Zgursk. My father-in-law's blacksmith, a gentile, just happened to be there, and when he saw the boy with the wagon, he went up to him in order to catch a ride home while helping him load the boards. The "*yegomotsht*," the senior priest, watched this through his window and this ignited his sense of piety: what was the meaning of this desecration of the Sunday? Was it not enough that the Jews worked so hard with the gentiles all week? Did the miserable creatures also have to engage in such drudgery on the Holy Sunday? No! He could not sit back quietly and let it happen!

He quickly and quietly dispatched someone to the municipal offices to bring one of the town's two policeman (the other was lame). He ordered the policeman to arrest everyone—the boy, the blacksmith, and even the horses and wagon—and bring them over to the municipal offices. It was a beautiful, warm afternoon, and half of the town was in the marketplace. When people spotted the policeman leading out the blacksmith and the boy riding a horse-drawn wagon full of boards, followed by the angry and agitated priest in his summer attire, the market became crowded with Jews, as well as peasants who had stayed in town after church.

My father-in-law, I, and several others were sitting at my grandfather-in-law's house in a room where the windows faced onto the manor so we were oblivious to what was going on in the marketplace. But a little boy ran in and cried out,

"Mordecai Dovid's blacksmith and the boy have been arrested!" We all jumped up and ran out of the house and made our way to the nearby municipality. We were barely able to push our way through the throng. We finally arrived just as the Priest was presenting his complaints to the Secretary of the municipal offices. He hotly demanded that the Secretary detain the blacksmith, the boy and the horses and wagon until the following day, when he would formally present his complaint before the courts about this great violation of the Holy Sunday.

The priest had barely finished stating his demands when my father-in-law, also agitated and as pale as a sheet, began to speak.

"The horses and wagon," he said, "are mine. The people whom *Pan Probotsht* seeks to arrest are my employees. I am no stranger here, but a homeowner in the town and an estate-holder in the region. If *Pan Probotsht* really wants to indict them, he can do so tomorrow. I guarantee that both of the accused will appear as summoned." The priest spoke again and restated his original demands. My father-in-law responded again until the Secretary stated his opinion:

"I have no right to hold these two accused men because a '*honorovi obievatel*' (honorable citizen) like Mr. Shtiglitz is pledging on their behalf."

The priest headed home, fuming, but nothing more came of the matter. He probably conceded the foolishness and pointlessness of his rash behavior.

* * *

I had another association with a priest, although this one was not actually a full priest yet but in the final course at the Seminary. The "*oglandatsh bilda*" (cattle inspector) and keeper of the "*katastre*" in the village of Yozefov was a peasant named Jan Korzhen. He considered himself something of a government official and could read and write. He often had dealings with the gendarmes and even with the *starosta* (lower government official) in Melitz. For this reason, some people even called him "*Pania Jania*;" it had not reached the point where people called him *Pan* Korzhen. (As was the custom *pan* was used to refer to him by his given name, but not his family name.) He was a well-to-do peasant and had a single son whom he wanted to turn into a priest. When I was in Yozefov, this young man was studying at a Seminary somewhere near Lemberg.

When he would come home during the summer vacations, his father would drive him around a show him off. Because I was good friends with his father and because he considered me a "*utshoni*" (learned man), he brought over his son and presented him to me. This priest–in-the-making was a tall, skinny young man named Stefan. People called him *Pan* Korzhen. He had one more year left at the Seminary and then he would become a vicar. Still, this boy was a real blockhead.

His father had barely introduced us when he began to tell me that he loved all of the people from the "*stari zakon*" (the Old Testament), that is to say, Jews. His love for them was so great that he really wanted them to become "*vierni*" (believers, Christians). He hoped to God—he was really only addressing God here—that he would become a great priest and then devote all of this time and energy to the holy goal of making the Jews see the truth and unite with the believers. He hoped that the government as well as the Pope would help him out. This half-baked priest visited me two or three more times over the summer. He had nothing else to talk about and kept restating his love for the Jews. In later years, I stopped seeing him around. He probably got some post as vicar or maybe he smartened up and gave up the priesthood. In any case, I never heard from him again and did not miss him much.

42

THE "WEDDING"

We were young and lived in "the lap of luxury" without a care it he world. We once commited such a nasty deed that even today, so many decades later, my face still burns with shame. The story might be a little long, but it is interesting.

Not far from the Yozefov Estate, where I had been living for a full two years, lay the Budzin Estate, which belonged to my wife's uncle, Shimen Sandhaus. He was the most refined and learned man in the entire family. Born in Ropshits, he was quite well-read in holy texts, could lead prayers nicely, and could write a pretty decent letter in *loshn-koydesh*. He was also known to occasionally crack a simple *seyfer*.

During his lifetime, he had always been the poorest man in the whole family. Everyone was always supporting him and helping him out with cash and merchandise. This, however, did not help much. First of all, he had a fairly small estate that barely provided him with a livelihood. On top of this, he had ten children to support (all of the members of the Kilkever family had a lot of children). He thus found himself in a perpetual state of need and in some embarrassing predicament that one of his brother-in-laws had to get him out of. Still, this Uncle Shimen was always a jolly man, cheerful in the extreme. I almost never saw him gloomy or worried. He might have the biggest problems and one could not tell. He always had a friendly smile on his face and was constantly telling jokes.

"Shimen is happily indifferent, totally unaffected by petty problems," the family was always saying about him, unable to understand how a person like him could always be bubbly and cheerful. As a father of ten children, one smaller than the next, he kept a *melamed*. For a time, he also kept an assistant for the really small ones who also helped out on the farm. These village-*melamdim* were usually not great scholars and did not really like to stay in one place: teach for a season, or two at most, and then find another boss.

* * *

Once, before the winter, Shimen Sandhaus had a *melamed* named Reb Sinai. He was a sturdy and hairy man, about 60 years of age. He looked like a noble Jew and he used to lead prayers. However, I never really had much to do with him. When I would come to the *minyen* every *shabbes* morning, I would chat with Uncle Shimen and Aunt Khaye as well as with the *melamed*, Reb Sinai.

Once, a week after Purim during prayers, the *melamed* told me that he wanted to come and see me in Yozefov with three of his older students so that I could examine them in a bit of Gemara and *Khumesh* with Rashi. I agreed, and he came with his students. I examined them and my wife received everyone with refreshments. At that time, our cook was a very fine and intelligent Jewish girl named Mrese from the nearby *shtetl* of Shtsutsin. She was an orphan, without a father. Her mother, a poor but decent woman, did not want to have her go and serve anywhere but with my wife, whose family had a very good reputation in the region. This girl was very pretty, tall, and extremely capable to boot. My wife thought very highly of her. When the *melamed* and his students were at my house, he was clearly attracted to her. He did not wait for her to come to us; he got up several times from the table to wander around the kitchen to get a better look at her.

At that time, a young man, a "*milkhiker* (dairyman)" lived together with my wife and me. He would collect all of the milk from the 50–60 cows and make butter and cheese, which he brought to Radomishla, Tarnow or Shtsutsin to sell. The dairyman lived in a separate little house in the yard proper, and he was a constant guest in our house. When this Khaim-Leyzer (or Harmuzin, as the gentiles called him) saw the *melamed* with the children, he soon came in and joined our conversation. This Khaim-Leyzer was a crafty boy as well as a prankster. When he spotted how the old man was constantly wandering around the kitchen and that he was simply devouring the girl with his eyes, he had a thought: let's get them engaged and have a wedding!

He called and my wife and me aside and told us that the *melamed* was lusting after the girl, and that if he could stage a wedding, we would split a gut laughing. When we agreed, Khaim-Leyzer got to work. He soon persuaded the girl to play the part of a bride and to be willing to do anything he asked. She agreed and promised to honorably and loyally play the role of Reb Sinai's bride. Then he got to work on the old *melamed*:

"How was it that a man like you, a scholar and respected gentleman, is without a wife? This is against the laws of the holy Torah!" Reb Sinai responded that there was nothing standing in the way between him and marriage and that he also owned several hundred gulden, but he had not found a *shidekh* that suited his stature. At this, Khaim-Leyzer took him aside out of earshot of his students, who were 15 year-old boys, and told him that he had a match for him, and that it was certainly divinely ordained that he just happened to come to the house where the bride was. Khaim-Leyzer told him that he had already spoken with Mrese about the matter, and that she was willing; because she stemmed from a genteel family, she wanted to marry a scholar, even if he was a little older than her.

When I saw the two of them standing and chatting, I went over. Khaim-Leyzer told me what it was about and I also approved the match. I assured the *melamed* that the girl had already collected 150 gulden towards her dowry. There was not much work left to do on Reb Sinai, and he soon agreed to the match. Khaim-Leyzer then called in the girl and asked her whether she was willing, and she nodded. She did the same when Reb Sinai asked her himself. As befits a quiet, Jewish girl, she did not say anything; she just nodded and returned to the kitchen.

Night had barely fallen when I sent a servant on a horse to Uncle Shimen. I briefly announced the happy match that had just been arranged and asked him to come to our house immediately with Aunt Khaye. Uncle Shimen was an intelligent and crafty man who never said "no" to a joke. He soon got the gist of what was going on and an hour later, he and his wife were with us in Yozefov. After we had congratulated the bride and groom, we began to discuss the date of the wedding. Those of us representing the bride, myself and my uncle, wanted to push off the wedding to the *shabbos* after Shavues, but the groom, Reb Sinai, would not hear of it:

"It is not the custom," he argued, "that the wedding be put off for so long in a second marriage. If God, blessed be his name, has sent me a match that suits me, I don't see why I should have to wait so long." He added shamefacedly, "I want to be a king for Passover and hold my own *seyder*."

We, representatives of the bride, acknowledged the legitimacy of his argument and gave in to his proposal. Khaim-Leyzer, the *shadkhen*, mediated and we decided upon a date for the wedding two weeks from Sunday. The groom hesitated a little: he really wanted the wedding to happen as soon as possible, a week from Sunday at the latest. However, Aunt Khaye pulled him aside and whispered something into his ear about the bride and the Jewish laws of *Nashim* (Women) that left the poor man no other choice but to agree to the date of two weeks from Sunday. We spent several hours like this, eating and drinking, with the groom dashing into the kitchen and hanging around his bride.

The next day was Sunday, the day when I usually rode to see my father-in-law in Zgursk, and oftentimes to Radomishla. When I announced, first in Zgursk and later in town, the news of the "engagement" that had been arranged between the old *melamed* and the young girl, everyone fell down laughing and got a real kick out of the joke. But it did not occur to any of us that the joke would be taken any further and be turned into some kind of "reality." We made this assumption without the groom, the old and smitten *melamed*, Reb Sinai.

When I came home that evening, my wife told me that the groom had come by to spend some time with his bride. Both she and the bride had had struggle mightily to get the passionate groom out of the house and back on his way to Budzin. We heard nothing from him for two or three days, but he was back on Wednesday night.

Every Wednesday was the fair in the *shtetl* of Shtsutsin, half a mile from Radomishla. Reb Sinai went and got hold of a fine gift for his bride. When he returned from the fair, he showed the bride his gift: a fine, satin kerchief that had cost him a whole five gulden.

"Here you go. Wear it well," he said to her with a goofy, romantic smile. "Now you have something to wear when you bless the *shabbes* candles after the wedding." The girl flushed deeply and refused to accept the kerchief. The matchmaker, Khaim-Leyzer, finally talked her into accepting the gift, in particular when my wife told her to take it and promised her that when the joke ended, she could return to the *melamed* the money that he had spent.

"If he is enough of a dimwit to actually believe all of this," Khaim-Leyzer kept repeating, "then I will make him a wedding that he will never forget."

My wife and I, and most especially the girl, did not want to suffer through the groom becoming a regular at our house. I was ready to let the cat out of the bag that it had all been a joke, and to tell him to get this foolishness out of his head. Khaim-Leyzer would not let the matter drop and argued with me and especially my wife until we agreed to take the joke to the next level: to stage a real wedding for Reb Sinai, with music and all of the frills. He pulled Reb Sinai aside and whispered to him that it was not appropriate for a scholar like him to visit the girl and chat with her so much before the wedding. The poor groom had to concede that Khaim-Leyzer was right, and promised not to return until the wedding day.

He kept his word and did not come back. He did send several letters to the bride during the period leading up to the wedding. He hired a boy at a cost of three kreuzer to deliver the letters, and promised him another two if he brought word from the bride. The boy waited and waited, pleading with the "*pania*" to give him some kind of response. But the bride was so "nasty and heartless" that she refused to allow the boy to earn his two-kreuzer bonus, and the groom did not get an answer from her. We read old Reb Sinai's love letters and laughed our heads off at how an old man could make such a fool of himself just like a young boy.

* * *

On the *Shabbes* before the wedding day, I was at my Uncle Shimen's for prayers at one of the three *minyonim* that served the three surrounding villages. The groom, Reb Sinai, was in an elevated position. He alone led the prayers. And when, as befits a groom, he was called up to the Torah, he made us all a *Misheberakh* blessing, first for the bride, Mrese, then his boss and me as those acting on behalf of the bride, and finally for Reb Khaim-Leyzer, the *shadkhen*. After the prayers, the "groom" provided the whole congregation with whiskey and honeycake for the Kiddush, and invited everyone to Yozefov for his wedding on Sunday. The jokes and hilarity that took place during that *minyen* were endless. People just mocked and ridiculed him. However, he was so blinded by love for the pretty girl that he took everything in stride: let them laugh, so long as I get the girl.

On Sunday, I rode to Radomishla and procured about 50 herrings, several large loaves of bread and some other provisions, and hurried home to be on time for the "wedding." When I arrived home late that evening, I encountered several wagons full of Jews—male and female villagers and their children—in the manor who had come to celebrate this unusual wedding. There were 50–60 people, and many others followed. Among them were inn-keepers who supplied a lot of whiskey along with several barrels of beer, and the crowd did not wait for the wedding to begin their revelry. The villagers included several individuals who could scrape out a few tunes on the violin as well as a gentile guy with a big accordion. They started drinking without even waiting for the groom. Men young and old along with their women and girls could not contain themselves and broke into a dance.

The cracking of "*tshvarnia*" (long, woven whips) announced the appearance of a big wagon led by four horses, "*na shpits.*" This was Uncle Shimen and Aunt Khaye, decked out in satin clothes and dripping with jewelry just like at a real wedding. They had all ten children in tow, with Reb Sinai at the head, as befits a royal groom.

Soon the technical difficulties began.

Some pretty village boy Mrese's size had been dressed as the "bride" in her actual clothes. This disguised boy sat between several women the entire time, his face covered with Reb Sinai's satin kerchief like a real bride. Uncle Shimen, and most especially Khaim Leyzer, wanted everything to go like a real wedding: Reb Sinai was to exchange vows with the boy using the ring he had brought, and then the couple was to be led off to "retire," according to the laws of Moses and Israel.

Reb Sinai had fasted all day, and he was told that the bride was fasting, too. He thus requested that there be no undue delays and that the wedding ceremony begin soon. But the villagers, who had had quite a lot to drink, would not hear of it. They weren't much interested in the "wedding" at this point, and they were dancing and skipping with their wives. The whole Yozefov manor was packed not only with Jews, but peasants with their wives and girls who had come to see the "*zhidovske veselia.*" They had a boy with a fiddle in tow and were offered several bottles of whiskey. While the Jews danced indoors, the peasants partied and reveled outside in the yard.

Meanwhile, it was approaching nine o'clock and the groom was pressing us to hurry up and write a *ketubah* and get on with the ceremony. It must also be borne in mind that although the "groom" was enough of a fool to be duped for so long, he was no stranger to Jewish practice and learning like the village Jews who were present, and he knew what the *ketubah* and ceremony entailed. Khaim-Layzer, who had it all figured out, found a solution: he pulled the groom aside and explained that since this was not an "official" (government sanctioned) wedding, they were prohibited from writing a *ketubah* and that the person officiating would have to recite the blessings quietly. The enamored groom went along with this, provided they would hurry up and get to the ceremony.

There were two Jews from a faraway village that Reb Sinai did not know: Reb Mendl Volyer and Reb Shmuel Volyer, both with fine, long beards. Reb Shmuel, who was basically a village butcher, was a big ignoramus. Several years later, incidentally, this same man was caught selling unkosher meat and was banned by the Radomishla Rabbi. Still, his remarkable beard lent him a stately air and he was the one presented to Reb Sinai as the Rabbi of Shtsutsin who was to officiate. The poor butcher got scared and complained of a terrible headache that would not allow him to fulfill his duty. We thus called over Reb Mendl Volyer, who thought highly of himself and was the prayer-leader of his *minyan*, despite the fact that he was as ignorant as the other Jews. He agreed to lead the entire ceremony.

The ceremony began at about ten o'clock. We took a big tablecloth and tied it to four bean poles to serve as our *khupe*. The ceremony took place in the large manor. Everyone held a candle in his hand. All of the peasants were present and splitting their sides with laughter at the thought of "Mendlo" (Mendl), the village errand-boy, playing the role of rabbi. After the musicians had finished playing a *freylakhs* dance "in honor of the bride and groom," the boy who was impersonating the bride was led to the *khupe* together with Reb Sinai.

Reb Mendl, who was "officiating," stood ready with his *siddur* in hand. But instead of reciting the blessing quietly like we had instructed him, he was suddenly overcome with the desire to show off what he knew and he began to chant them in a loud voice. Here it where things went awry. Because he was afraid to utter the name of God in vain, he said "*adoshem elokeinu*" instead. Also, starting with the first blessing, he made some really obvious mistakes that were too much for even the besotted Reb Sinai. The truth began to dawn on the "groom." He abruptly tore the satin cover off of the bride's face to reveal the face of Shloyme, whom he knew very well from the Budzin *shabbes minyen*. Now the real "wedding" began.

I was a young guy of barely twenty at the time, and I had never in my life seen a face as contorted with wild rage as that of the thwarted groom. When the "joke" that had been played suddenly dawned on him, and he realized that he would not get the pretty girl, he went wild and completely lost control. The fact that he was exhausted from the long fast that had lasted from early in the morning to late at night did not help. He began to shriek and rant as if possessed, like a man gone insane. Then he began to curse me, his boss and his wife, and especially the "*shadkhen*," Khaim-Leyzer, with the most awful, horrible obscenities, the likes of which like I had never heard before coming from a Jewish mouth. Finally, he tried to throw some punches, but found himself face-to-face with the frenzied and riotous crowd of village Jews that wanted to grab him and tear him to pieces. A few of us barely just managed to wrest him out of their hands and bring him inside the house. My wife and Aunt Khaye implored him to calm down a little and to have something to eat have such a long and agitated fast. However, he sat in silence and refused to listen to them. He certainly was not going to eat anything. Suddenly he jumped up and darted out of the house. He ran through the entire yard full of Jews and peasants, and disappeared into the dark on the road to Budzin.

The crowd moved back into my house and resumed drinking, carousing, and dancing as if nothing had happened. Some of us, however, were unable to calm down. We had seen the man's wild despair and we were afraid that he might have gone so far as to take his own life. We sent a servant on horseback to Budzin to find out what had happened to him. An hour later, the servant returned and told us that the "rabbi" was lying in his bed, snoring, with a bottle of whiskey next to him. The "wedding guests" partied until about three in the morning and we were barely able to get rid of them.

The next day, when I rode to Budzin to get the latest news, there was no trace of Reb Sinai. He had settled accounts with his boss, collected his bit of pay for the season's work, and without a goodbye, left the court and vanished onto the road towards Radomishla.

* * *

"That wonderful and gay wedding" was the talk of the town for years. Still, today, some fifty years later, my face burns with shame when I think back to the horrible stunt that we pulled off. I only have one defense: we were young, lived in the lap of luxury, and had no troubles. We were in high spirits so we had a little fun. We did not take into account his heart and feelings.

43
SHIMSHEN ASHEIM

One of the most interesting and peculiar personalities residing in our area was the very wealthy and very stingy estate-holder, Shimshen Rzshempniover, or Asheim. His name was famous for miles around. Everyone knew him and had to admit that there was no one like him.

Shimshen Asheim stemmed from a middle-class, stylish family. A brother of his was the chief *shoykhet* in the *shtetl* of Shendishov, near Ropshits. Shimshen was a learned man, had beautiful penmanship, and used to write Hebrew letters full of flowery rhetoric as well as very apt Biblical verses and Gemara references. In his youth, he had been a tenant-farmer in the village of Rzshempniov, about half a mile from the village of Yozefov, and some of our fields bordered each other. I don't know how he came to this village or how he married his crass and ignorant wife, Kreyndl. From what I heard, he was an assistant in her father's inn and subsequently married the daughter.

He lived in this inn for some time until he purchased a full estate from the *porits*, who was half-Polish, half-German, but a complete wastrel. A few years later, he paid half-price, a pittance, for two smaller estates that the *porits* still owned: a total of 700–800 acres of prime fields, with a whiskey distillery to boot. Shimshen also had a hand in money-lending. He offered larger loans to Polish *pritsim* and smaller ones to well-to-do Jews, always at substantial interest rates. When I got to know him in the 1890s, his fortune was valued at a quarter of a million gulden, which was a conservative estimate.

However, this rich man was horrifyingly stingy, and not only with strangers but with himself and his own household. He was always dressed in the most awful clothes, like a pauper or vagrant. He did not care what he wore in social settings. He gave no charity; this was considered throwing money away, and he avoided these types of unnecessary expenses. When a poor man did come to his manor, especially one of the "*sheyne yidn*" or a descendant of some Hassidic leader, the wealthy Reb Shimshen would make a dash for a stall or granary as soon as he spotted the visitor, and hide out until the "descendant" had gotten tired of waiting and left empty-handed. Sometimes it happened that a "descendant" arrived without warning and Reb Shimshen found himself unable to run and hide fast enough. Then he would approach the man, greet him, and say that the Boss had just left for town half an hour earlier and would not return until late that night. The visitor, usually a stranger to the area who did not know Reb Shimshen personally, took him for a servant, believed his story that the Boss was not home, and continued on his way. During the summer, on the hottest days, this wealthy man had the habit of wandering around in his fields without a coat and even without shoes.

He behaved the same way in his fields and in his business affairs as he did at home. The fields in Rzshempniov and in its three farms were fine but terribly neglected. There were far fewer teams of horses and oxen in the stall than were needed for an operation of this scope, and they were small, thin, and weak. He begrudged them the bit of hay and oats that they needed to have the strength to work. He did the same with the farmhands and other servants in his business. He never had a decent farmhand, only scruffy guys or half-grown boys whom he never paid the standard wages. He was always looking for bargains. No one wanted to come to him for a job, because working at Rzshempinov rendered it very difficult to find another, better position later. His farmhands and other servants had a very bad reputation, and no decent estate-holder wanted to hire them. His miserliness reached the point that oftentimes, especially in the summer when the horses had a lot of work, he would travel the two miles to Radomishla or half-mile to Shtsutsin on foot. He counted on meeting a gentile acquaintance or Jewish estate-holder on the way to offer him a lift.

As was already said, his fields bordered on ours in Yozefov.

Because he never had a full-fledged, responsible herdsman or *parobek* (farmhand), and only had small, half-grown kids, his livestock—in particular the horses—would sneak into our fields at night and caused terrible damage. We often wound up in court with him in front of the village judge. He routinely avoided honouring the verdict and paying compensation for damages. We did not want to enter litigation, and so we constantly absorbed damages.

My brother-in-law and his wife, Aydl, first became acquainted with Shimshen Asheim because of damage to our fields. It was summer and the fields were ablaze with activity. Before daybreak, the *parobkes* who were tending to our horses in a meadow, brought in Shimshi's (the gentiles would call Shimshen Asheim "Shimshi"), six horses that had caused severe damage to a wheat field. Aydl ordered the horses locked in a stall, with the intent that whoever claimed them would be ordered to pay for the damages.

No one came for the horses all day long, and Aydl was making plans to summon the judge and his official evaluators to assess the damage. However, at dusk a man in his fifties appeared in his shirtsleeves without a coat and barefoot to boot. His boots were slung over his shoulders. He entered the manoryard quietly and respectfully and stood by the door in the same manner as the poorest of the poor. Aydl, who did not know him, gave him a "*firer*" (a four-kreuzer coin) and offered him some food.

"I have not come here for money," the man answered. "I am your neighbour, Shimshen Rzshempniover, and I have come to ask you to release my horses to me." Poor Aydl was so horrified that she ran into another room and let her husband deal with the question of damages. Their neighbour promised to pay, but never did.

Shimshen Asheim really did not like to enter litigation in the courts, and he liked a lawsuit before a rabbinical court even less. If someone—whether it was me, a farmer, or a *porits*—owed him money, he almost never brought him to court. He allowed the debt to accumulate until the other party paid up. In most cases, the money was lost. Still, his name often came up in the courts as the guilty party.

If he had dealings with someone in his many business ventures or in the whiskey distillery that required disbursing funds to another party, he never paid up willingly. His heart simply would not allow it; he had to be forced in court. However, accusing him and receiving a "*virok*" (verdict) in one's favour was not enough. He still refused to pay until his animals were seized and being hauled off to market or to a public auction to be sold. Only then would he grudgingly pay the principal as well as the legal costs, which often amounted to more than the original sum. There was no other way to get him to pay up. He openly admitted that the other party was justified, but his heart would not allow him to behave like other people.

You would think that his poor management would have made him a poor man, but it was the opposite. His wealth increased, and every year we would hear that Shimshen had acquired a new estate or extended a sizable loan to a Polish *porits* at high interest.

He had eight or nine children, all of them rich and well-provided for. They fell into two categories: the eldest four, who had been born and raised before he became extremely wealthy, were boorish and uneducated and married off to rich but uncouth villagers. The younger four or five were slightly better educated and matches were arranged farther afield, from the larger cities of Kolomea and Krakow. He did not care about *yikhes*. Although he was essentially a refined person and it was a pleasure to spend time with him, his great love of money outstripped his good qualities and turned them into faults.

Shimshen Asheim was a rare type. There were enough stories, witticisms, aphorisms and legends in circulation about him to fill a book. I, who was his neighbour for a number of years and, with my father-in-law, had many business dealings with him, have a lot to recount. I think that the bit that I have written about him offers a fair impression of what kind of person this Reb Shimshen Asheim was.

44
THEFT

In a previous chapter, I wrote that our area was very safe and that major theft was almost unheard of. It is true that large-scale big city crime did not touch us: there was simply nothing to steal, and we lacked experienced and gifted thieves. However, we did have small-scale crime as was usual.

Jews in our area used to say, "Every peasant is by his nature a thief. If he does not steal, he is either lazy or is afraid of a beating."

A peasant accused of a theft that fell into the hands of a gendarme was not to be envied. If he did not confess fast enough, he received his share of blows, slaps, punches, and other physical treatment, although by law the gendarme had no right to beat him during an arrest. Regardless of the "treatment" that awaited him, the peasant was unable to go against his inborn nature: he had to steal wherever the opportunity presented itself, in particular from the Jewish estate-holder. For a peasant, the smallest stolen article was an asset. He would even delight in stealing a nail if he had something to tear it out of the wall: "*pshida shie*" it'll come in handy.

A Jewish estate-holder and his household had to have eyes in the back of their heads in order to make sure that his workers were not stealing from him, summer in the field, and winter in the stable, in the granary, or in the stall.

For example, one farmer hatched a plan to get his hands on a lot of hay and grain from the estate-holder and other farmers. His method is worth sharing as an example of gentile craftiness. Not far from the Yozefov manor there lived a gentile called Shimek. He had about three or four acres of land and would ordinarily have been counted among the poorer gentiles. However, because of a clever idea, he was quite wealthy. He had about a dozen good animals as well as a lot of hay and straw. This hay and straw did not cost him anything. With minimal effort, he collected it, not from his fields like everyone else, but from the trees that grew near his field.

The whole area around Yozefov is low-lying and there are many meadows. Farmers from many surrounding villages would go there to buy hay and clover for their livestock. Shimek's field was narrow but long, and was bordered on both sides by a road that was used to transport hay, clover and grain. Traffic was heavy: without exaggeration, about 1,000 loaded wagons would pass through every summer. This Shimek hatched a plan: on both sides of "his road," he planted some fifty willows, about twenty-five on each side. When a wagon would pass through this field, the branches—and he knew at what height to keep them—would catch hay, clover, and ears of grain. Shimek, his wife, and their little brats would go out with long rakes and remove everything from the branches, collect it, and carry it to the stable.

With this method, he would amass some thirty to forty wagon-loads of hay and clover, as well as a tidy quantity of grain. He became prosperous and acquired much livestock, but no one could do anything. He was a robber, but within the law.

* * *

To speak of all of the petty peasant thievery that transpired in Yozefov and that cost us several hundred gulden a year is besides the point. I wish to write about two really interesting thefts. The reader can imagine the rest.

I have already written that we worked extensively with Timothy seeds at Yozefov. This is the kind of product that can bring in a hefty income. However, it also requires constant, slow and painstaking work. I do not wish to go into detail about the care that must be applied starting in the process of cutting the stems and harvesting the bundles so that the precious seed is not lost in the process; I will simply recount what is involved during the product's threshing and cleaning. The Timothy seed is similar to poppy, but it has a silver membrane, and the lighter its colour, the greater the selling price, oftentimes up to forty gulden per hundred kilos. It cannot be threshed by machine because the silver membranes would be lost by contact with the iron tines and its value would be very low. The seeds must therefore be threshed by hand. The straw is very thick and the average farmer cannot thresh more than fifteen to twenty bundles a day. This process produces endless mountains of chaff and straw. If six farmers are threshing all day, three women are at work at the cleaning machine (*mlinek*) in order to extract the small, silver seeds from the heap.

One year we had an excellent Timothy harvest, over a hundred sacks for sale, and at a very high price. This required a whole winter of uninterrupted work. Aside from twelve threshers in two stables, there were five or six women at work cleaning and sifting at the granary. I was busy all day, running back and forth. Ordinarily, the same threshers and women were at work every day at the same task. We assumed them all, in particular the women, to be honorable people, and did not guard them closely. When one only has two eyes, and one can only be in one place at a time, and one's times is split between locations and one's wife and children are in the house, even with the best of intentions, one cannot guard everything.

* * *

I cannot remember exactly how the truth came out: whether we become suspicious of one of the women, or one of her co-workers informed us that she had been stealing Timothy seed and pouring it into a little sack fastened to her body under her clothes during clean-up time.

I do recall, however, that I, my wife and our farming manager decided not to confront this woman; we would simply surprise her so that she would not know what had hit her. The farming manager and I entered the grain elevator where the women were at work cleaning the Timothy. I went up to one of them, and without saying a word, I hoisted her dress over her head. The shocked woman was left standing in her undershirt, naked from the waist down, the theft revealed! A linen band was firmly fastened around her bared skin, to which were attached two small sacks, both already half-filled with Timothy seed.

Soon there was a terrible screaming and uproar. The woman threw herself on the ground and bellowed like a slaughtered cow. The other women began to scream along with her, and I, white as a sheet, added to the racket. It took all of a few minutes until many workers ran over to the granary to see what the commotion was about. My farming manager, a highly intelligent and cunning Jew and former estate-holder named Reb Mordkhe Brand, kept his wits.

Before much time had passed, he had two horses hitched to a waiting wagon. Together we hurried into town, and brought the village judge and one of his "*pshishenzshnikes*" (jurors) back to the house of the woman's parents and began a search of the premises. All of this transpired so quickly that the village did not know about the woman's theft. The result of the surprise search was impressive: it was not long before two sacks of Timothy seeds were located stuffed into a corner in the attic among the hay. These sacks weighted approximately 150 lbs, and were worth about forty gulden.

It would take too much place to recount in detail how this fascinating house inspection proceeded and how we had to go through women's "*spodnitses*" (dresses), and listen to the "fascinating" and absurd contentions of the farmer and his "*baba*" (wife) when we uncovered the stolen goods. I will simply recount that I asked the judge to seal the two sacks of Timothy with his seal and have them held by the Community. I then threatened the farmer that I would take him, his *baba* and their daughter to court.

In the end, it did not come to that. The judge and several homeowners appealed to Efraim, the Jewish tenant farmer who ran my inn, to get me to reconsider. They wore me down with their efforts and pleading—they even went so far as to travel to Radomishla to the "*Stari Pani*," Bobe Nekhome—until they finally managed to convince me not to take the family to court. I did not want to provoke the entire farmer "*gromada*" (Community). Moreover, the estate of Yozefov was located in the middle of an open field and the road from our manoryard into the village was exposed on all sides; one had to travel at least a kilometer to the next human residence.

"One should not provoke a gentile too much," we would say in the area, "he is like an 'malicious worm.'"

The woman, however, left the village and was packed off to relatives somewhere, and we never saw her again.

* * *

The second theft, which occurred several years later, was even more remarkable and thus much more exciting. It cost us a lot of effort to catch the thief.

In addition to Timothy seed, which I have already described, the Yozefov fields generated a lot of wheat and oats—they were not well-suited to other grains—and in a good year, we would produce 500–600 bags of surplus, on top of what we needed for internal use. Both types of grain were threshed and cleaned by machine. One floor up stood the big thresher. The grain fell into the "*mlinek*" (cleaning machine), where there stood a woman who shoveled the clean grain into a pile. Both machines, which were connected, were driven by a single "*kierad*" (horse wheel) turned by four horses.

At dusk, an hour before we stopped work, the "zbiorke" (collection) began in the stable. The grain was poured into sacks, placed on a wagon, and brought to the granary in the manoryard, a hundred yards from the stable. The "zbiorke" was not the same every day. However, usually there were some twenty bags of wheat, or forty or fifty bags of oats, depending on the yield of the bundles.

Between noon and one was lunchtime. The workers left the stables, ate their lunches and the horses were brought into the nearest stalls. During this time, the three large stables were completely deserted.

129

One time, my highly capable wife who was everywhere, and the farming manager, Reb Mordkhe Brand, began to notice that the pile of grain in the stable—at that time, oats—appeared smaller in the afternoon than it had before lunch. They began to suspect that someone was sneaking in at lunchtime when the stable was locked and helping himself to the pile of grain.

As I have already written (in the chapter about Velvele Damask), the buildings in the Yozefov manor were not in good repair. This was also true of the stables: there were three spacious buildings, but instead of having wooden walls as was usual, their walls consisted of woven willow branches. This was an advantage because the air could circulate easily. Much greater, however, was the disadvantage: these walls were no real deterrent to thieves.

When my wife and the farming manager began to have suspicions about the pile of grain in the stable, they doubled their vigilance: they left certain signs when they went for lunch and then checked whether these same indicators were still there when they returned. It only took a few days until we were convinced that grain was being stolen from the pile, on average a sack of oats each time. Knowing was not enough: we decided to do everything possible to catch the thief. Reb Mordkhe the farming manager took on this difficult but exciting task.

When everyone was away from the stable for lunch, eating outside or in the nearby yard and stalls, he remained inside, hidden among bundles of grain not far from the room where the pile of threshed and cleaned grain lay. For two or three days, his vigilance was for naught: the thief did not appear and the grain remained untouched. We were afraid that the thief had figured out that we were guarding the grain at lunchtime, and had stopped coming. However, subsequent events indicated that this was not the cause of the thief's absence. Evidently he was not suspicious as all, and had simply not come by because he was busy elsewhere. He had no clue about the watchfulness of the farming manager.

On day four, with Reb Mordkhe hidden among the bundles, he suddenly spotted a tall peasant with a kerchief over his face so that he would not be recognized, and with a sack in hand, approaching the pile of grain. If Reb Morkhe had not been so shocked, the most practical response would have been to allow the man to fill his sack and throw it onto his back, and then to surprise him and tear the kerchief off his face. However, Reb Mordkhe had received such a shock at the onset that he immediately let out a loud scream that alerted the thief, who did not enter the pile of grain. Rather, he ran out of one of the holes in the wall. The walls of the stable had enough holes that a savvy thief could escape. He ran to the part of the field that was furthest away from the manoryard.

Reb Mordkhe's scream was not wasted: it soon brought all of the workers in the stables, farmers, male and female workers, about thirty people in all, and together with the farming manager, they began to chase the thief. They ran too slow, the thief had gotten too much of a head start, and they could not—or would not—catch him. Our fields reached the Bren River and this is where everyone stopped.

Right at the edge of the river lived an elderly and wealthy farmer called Saidok. He owned an enterprise of several buildings, stables, stalls, and the like near the water. The thief fled in the direction of Saidok's property, with everyone in hot pursuit. Then he suddenly vanished without a trace, although everyone was certain that he had to be hiding out somewhere nearby.

Reb Mordkhe first ordered all of the workers, including our *parobkes* who had followed, to position themselves around the perimeter of Saidok's property and keep watch that the thief could not escape. Then he ordered two *parobkes* to ride to the village judge and bring him back with his assistant jurymen (*pshishenznikes*). He also ordered these two *parobkes* to find any available gendarmes and send them to him. His orders were carried out immediately and, before an hour had passed, the judge was there with his people, and soon after a gendarme, whom the rider had found in a nearby village, arrived. He soon took over the whole operation and then the real inspection began.

While all of this was happening, I was at not home. It was Wednesday, market day in the nearby town of Shtsutsin, and I had some dealings there. When I returned home, it was beginning to get dark outside. I ran over to Saidok's. I found everyone still assembled around the buildings. Several held lanterns with candles in their hands and stood guard so that the thief should not be able to escape in the growing darkness. My wife and the farming manager were distributing glasses of whiskey, pieces of bread, herring and cheese to everyone to discourage them from leaving before the thief was finally found. It is very likely that the workers would have left us alone if not for the gendarme, who threatened sternly that whoever dared to leave would be arrested first thing the next morning for not following his explicit orders. Everyone trembled at this; they knew the gendarmes all too well: they would carry out their threats and arrest all transgressors.

The search of all of the buildings took several hours. All of the stables were searched, and the grain and hay in them was tossed around. Wherever access was difficult, the gendarme would jab with his sharp bayonet, which he had placed on a rifle and that reached about two meters.

Truth be told, my wife and I were getting sick of the whole matter. We simply could not watch the huge commotion and terrible disorder that was being caused to the property of old Saidok, who was standing with his *baba*, watching everything helplessly with bleak eyes. Although we kept promising him that we would compensate him for any damage, this did not keep this wealthy and quiet man from being deeply saddened and vexed.

We began to request that the gendarme call off the inspection, but he was like a dog who had been taken on the hunt and had smelled a wounded animal.

He would not hear of it, and insisted that he was certain that the thief was hidden and it was therefore his duty to continue the search; if he became tired, he would send a messenger to the sergeant to provide other gendarmes to help.

It was about 9:00 pm and we were all exhausted. The gendarme was still spearing the pile of hay with his long bayonet when suddenly we heard a scream, "*dla boga!* (For God's sake!)" The shout came from the thief, who was hidden deep in the pile of hay but whom the gendarme's long bayonet had somehow reached. We all trembled with shock and fear: what if the gendarme had stabbed the boy to death? All of the workers ran to the pile of hay and began to tear it apart. After a few minutes, the thief was found. He crawled out intact and uninjured. The gendarme's bayonet had only grazed him.

I cannot describe what ensued when we discovered the identity of the thief. It was Michal Sova, one of the most important and respected farmers in the whole village! He was one of the jurors and there was talk of naming him village judge. He could read and write a little, and was on the whole a lot more intelligent than most of the other farmers in the village. All of the village's farmers where present when Michal Sova crawled out of this hiding place in the pile of hay. Everyone was filled with shame and could not look him in the face. They felt the disgrace as acutely as if it was their own and the thief was a close relative.

The gendarme was in seventh heaven. His whole face turned red and he kept saying to me or to the farming manager, "*poviedzshalem panu* (I told you)!" The workers received more glasses of whiskey and the gendarme ordered them to return home. He shackled the thief's wrists in iron chains and brought him to our manoryard to get an official statement. When we arrived, he bound his ankles in chains and threw him into the corner like a bound animal. He then sat down to eat and speak with us. He kept extolling his brave deeds in catching thieves. When he finished eating and drinking, he turned his attention to Sova. First, he gave him a couple of good whacks. He would have given him many more, but I and, especially my wife, pleaded with him and held him to keep him from beating Sova too much. We simply could not bear to watch it.

He began a serious interrogation. The thief insisted that this was the first time that he had come to steal in the stable. Although we all knew that this was a lie and the gendarme wanted to extract a true statement from him through a good beating, we could not allow him to be beaten any more and the man never confessed.

That same night, the gendarme brought him to court in Radomishla. Statements and investigations followed. We did not want to press the matter too much, and did not want to provoke the entire *gromada* of farmers. However, the district attorney in the Tarnow criminal court persecuted the case very strongly and Sova received three full months in prison, on top of the two months that he had already served before the sentencing, plus extensive court costs that I had never requested.

When Michal Sova returned from prison, all of the farmers avoided him and would have nothing to do with him. They refused to forgive him the great shame that his theft brought the entire village, where he had previously been one of its most important property owners. Within a couple of weeks, he had taken to wandering around the village, alone and isolated, until he was found one morning, hanging from the door of his stable.

Years later, whenever farmers spoke about him, they always agreed that a devil must have entered him and forced him to act so foolishly. In my mind, they came to the same conclusion about these matters as the Gemara, which states: "No man sins unless a spirit of madness enters into him."

45
SHTSUTSIN (SZCZUCZYN)

About ten years ago I heard that Shtsutsin has become a real metropolis with a train station and a bridge over the Vistula River; the town has come to life, became a real commercial centre, and is not to be recognized. However, some forty years ago, it looked very different. At that time, Shtsutsin was unlike the larger neighbouring towns of Dobrov and Radomishla. There was no courthouse, no tax office, not even a *starost* (village chief). Aside from the post office and telegraph office, there was nothing to connect the town to the outside world.

Shtsutsin, located two miles from Dobrov and four miles from Tarnow, lies right by the Vistula River, which has always marked the border between Galicia and Tsarist Poland. There was even a booth of sorts with officials (a border guard), and one could travel between Poland and Galicia by ferry. However, the traffic between the two countries was negligible, and so rare in Shtsutsin that it went almost completely unnoticed. When a stranger did appear wearing a Polish-style hat—a cap with a peak—everyone stared at him like a novelty. There were also not very many Jewish estate-holders like around Radomishla, and so aside from market days on Wednesdays, you saw almost no one in the streets.

About fifty Jewish families lived in the whole town and none had anything close to five thousand gulden to their name. By the same token, there were no paupers in the town who depended on charity. Almost everyone possessed his own little house, although the town did not have a single brick home. Many of the Jews also had a field or, at the very least, garden plots to cultivate. The wealthier among them had one or two cows and between the dairy products and field, they could earn a decent income. The area around Shtsutsin was rich and the Jews had little to do with the farmers when it came to loans. The town's

Jews were not moneylenders, and the farmers did not need to come to them for money. The Shtsutsin Jews owned stores and also traveled to the surrounding villages to handle all sales and purchases among the farmers; they made a good living off this. The Jews of Shtsutsin lived quietly, peacefully, and worry-free. They did not seek out great fortunes or show enormous initiative, and were satisfied with what they had.

* * *

The Yozefov estate where I lived was a lot closer to Shtsutsin than to Rado-mishla. A mere two kilometers' travel on the Polish road through Sluptse put one on the Kaiserweg and a single mile from Shtsutsin. It did not take more than an hour and a quarter to travel from Yozefov to Shtsutsin, whereas getting to Radomishla required two hours' crawl across muddy and sandy roads.

The town of Shtsutsin had a much greater attraction than Radomishla for me. When I would go to the fair in Radomishla on a given Wednesday or Sunday, I had to stop off in the Zgursk manor at my father- and mother-in-law's at some point. This visit usually involved an interrogation, in particular from my mother-in-law, as to why I was coming to town so often when it seemed to her that I had just been there.

"Such a man who can't stay in one place," she would retort irritably, "and works the horses for nothing..."

In Radomishla there was no shortage of relatives. First, I had to stop by my grandfather-in-law's, Reb Yudel. He did not bother much with me: offered a perfunctory greeting, forced out a couple of words, and I was dismissed. How-ever, escape from my grandmother-in-law, Bobe Nekhome, was not so simple. She was an intelligent and practical woman, but she had a tendency, like many older women, to offer unsolicited advice. Then there were my uncles and aunts and their children. Everyone said hello and often insisted on a visit to their homes, which was a serious burden.

Travel to Shtsutsin, on the other hand, freed me of all of this unpleasantness. I was free as a bird, liberated from obligations and itineraries. However, truth be told, the town of Shtsutsin did not have a positive effect on me morally. There I learned things that I would never have known about in Radomishla. First and foremost, I learned how to play cards.

In my youth in Lemberg, I never played cards, except for the innocent childish games with the two girls from the wealthy Horovitz Family. At most, there were occasional domino games with my mother or lotto played with little bits of glass. Card-playing was likewise unheard of in my father-in-law's house. Everyone was always so busy with work, both in the winter and even more so in the summer, that there was simply no time for folly of this type. In Radomishla, I never had the time or the opportunity to sit down to a game of cards. The first few years after my wedding thus passed without me touching a single card.

After I began to come to Shtsutsin frequently and became acquainted with several young gentlemen, they converted me. Over time I was as adept as my teachers and became a real devotee.

Sin breeds sin.

Liquor, wine, beer, and especially whiskey had never touched my lips until my wedding day. In my house on Friday nights, a morsel of bread dipped into a drop of liquor was served together with the fish. There was always a lot of whiskey at my father-in-law's, and both he and my mother-in-law would drink whole glasses-full, as did their young sons. This alcohol was very coarse, raw, and unrefined, and I could not get used to the taste. It was only when I set up my own household in Yozefov, and became a frequent visitor to Shtsutsin, and a pretty passable card player, that I became a convert to alcohol consumption and soon became as adept as any villager. Initially I only drank sweet liquors, Rosolias, but with time, drinking became second nature to me and I consumed whatever was available: coarse whiskey and a lot of Okocim beer.

At the time I was young and carefree. I never lacked cash and so, whenever time and circumstances permitted and under various pretexts, I would make my way to Shtsutsin and while away time at the "green table" (although there was no actual such table) with a couple of glasses of whiskey. There was no one to disturb me or make a comment. My father-in-law paid no attention, and remained unaware of all this. Even later, when I left the Yozefov estate and lived some four miles further away from Shtsutsin, I did not sever my ties with the town. Quite the opposite. My dealings with the "Shtsutsin Meadows" (which I will discuss later) brought me even more frequently to Shtsutsin; my business required it.

* * *

It goes without saying that I knew everyone in town and everyone knew me. However, I only established close ties, as card- and drinking-buddies, with a couple of people. Two were estate-holders who lived close to town, and two were young residents of Shtsutsin.

The eldest of the group, and the richest, was Alter Schnur. At the time that I got to know him, he was in his forties. I don't know what he did when he was younger, but when I knew him he owned his own estate. This property was not large, about 200 acres, but contained very fertile fields as well as considerable meadows that generated a lot of money without any work. He was not a man with a generous nature, but rather a bit of a braggart and when it came to his honour or the claiming of a personal victory, money was no object. His fortune was estimated to be vast, in the range of 30,000 gulden. He always had cash on him, and when you needed a couple of hundred gulden, you always got it.

Aaron Wechsler was a few years his junior, the holder of an island estate, about a Shabbes journey from Shtsutsin. He stemmed from a wealthy family in Poland, but because he did not want to serve in the tsarist army, he fled to Galicia and settled in the nearby town of Shtsutsin. He married a daughter of the wealthy Shimshen Asheim Rzshempniover. His estate was small—150 acres in all—but it was right on the Vistula River and was thus the best piece of land in the entire region. He became wealthier year by year there. Being the son-in-law of Shimshon Asheim with his daughter as wife, one can surmise that he was no generous spirit. But he was not as miserly as his father-in-law. He coveted honour, and in particular wanted people to think him wealthier than Alter Schnur. This resulted in many comical incidents, and once (as I will describe later) their rivalry got to the point between them that it set Aaron Wechsler back over a thousand gulden and made him into a laughingstock.

The third in our regular gang was Chaim Dovid Fertziger, also known as "the Rebbe." He stemmed from Dembitz and was living in Shtsutsin. He was a bit of a scholar, and liked to peruse *loshn-koydesh* volumes, but always borrowed them so that he did not have to spend any money on them. He made a late marriage with one of the daughters of the innkeeper in the town of Volye, which was not far from Shtsutsin. For years, he lived at the inn with his father-in-law. Because his wife was sickly and they had no children, he lived quite frugally and also had financial dealings with gentiles, lending them money and charging healthy interest rates. He was thus able, bit by bit, to accumulate a fortune of several thousand gulden. He then relocated to Shtsutsin and lived on a back street in a small house with two rooms and a kitchen. This is where we would gather to play cards.

Chaim Dovid was the only moneylender in the entire town, and Jewish merchants who needed fifty or even a hundred gulden—he was too cautious to deal with larger sums—had to come and deal with him, and he knew how to negotiate. He was likewise the lucky one in our card games. He was virtually always among the winners and rarely lost. It's not that he was a card shark, or that he knew how to stack the deck. By no means. His luck lay in his cold and calculating character. He never got excited during a game. He could be losing a lot of money—often fifty or more gulden—but he never lost his head. The same was true when he was on a roll, and he won a lot of money. He was always cool, thoughtful and calm. This trait is a great advantage in card playing and whoever lacks it will always be a loser.

The fourth member of our crew was the much younger (roughly my age) Aaron Hoyzer. He stemmed from Dzikov (Tarnobrzeg), where his grandfather, Reb Moshe Hoyzer, had been a very wealthy man with very large family and about 300,000 gulden to his name. Old Reb Moyshe had about ten children, but several of them were big ne'er-do-wells and he had to support them and their families. When there was a grandchild, he had to marry it off and provide some sort of dowry. Hershele Hoyzer was among the ne'er-do-well sons, and his father supported him with ever larger sums of money. This did not improve matters, however, and he remained a burden to his father. This Hershele had a tall, skinny son called Aaron. He arranged a match for him with a wealthy innkeeper, Shoyl Rappoport, who managed an inn off the Kaiserweg a half-mile from Shtsutsin.

This Shoyl Rappoport was not particularly wealthy, but he was genteel. He only had one daughter and a profitable business. Hershele Hoyzer seized this opportunity. The match was sealed and the young Aaron soon embarked on a state of permanent financial dependence. Aaron Hoyzer was not well educated, but he was nonetheless a sophisticated young man raised in a big city and in a rich family, and he was unable to accustom himself to the simple, though prosperous, village life of the innkeeper and his very simple daughter. The young man took after his ne'er-well father more than his energetic and diligent grandfather, and everything that he touched turned to dross.

If Shoyl Rapoport had not dabbled with this rich and prestigious match and if Moyshe Hoyzer had not been both such a wealthy and elderly man who would not be around forever, and who would leave his son Hershele 30,000 gulden (and this did happen a few years later)—if not for all of this, Shoyl Rapoport would certainly have sent his son-in-law packing back to Dzikov. But in the meantime, he stuck with him, and Aaron Hoyzer was taken care of. And because he had nothing to do at the inn, he would drive into town every day in the morning and in the evening. He claimed that he was going to pray, but in truth he went to hang out with the town folk and with our gang.

On Sundays or Wednesdays, I would usually arrive in Shtsutsin for the market at about 11:00 AM. I almost always had something to attend to in town that took up two or three hours of my time. However, because the town was small, tiny in fact, we would meet up during these three hours and stop in at Levinger's *propinatsye* (bar), sip sweet liquor and make plans to meet at Chaim Dovid's between 1:00 and 2:00 PM. Chaim Dovid's wife, a weak and quiet woman, was always sitting in the kitchen, hard at work with darning needles and some socks, and never exchanged a word with us. A bottle of whiskey or a couple of bottles of beer alongside two or three herrings to snack on always waited on the table. The master of the house, Chaim Dovid, always took a cut of the card money to cover his expenses, along with a little extra.

We always played Oko, with fairly low stakes, usually at 20 to 30 kreuzer per card. Before we sat down, we decided how long the game would last, usually two to three hours. Nevertheless, if your luck was bad, you could lose over 20 gulden in a single sitting. Both I and Aaron Hoyzer, and him more than me, were almost always among the losers, and if we were left with five gulden at the end of a session, we considered ourselves fortunate. Aaron Wechsler and, especially, Chaim Dovid almost always won, and because Aaron Dovid was not much of a customer, we would say that our card games brought in most of his earnings.

46
THE SOLD-OFF ESTATE

I want to describe a very interesting event that shook up the entire region and that everyone talked about for a long time after. It went like this:

At every possible opportunity, Aaron Wechsler loved to boast about his wealth. He did this in a really strange way, not like other people. Instead of bragging that he owned so-and-so many gulden, he would complain that his business was bad: he was losing money hand over fist. He did this intentionally, knowing full well that he was considered something of a liar and someone who liked to complain, and hoping that he would not be believed and in fact reckoned to be richer than he actually was. But one time, he got ensnared by his behaviour and it wound up costing him dearly in money, health and aggravation.

One day, a couple of us were sitting in a separate room at Levinger's bar drinking a little whiskey and talking about various things. As usual, Aaron Wechsler turned the conversation to the bad times that were getting worse and the fact that he was constantly losing money. This irritated the sly and crafty Alter Schnur. Everyone knew that the person in question had pulled in a tidy couple of thousand gulden that year. He asked Wechsler why he was complaining so loudly at a time when everyone knew that he possessed at least 25,000 gulden.

Wechsler replied in a pathetic voice, "If only that were true," and added that he knew that his entire fortune was, in fact, worth far less than 15,000 gulden.

"If so," retorted Alter Schnur, "I will give you 20,000 gulden for everything you own!"

"Are you serious?" Wechsler kept repeating, and when Schnur assured him that he was, Wechsler called out, "Agreed." He did this with the countenance of someone who had just struck an excellent business deal. We all took up the matter and encouraged the two men, who were becoming more and more heated. We incited each of them and cheered them on not to have any regrets. The result was that Alter Schnur took a whole 500 gulden out of his leather wallet and demanded that Aaron Wechsler immediately do the same, and leave the sum as a pledge. Now Wechsler could not pull out of the deal. Out of his pocket he extracted a roll of cash held together by a thin string—he did not carry a wallet—peeled off the bills and placed them on the table. Chaim Dovid was selected by both sides as the arbiter who would hold the money in trust until the deal was carried out.

The Christian Community notary was soon summoned and he worked out an agreement whereby Aaron Wechsler would sell everything that he owned, aside from clothing and furniture, to Alter Schnur—assets and liabilities, the estate and absolutely everything connected with it—for the sum of 20,000 gulden. Wechsler had a total of three months to give Schnur his entire capital and to receive the agreed-upon sum in cash. During this period, he was forbidden from selling anything except for dairy products and other minor things. If either side renaged on the deal, he had to pay the other party a sum of 5,000 gulden.

The agreement was signed and sealed in front of witness, and Chaim Dovid took and stashed away the pledged 1,000 gulden. The crowd, which had grown to half the town, had taken to drinking and munching on bread with sausage on this account. However, the next day, when Aaron Wechsler had sobered up, he began to grasp how badly he had been had. The first thing he did was to drive to a lawyer in Tarnow and show him the unfortunate contract that he had signed. However, the lawyer informed him that the document could not be annulled unless he paid Schnur 5,000 gulden. Then Wechsler adopted a different approach. He began to whisper to us, and in particular to Chaim Dovid and to me, that we should work on Alter Schnur to rescind "that silly piece of paper." He knew, Wechsler claimed, that Schnur would focus all of his attention on this, and would never be able to raise 20,000 gulden in cash. He, Wechsler, would be able to earn a tidy sum in the transaction, but because he was an honourable person, his conscience would not allow him to swindle someone. He would throw a little party for us all and toss the little piece of paper into the fire over a glass of whiskey.

But Alter Schnur would not hear of it. He would stick to his end of the bargain and to the contract! He told someone that he was already in negotiation with a bank in Lemberg about getting a mortgage on his own estate. He was also dealing with a couple of moneylenders in Tarnow so that he would be in a position to meet his financial obligations and have the entire sum of money ready on the designated date, in cash. Moreover, he kept insisting, he could not understand what kind of person this Aaron Wechsler was: when one draws up a contract and signs it, one has to stick to it! Aaron Wechsler certainly had his share of troubles during these first few weeks.

Wherever you went in the area, the talk was about this outrageous business deal between the two merchants. No one had every heard of anything like this; when had it ever happened that a person willingly sold his entire state so suddenly and without any reason? People also started to seriously exaggerate the value of Aaron Wechsler's estate, which he actually really enjoyed. He was valued at 50–60,000, 75,000 and up to 100,000 gulden.

Soon his wife and family got involved. His two brothers, two very distinguished gentlemen, came over from Poland, and they tried everything possible to get Alter Schnur to terminate the bizarre arrangement. This went on for about four weeks. Aaron Wechsler was willing to lose his initial 500 gulden, which were being held in trust by Chaim Dovid. But Shnur would not hear of it.

The short of it is that the sly and cunning Schnur triumphed. After much argumentation from our side, we just barely managed to persuade him. He then tried to convince us that he had accumulated several hundred gulden in expenses and that he wanted to take the initial 500 plus another 500 gulden. This little episode thus cost Aaron Wechsler a hefty 1,000 gulden.

A group of us, plus several gentlemen from the city, sat ourselves down in a separate room in Levinger's bar. We ate and drank, and the whiskey flowed freely. The two parties who had not spoken to each other during the entire period, shook hands and became "best buddies," like before.

For a long time afterwards, people talked about the story, and the braggart Aaron Wechsler delighted in hearing how his worth was valued at much higher than its actual value.

What a bunch of rascals we were!

47
WET AND DRY YEARS

The soil of Yozefov was quite good on the whole, though fickle. Only when the conditions suited it did it yield its bounty. If one year it was too wet or too dry, Yozefov suffered much more than the other estates in the region.

At one time, years and years ago, Yozefov, which lay in a valley between two rivers, consisted of grassland. It was completely covered with grass where cattle pastured. The grasses in the higher meadows were cut to make hay and feed the cattle in the winter. When there was a rainy year, the lower meadows suffered; they were completely submerged by the two rivers that passed through Yozefov: the larger Bren and smaller Ribnitsa. However, over the course of time, people became more savvy and found ways of dealing with the water.

Velvele Damask, the owner of Yozefov, purchased the entire estate of about 450 acres from an old *pritse* (noblewoman) for under 20,000 gulden. In addition to erecting buildings, he invested several thousand gulden in the property. He dug a lot of *pshikopes* (drainage ditches) to divert water from the grassland into the Bren or Ribnitsa, which improved the grasses in the meadows. Furthermore, many of the higher-lying meadows were ploughed and transformed into grain fields. To plough a field that has been used as grasslands for centuries and has been packed down by the feet of thousands of cattle is no easy task. It requires very strong oxen and special plough implements. The work, however, always pays off. For the first few years, the meadow produces an abundance of wheat or oats and the field does not have to be fertilized. This is how the estate of Yozefov came into being. When my father-in-law leased it under less than ideal conditions, as I have already described, the estate already contained about 300 acres of grain fields, with the rest consisting of grasslands.

However, despite all of the drainage ditches, the Yozefov soil remained shallow and wet. Over the course of the years, these ditches fell into bad repair and became overgrown. Damask did not concern himself with this, and if we had wanted to keep all of the ditches in good condition, it would have set us back a thousand gulden a year in expenses. We did the minimum in maintenance every year, but to keep everything in working order was beyond our capacity.

The result was not good. The fields suffered doubly: when it was a wet year, entire areas of field and meadow were submerged, and when it was a dry year, they suffered too. However, in the twelve years that we held the lease in Yozefov, we experienced the most hardship during two particular years: one was too wet and the other was exceptionally dry.

I am now going to recount a little more about these two years.

48
THE WET YEAR

I do not remember exactly when it was, but I think the year was 1887. It was during the month of June, when all of the spring labour had been completed and the fields were flourishing. Some grain had already bloomed and the others were in the midst of blossoming. We had great hopes that the year would be very fruitful and we would earn a tidy few thousand gulden.

One Sunday it suddenly began to rain. It rained for one day, a second, and then a third. We had become accustomed to this sort of thing, in particular during the months of May, June, and July. We—myself and my farming manager—headed out with several peasants in the middle of the downpour with shovels to redirect the water to the lower-lying areas or into already half-filled ditches. It did not occur to any of us that we would have an enormous flood this year. The rains did not justify this fear.

By Wednesday morning we saw, to our great horror, that the Bren had begun to swell heavily and that the water had begun to overflow the dikes in some places. Those of us at Yozefov, plus almost all of the peasants from the surrounding villages, worked hard all day to protect the lower dikes. We made one serious miscalculation: we thought that it had only rained heavily in *our* region. However, it turned out that the mountainous regions around Sanz and Yaslo had experienced several major downpours. These torrents did not drain quietly: with a terrible force, they tore down to the Vistula River. The Vistula soon became so full that not only could it not absorb any of the overflow from our region, but it began to back up into the surrounding rivers.

On Thursday morning, Yozefov experienced a torrent: the Bren and Rib-nitsa Rivers could not longer travel along their usual courses into the Vistula. Instead, their swollen and roiling contents overflowed their banks and flooded the entire region. The whole estate of Yozefov and several surrounding villages were completely submerged. There was no land to be seen, only water and sky. The village and farmers' homes were visible from afar, but they could only be reached by boat. In some places, the water was over a meter high.

In Yozefov our lives were in no great danger because the whole manor and all of its buildings were surrounded by a high dike—a safety measure from earlier times—that kept everything from being submerged. We also worked hard to reinforce and strengthen these protective dikes.

For three full days and nights, we were surrounding by raging and churning water that was terrifying to behold. All of our animals, which were safely locked away in their stables, roared and bellowed horribly, even though they did not lack food or water. They instinctively sensed the looming danger and this made them fearful and agitated. We had no shortage of food. We had our own boat that we rowed around the fields and into the nearby village, and several of our neighbouring farmers came to visit us by boat to check in on us and find out whether we needed anything.

On the fourth day, things began to clear up. The waters began to recede and the earth reappeared. It took two or three days for the water to retreat completely except in the lowest meadows. We now had the opportunity to really assess the massive damage that the flood had caused. Many fields and their grain were ruined and had to be reploughed and reseeded with millet and buckwheat, both of which can be planted late and also ripen last.

* * *

The weather turned beautiful again. There were several warm and light rains that rinsed off the sand and "*mudlines*" (tamped-down grasses) that the waters had brought. Some of the stalks that had been flooded and squashed by the rushing water straightened themselves up and sprouted anew. Overall, however, the damage was extensive. A lot of grain suffered too much water damage and turned yellow and shriveled. Almost all of the beets and potatoes underground rotted and could not be salvaged.

When the harvest finally came, we able to assess the full extent of the damage from the flood. Aside from the fact that the stalks contained very little grain, we had to cut them high because the lower stalks were full of sand, and the hay and chaff would have been unusable for the cattle. In the end, this did not help much because, even in the higher stalks, too much sand and tamped-down grasses remained. When we threshed the grain by machine, or even by hand, the dust was so thick that it was almost unbearable. The cattle had no desire to eat this sandy straw or hay, which caused us no end of trouble. We had to thresh everything over again and shake it with rakes and pitchforks to get the sand off. We also came up with another solution: we bought a lot of cheap, coarse salt, ground it very fine or dissolved it in hot water, and sprinkled it over the sandy hay, straw and chaff. The cattle munched on this with enthusiasm and then drank a lot of water.

However, the end was wretched: at the end of the winter, a lot of our cattle, in particular the young ones in the two-to-three year range took sick with dysentery and died. We had sold quite a few of them in time, but the damage just from the loss of the cattle alone amounted to several hundred gulden. It was an unfortunate year for us. Aside from financial losses, we had undergone more trouble, distress and extra effort than in our best and highest earning years, and all for nothing.

* * *

Only once, some three years later, did we have another, though smaller, flood. However, it took place during a time that caused no damage except for the shock. It was during the month of February or the beginning of March. The ice on the Vistula was very thick that year, and its shift coincided with heavy rains in the mountainous regions. The fast-flowing water was unable to break up the great masses of ice in the Vistula. Then came the torrent: the waters of the Bren and Ribnitsa stopped flowing along their usual courses into the Vistula, and backed up and flooded the surrounding low-lying villages and our estate of Yozefov. But because the fields were frozen solid and snow-covered, the water did not do any damage. A few warm rains soon followed and completely rinsed away the sand and tamped-down grasses. In the end, we went on to have a very good year.

49
THE DRY YEAR

We had another year in Yozefov where we did not suffer from too much water, but from the opposite: extreme drought. The end result was almost identical: we lost a lot of money and our cattle-count diminished considerably.

There is no question that if anyone else had been holding the lease to Yozefov, he would not have been able to maintain it. He would have, as they say, fled by the light of the moon However, my father-in-law was extremely wealthy, with excellent credit and a profitable business to boot, so he didn't really care if Yozefov had a bad year and a few thousand gulden had to be poured into it. His own large estate, Broniovski's Zgursk, covered everything.

I do not remember exactly when the drought took place, but I think that it was 1888. It hardly rained all summer, from the beginning of May through the end of August. When a little rain did fall, the parched fields did not even notice. Even when the sky turned completely overcast, it stayed completely dry. It was the fulfillment of the verse, "Heavy cloud and wind but no rain." [Proverbs 25, 14]

We in Yozefov suffered much more from this dryness than the surrounding estates, and in particular than my father-in-law's in Zgursk. An old agricultural rule states that low-lying fields are particularly vulnerable to drought and they are also much harder to cultivate than those on higher ground. The grain that we had planted—oats and barley—scorched as the sun beat down on them mercilessly. Each day the earth became more parched, and choked without any opportunity for respite. Even the winter grain, wheat and rye, which had been growing so lushly, suffered. Because of the lack of moisture, with even the dew scant, the stalks lacked the strength to grow. Their blossoming was weak and everything ripened and dried out before its time. The same thing happened to the clover and Timothy in the fields, and to the grasses and hay in the meadows. The drought cut their production dramatically to about a quarter of the usual yield.

The results were disastrous. Instead of the usual 500–600 sacks of wheat that we produced in an average year, we only sold 130, and at the end of the year, when there wasn't enough to feed us and our servants, we had to buy back about 20 sacks of wheat at a high price. Moreover, our fields were so parched and hardened that it was almost impossible to plough them for the coming year. The arduous exertion of four large and heavy oxen—horses are always weaker and not suited for such heavy labour—was barely enough to break up the hard, flinty earth.

All of this would have been manageable; we at Yozefov were accustomed to big losses, and a few more thousand gulden would not have made us (that is, my father-in-law) any poorer. The worst part, however, was this: when we collected the little bit of parched grain from the scorched fields, we realized to our horror that it would be impossible to maintain all of our cattle, cows, horses, oxen and all of their young, which totaled about 100 in number. Our justified fear was that we would not have enough straw and hay and that they would die of hunger. Selling horses or oxen was out of the question: we desperately needed all of them to work the fields. We could not sell our cows and calves; because of the drought, everyone was selling off as much cattle as he could. Their price fell to the point that an animal that had been worth about forty gulden barely fetched ten. We concluded that we had to reduce our cattle count by half. My father-in-law took 20–30 animals to Zgursk.

About forty cattle remained to get rid of and we decided to put them on a *"brave"* regimen and fatten them up so that they could be sold to butchers or all the way to Krakow or Vienna. In every distillery, spirits are made out of grain (rye or corn), and in our region, out of potato. The sugar content is converted into alcohol, and the waste, or *brave*, is fed to cattle. When clover, the poorest of fodders, is mixed with this byproduct, it makes the cattle fat and puts a lot of meat on them. There were several distilleries (*gorzshelnis*) of this kind in our area, and one of them belonged to my father-in-law's brother-in-law, Moshe Lind in Dobrov, a mile from Yozefov or Zgursk. His stall could hold a hundred big oxen or some two hundred smaller cattle, so we rented stalls plus *brave* for a hundred animals from him. My father-in-law and I placed about seventy, and we also brought in about thirty from two or three of our relatives who were estate-holders nearby. In the end, this venture did not amount to much, with large expenses and few returns. When everything was said and done, we did not get much more for our animals than if we had sold them at throwaway prices at the beginning of the winter.

As a result, however, we lived it up all winter, eating and drinking and playing cards.

50
UNCLE MOSHE LIND

In those years, Moshe Lind had "made it." He was reasonably affluent, had excellent credit, and liked to live in style just like a Polish *porits*. He was not even the richest of the family: in the Kelkiov family there were two or three members who had a lot more than he did. But he liked to carry himself like a true *shliakhtsits* (*szlachcic*, Polish noble). He had ten children, and kept a teacher (not a *melamed*) for the boys and a governess for the girls. They studied Polish, a little German and French, and they were the very first Jewish girls in the whole area to learn to play piano. He and his wife, Aunt Soretshke, were friendly and dependable people who liked to entertain guests, in particular from the family. The kitchen was always busy, with two cooks always at work cooking and baking for the large household and guests. Two or three roasted geese or ducks, along with a couple of cases of beer were always ready and waiting. You knew that when you came to Moshe Lind's in Dobrov, you would not go hungry.

When we rented out the *brave* and boarded our cattle, it became our regular custom to drive over two or three times a week "to check in on the animals." There was nothing to check: we had a Jewish overseer and some of our gentile workers there to keep watch. Still, we passed by often to "check up on the animals." Saturday nights after *havdole*, I drove right over from Yozefov to my uncle Shimen in Budzin, who always accompanied me to Dobrov to "check in" on his few animals that were boarding in the stall with mine (and for which he did not pay anything). My father-in-law and a relative of ours, Shimen Yas, or some other family member, would soon follow.

First, for duty's sake, we would drive up to the stall and one by one, or all together, survey the cattle and spout wisdom about them: who was gaining more or less weight, and for whom the *brave* with clover "was being wasted." We chatted a little with the Jewish trustee and the workers, distributed a bit of cash among them, and asked them to guard the "beasts." When this was over and done with, we checked in on our horses in the adjacent stall: the one-horse carriage that was my preferred mode of transportation, and the carriage and "Zugov" horses of my father-in-law, who considered anything else beneath his dignity.

We would then descend on the house of Uncle Moshe Lind. There was never a shortage of food and drink, and it was the best of the best. As soon as we finished eating and drinking, we would sit down at a green table to play cards. When there were a lot of people, we played at two separate tables. In addition to Saturday nights, we soon got into the habit of coming by midweek and playing cards until about two o'clock, when everyone headed home.

This is how we "suffered in agony" all winter long. We did not gain much from the *brave* stable, but in the process we enjoyed a nice bit of luxury and had a great time.

* * *

With Passover approaching, the activity in the distillery came to a stop. We sold our cattle and the drivers were dispatched by the merchants to collect them. I, my uncle Shimen Sandhaus, and our relative Shimen Yas were all in attendance. When everything was over and done with and we were ready to head home, Moshe Lind invited the three of us to accompany him into the nearby town of Tshermin (Czermin), about a half-mile away from Dobrov.

Tshermin was a big village, not unlike a town. It was almost entirely inhabited by German colonists. It had a post office, and there was a tax office and gendarmes. Our Moshe Lind, estate holder and distillery-owner, often had to depend on the services of these financial offices and gendarmes. And although he was a proud *porits*, a real *pan*, he had to swallow this pride and live with everyone in a friendly manner. So with all work in the distillery having ended, he wanted to offer everyone a bit of fun and have a good time with them, and he invited us along as well.

The Tshermin Inn, or Wirsthaus, as it was called by the local Germans, was a spacious and comfortable building. It belonged in a German village. The Jewish leaseholder, Moshke Tsherminer, a relative of my mother-in-law's, was a fine man and very fastidious. His Wirthaus was run in big-city style, not like a rundown village tavern.

146

We arrived in front of the building in two carriages, and Moshe Lind went off to the tax office and the gendarme posts to invite everyone who was not on duty to be his guests that evening. It did not take long before everyone arrived, 10–12 people in all. We were soon seated in a separate spacious and comfortable room, and began to eat and drink. The inn was connected to a very fine delicatessen and they had the very best food including a selection of the finest kosher Krakow sausages. We drank the best beers and foreign schnapps until we were dead drunk.

At about two o'clock in the morning, we were ushered out by Moshke Tsherminer. The gendarmes and financial officers dragged themselves home. Moshe Lind was the most sober among us, and was the only one who had not completely lost his head. He sat me and Shimen Yas on a wagon, stuck the whip into the shank of my right boot, and had the horse follow his britzka.

I swear that I have no memory as to how I arrived at Yozefov, about a mile away. I was oblivious to Shimen Yas crawling out of the wagon, and have no idea where it happened: probably at some well-known tavern. To this day I do not know how my horse crossed the Bren, which had no bridge, or how we made it in one piece across the narrow bridge over the Ribnitsa, which had no railing at all, was pretty high above the water, and had to be carefully negotiated under the best of circumstances.

At one point, I was awakened by the cold and saw that the wagon was in front of my house in the Yozefov manoryard. I staggered into the house and when I fell into bed, I slept for about twenty-four hours.

This is how we served Bacchus, the God of drinkers, in our youth.

51

OUT OF YOZEFOV

Time did not stand still. Our twelve-year lease period was due to end on March 15, 1894, and there was no talk of renewing the contract. Old Velvele Damask had passed away and the authority over Yozefov had passed to his eldest son, Yosef Damask.

Because the conditions under which we had signed the lease were so difficult, my father-in-law was certain that there would be no takers. He was not prepared to pay more than 3,000 gulden a year, which amounted to a full 1,000 gulden less than the current lease. However, while we were in negotiation with the young Mr. Damask and showing him how much money we had poured into the business, another taker entered the picture, which we had not counted on. This was Meyer Asheim, son of Shimshen Asheim, our very rich and miserly neighbour described in an earlier chapter. It did not make financial sense for us to pay the same price for the lease as before. He had his own considerations, however, and he grabbed the great bargain from us.

Before Mr. Damask sealed the deal with Asheim, he wrote a letter to my father-in-law telling him that he had a new lessee, but that he would prefer to continue to keep us on. My father-in-law replied and offered a detailed account indicating that he had poured over 25,000 gulden in Yozefov over the last dozen years, and could thus not offer any more than 3,000 gulden. About two weeks later, we found out that Meyer Asheim had leased Yozefov for the same 4,000 gulden that we had paid. This did not cause us too much heartache. Yozefov had caused me and my wife enough trouble and we wanted to leave for another estate. Although my father-in-law was not too difficult a partner and we had all kinds of freedom, we were pretty tired of the arrangement, and wanted to be our own bosses and stand on our own two feet.

Meyer Asheim leased Yozefov in the spring of 1893, which left us a full year to harvest the fields. As we did not have to plough or seed, we had plenty of time to look around and figure out where we were going. We were offered several large estates that we could have acquired easily had we remained in partnership with my father-in-law. However, we looked into much smaller ventures so that we could function alone and without partners.

A full summer and fall passed in this manner. We were very busy at Yozefov with the grain harvest. We had a large crop and grain prices were quite high.

52
THE SHTSUTSIN MEADOWS

Clover, hay and pasture has been a Jewish business in Galicia for many years. Because this is not a well-known fact and I have not managed to find any description of it, I will go into a little more detail here, with a focus on Galicia.

As everyone knows, Galicia was under a system of "*pantshizne*," or serfdom. Every peasant, his wife and children were eternal slaves of the *porits* and had to perform all necessary labour in his fields, forests and in his manor, without any compensation. So that the peasant would have a means of subsistence—slaves also have to eat, after all—the *porits* gave every peasant several acres of land to work for his own use, and this is how they eked out a living.

The revolution of 1848, which caused major upheaval in many European lands, also brought freedom to several million peasants in Galicia. Eternal slaves became free people over whom the *porits* had no more rights. However, since the peasants no longer had to work for the *porits*, he was conversely under no further obligation to support them or allow them to earn a living from his fields for free. How would these millions of people survive? The Austrian government, which ruled Galicia, found a solution: it purchased from the Polish *pritsim* (or, more precisely, forced them to sell) a large proportion of their fields, and distributed this land among the peasants. To this end, the Austrian government distributed bonds called *Grundentlassungs-obligation* [Soil-Release Bonds] for a total of about forty million gulden, and paid the money to the *pritsim* for their seized fields. The peasants stayed on the fields that they had originally received from the *pritsim*. However, they also had to pay taxes to cover the cost for the bonds, including the principal plus interest. I do not know exactly how many acres every peasant received at the time. What is clear is that not everyone received the same number: some had 15–20 acres, which others barely had two or three. There must have been some system of calculation in place.

After a mere thirty years, the peasants increasingly suffered from a serious land shortage. Their many children grew up, married, and had to be helped to establish themselves. The peasant father had no choice but to give up part of his own landholdings, even a small portion of two or three acres, to any newly married son. As for the daughter, in our region, they received cattle or cash in lieu of land. The peasants especially lacked feed for their livestock. Galicia has always been a land of livestock raising, with a great number of beef cattle shipped to Austria or the surrounding lands each year, as well as many thousands of horses. These cows and horses accounted for a large proportion of a Galician farmer's annual income. In the summer, cows and horses are pastured in the fields and left to find their own food. But for more than six months of the year, they are kept in stalls and eat whatever their owner can provide for them.

Not every peasant had fields that produced enough feed for his livestock. He thus had no other choice but to open his tightly sealed purse and buy food for his "beasts." This vital item was not to be purchased in a ready-to-use form; this would be too expensive. The peasant would only resort to it if his earlier supply had completely run out and he had no choice, in particular in the spring when he had to provide his horses or oxen with better feed so that they could work his fields. Most peasants that raise livestock prepare enough feed during the summertime to suffice for the time that the animals have to be kept in the stall. During the months of June through August, the peasants thus go around to the *porits*'s manors or the wealthier farmers and buy clover or entire sections of grassland from them, which they then cut down, dry and transform into hay. This was brought home and kept in the hayloft or in special stacks in preparation for the cold months.

During the 1870s, a new plant called clover was introduced into Galicia. It adapted very effectively and grew well. In the first year after the clover is planted, it can be harvested twice and the yield, in particular in better fields, is five, six or more overloaded wagonsfull per acre. In year two, the clover does not have to be seeded; it grows by itself and still produces two to three wagons of feed per acre. About ten years later, Timothy seed was introduced from the United States. It grows best in low, hard fields, and has characteristics similar to clover. Enterprising leaseholders, especially in our area, began to seed many of their fields with clover and Timothy and it got them back on their feet.

The Jewish leaseholders were busy people and most of them had neither the time nor the will to deal with the peasants, who could be very tough and frustrating customers, in individual sales of clover, Timothy or grasslands. These leaseholders thus preferred to sell the entire enterprise to a Jewish merchant, take his money, and have him quibble with the peasants. Our region eventually had several city Jews who had these types of business dealings with the estate holders during the summer and turned a tidy profit.

When I was on my way out of the Yozefov estate and on my way to becoming my own boss without my father-in-law as partner, I thought up a new business venture. As I have already described elsewhere, Yozefov was a little more than a mile from the town of Shtsutsin. The whole town—including several estates of very fine fields by the Vistula—belonged to an old countess who lived in Krakow and managed the business on her own. This old lady did not like Jews, and except for two or three innkeepers, no Jew was allowed to set foot on her properties. All of her grain and other agricultural products were shipped to a Christian bank in Krakow, and although she could have gotten much better prices from Jews, she would not hear of it. Jews were *persona non grata* to her. When the countess died, her will stipulated that all of her holdings be transferred to one of her grandchildren, the wife of Prince Lubomirski von Pshevorski, a very wealthy man who was more occupied traveling the world and hunting than in handling business matters. His representative and the manager of all of the estates as well as the sugar factory in Pshevorsk was a certain Count Mitshelski, an impoverished *shliakhtsits* from Prussia who had been forced to expatriate because of his strong Polish patriotism. He had became the manager of wealthy Count Lubomirski's commercial affairs, and representative of the newly inherited Shtsutsin estates.

These estates included one very prime property called Zabrine. This estate was virtually unploughed as it was too low and damp for grain. It consisted of many grassy meadows that produced a lot of good hay. The whole estate consisted of about 650 acres, aside from a small farm with its own meadows and a bit of ploughed field.

While the old Countess had been alive, these meadows were leased to peasants and the total income was a pittance. The Christian vendors squandered everything, letting it go practically for free. Whatever money was left, they stole and drank away so that almost nothing was left for the Countess. Jewish merchants repeatedly tried to lease these Shtsutsin Meadows, which were renowned in the area, from the Countess. They offered a price that was several times higher than what she got from her Christian vendors, but she would not hear of it: she did not do business with Jews!

When Prince Lubomirski, or better put, Count Mitshelski, took possession of the Shtsutsin estates, there was a rumour that change was in the air, and that Jews would now have better access to these goods. Lo and behold, dealings with Jews did take place on one of the Pshevorsk estates, and the Pshevorsk *proprinator*, Reb Yitzhok Engelhardt, was a big shot with Count Mitshelski and was engaged in all kinds of business ventures with him.

It occurred to me that it would be a good plan for me to lease these Shtsutsin Meadows, which were in my area and whose flaws and attributes and I was familiar with. I penned a letter to Count Mitshelski, inquiring as to whether he would be prepared to lease out the meadows for a period of several years. A few days later, I received my answer from him: he was planning to be in the Shtsutsin Manor a few days later, and I should come to see him to discuss the matter more thoroughly. I should, however, be aware that he would not take less than ten gulden per acre. When I received this letter, I was ecstatic. I knew the value of the Shtsutsin Meadows and was aware that if I managed to lease them for a period of several years, it would make me a very wealthy man.

That same day I sent to see my father-in-law in Zgursk and told him about everything. He was very happy; he also knew the Shtsutsin Meadows and praised me for my smart idea. It did not occur to me to strictly instruct him to keep the matter secret, and he would have been insulted it I had. A young pup like me telling him how to run a business! But my father-in-law was, may he forgive me for saying so, something of a braggart, and he liked to recount things to his buddies, the wealthy Radomishla men, that should, by all rights, have been kept secret. As usual, he was unable to keep the news to himself and could not refrain from telling a few people about the very lucky venture that his son-in-law had hit upon.

On Thursday, when I came to Radomishla for the market, I encountered the two wealthy moneylenders, Reb Avremele Aberdam and his brother-in-law Reb Moyshele Rappoport. Rappoport was, incidentally, a great scholar and a son of the Dombrover Rabbi, Reb Shepsl Rapoport. They greeted me warmly and smacked me on the back as if to say, "you are well on your way!" Although they did not say anything about my new business dealings, their expressions told me that they knew everything. I was upset at my father-in-law's indiscretion and chatter, and my instincts told me that his talk had seriously harmed me. The next week proved me correct.

When I arrived at the Shtsutsin Manor on Tuesday and presented myself before Count Mitshelski, who had just arrived that morning, he received me warmly and then got right down to business like an experienced businessman. He told me right from the onset that he very much regretted having quoted me a price of ten gulden an acre for the meadows. During the week, he had made inquiries and determined that they were worth much more, at least 15 gulden. On top of this, he told me with a derisive smile on his face, he had received a letter that very day from two Jews offering thirteen gulden per acre. With these words, he handed me the letter from the two Jewish merchants.

A quick glance convinced me of the truth of his words. The letter was from my "buddies," Alter Schnur and Aaron Wechsler. Their short letter stated that word had reached them that the Count planned to rent out the Shtsutsin Meadows, and as such, they were informing him that they were close neighbours who knew the value of the meadows and were willing to pay 13 gulden an acre. They were also prepared to pay their annual dues in advance, on June 1, before beginning their sales of the meadows to individual buyers.

I was stupefied when I read over this short letter. But the Count did not let me ponder for long.

"Do you see, merchant," he said to me, "the offer that I have in my hands? I checked up on them with my manager, Pan Lewandanski, and he gave me favourable reports on both. But because you were the first to write me about the matter and you seem to be a decent fellow, I would rather deal with you, but with the understanding that you match their conditions."

What choice did I have? I knew that I was up against these two lions, each of whom was worth a lot more than me and were not dependent on the Shtsutsin Meadows for their livelihoods. They had their own successful businesses. They put a major kink into my business deal and future plans. The major issue was not the three gulden per acre, which would amount to about 2,000 gulden a year, but the actual conditions of the contract. I had already generated plans on how the contract should be drawn up so that I would only have had to invest a minimal amount into the business. To this day I remain convinced that if these two individuals had not mixed in and presented themselves as competitors, I would have been able to convince the *porits* to agree to my conditions while still earning a lot more from the meadows than they used to bring the old Countess. Now, however, the tables had turned. He had the advantage, and I had to agree to his demands. I was barely able to persuade him to let me pay my annual dues in two installments instead of in a lump sum, with half due on June 1 and the balance six weeks later. I gave the Count 500 gulden as a deposit and we agreed that I would come to Lemberg two weeks later to sign the contract with his lawyer, and pay him an additional 3,500 gulden. This 4,000 gulden in cash would be held by the Count as collateral at 5% interest during the four years that the contract was in effect.

About two weeks later I received a letter from the lawyer summoning me to Lemberg to sign the contrast and to bring the 3,500 gulden, which, with the initial 500, would complete the surety of 4,000 gulden. When I arrived, the contract had already been drawn up and signed by the Count. All that was left for me to do was hand over the money.

The contract, which was to last for four years, was very short, a mere two pages in all. However, when I read it over, I soon noted that it was not at all favourable to my needs. During the time that had passed since I had made the agreement with the Count, I had been thinking and rethinking the matter, and had noted on paper all of the conditions that I wanted to include in the written contract. First and foremost, I wanted the contract to run for a period of twelve or at least nine years, like they did for all estates. I had also wanted to press for permission to plough the grasslands that lay higher up and did not have much grass growing on them and transform them into grain fields. For this I would need plough animals—oxen and horses—as well as buildings for them and for the grain that would be produced. On top of this, there would have to be a comfortable home for the lease holder and his servants. The ditches that ran through many of the meadows were in such bad repair that it would cost at least 1,000 gulden for the most minimal repairs. I also planned to add a number of other points and conditions to the contract such as bridges, roads and so on. I wanted to turn the Shtsutsin Meadows into a large estate, with many ploughed fields like other important properties. I harboured the hope that if I could only manage to convince the Count that my requests were just and practical during the writing of the contract, he would surely agree.

Nothing came of any of it. I did not see the Count again. The lawyer handed me the contract and told me to sign it, telling me in a businesslike tone, "That's it!" In other words, no new conditions could be added. He also told me that he had instructions from the Count that if I demanded the addition of any new points, he was to immediately return my 500 gulden to me and the deal was off. Together with the contract, the lawyer handed me a map drawn up by an engineer showing that there were 650 acres in all.

I was deeply upset when I saw that nothing would come of my future plans: they had come to naught. For one heated moment, I considered withdrawing from the whole deal and taking my 500 gulden back from the lawyer. But then I reconsidered: the Shtsutsin Meadows were still, even without all of my conditions, a very good business proposition and if I backed out, someone else would snatch it up immediately like a precious gem. Furthermore, I did not want my competitors—Alter Schnur and Aaron Wechsler—to have the satisfaction of getting the meadows so easily and painlessly. The points that were so important to me did not matter to them at all; they had their own estates and buildings in which to live with their families.

With no other choice, I signed the contract and handed the lawyer the 3,500 gulden as collateral. I got his pledge that he would persuade the Count that he would erect a small house—not a real dwelling—on the meadows so that

I would have somewhere to live during the months when the hay was sold, as well as a small stable for one or two horses.

Within a year, I became the lucky leaseholder of the great Shtsutsin Meadows. Everyone was really jealous of me and of the good business deal that I had managed to make, in particular because I had gotten "a foot in the door" in the Shtsutsin Manor, which had been free of Jews up to that point.

53

OSHITZ

All of this took place in winter of 1894. Our contract at Yozefov was to end on March 15, and I had to leave the estate after having spent over nine years there and with five children (thank God) in tow. After my plans to erect a house and other buildings and to keep cattle on the Shtsutsin Meadows fell through, the question of another estate and an occupation for my very capable wife came to the fore. I had been supplied with a business that would keep me very busy almost all year round. My wife did not, under any circumstances, want to move to town and sit idle. She simply could not live without an estate to run; this was her entire existence. So we decided to rent another estate, but not a large one: one in the 200-acre range that my wife could manage without my help and that would provide income, an occupation for my wife, and, above all, somewhere to live. When we began to search for an estate of this kind, we soon found exactly what we were looking for.

In Radomishla there lived a very wealthy Jew, Reb Mordkhele Gorlitzer, who was valued at about 300,000 gulden. Years earlier, soon after the insurrection, his father, Reb Leyb (Pozik was the family name) had bought the large estate of Yashtshombke from a Polish *porits*, probably for a pittance, along with two smaller farms and over 800 acres of very valuable, dense forest. When Reb Leyb died, he left behind just two children: Reb Mordkhele and a daughter, who was married to a scholar of very distinguished lineage, Reb Lipele Weinberger from Dukla. Initially the two brothers-in-law managed the large inheritance together, which was valued at over 500,000 gulden. Reb Lipele resided at the estate in Yashtshombke—over 700 acres of fields with a big distillery—and worked in agriculture. Reb Mordkhele lived on the estate in the nearby town of Radomishla and was involved in business: loaning money for interest. When the sister, Reb Lipe's wife, passed away, disputes arose between the two brothers-in-law, and they fought it out for a couple of years until their relatives and friends intervened and the sizable assets were divided between them. Reb Lipele kept the large estate and one farm, and 100 acres of forest. Reb Mordkhele got the big, 600-acre Yashtshombke forest, as well as the Oshitz farm made up of 180 acres of fields and some meadows.

This farm of Oshitz, which was just a mile from Radomishla en route to Tarnow, had previously housed a Jew named Moyshe Kshonz for quite a number of years. Initially he had paid a trifle, something like 200 gulden. Later, the price was gradually raised until he eventually paid something like 500 gulden. When the division of property took place between the two brothers-in-law and Reb Mordkhele became the sole owner of the Oshitz Farm, he reconsidered the arrangement and upped the price to a whole 800 gulden per year. Moyshe Kshonz, the previous leaseholder of Oshitz Farm, had amassed a large sum of money over the years, and was a big miser. He had dealt in money lending with the village gentiles and had managed to save about 20,000 gulden, a lot of money for someone as coarse as he was. This made him self-confident, and when he realized that he would now have to pay a whole 800 gulden for the estate, he gave it up and leased himself a much larger property, the village of Diltsch, also near Radomishla, from another wealthy man in Radomishla, Rafael Gutvirt, for an annual fee of 2,500 gulden.

Oshitz was thus available for lease. And although the fields were not very good—with soil that was sandy with areas of wet clay—there were still several interested candidates. First, it was a mile from Radomishla, and barely 2.5 miles to the large town of Tarnow. The farm itself also had certain advantages: the pastures that were sold off and the acres that were rented out to peasants brought in an income of about 500 gulden alone.

But the owner, Reb Mordkhele, was in no hurry to lease it out. He was, may he forgive me for saying so, a big miser and he disliked poor people. He was afraid that if his new leaseholder was unable to pay the high asking price, he would have to knock off fifty gulden, or maybe even more. He was looking for a taker who was a very wealthy Jew from whom he did not have to fear such things. At that time, there was no such person knocking at the door. Jews with a lot of money were seeking and finding better and larger business deals and did not want to be bothered with such a small farm. When a business acquaintance proposed to him that he lease Oshitz to my father-in-law for me, he accepted with open arms. He soon agreed to concede to conditions that he would never have agreed to with someone else. He had known my father-in-law as a boy and me since my wedding, and he knew who he was dealing with. He knew that we would not ask him to lower the price of the lease, and that was the main issue for him. The deal was sealed for a period of six years for 800 gulden, beginning on March 15, 1894, that is, on the exact day that we had to leave Yozefov.

Because the old leaseholder, Moyshe Kshonz, had to remain there until June 15, when his lease in Diltsch began, we were given temporary lodgings in an old building. There were plenty of stalls and there was place for my livestock as well as the previous owner's that he was in the process of transferring to his new estate.

Now everything had been attended to, thank God: both a large and very promising business, the Shtsutsin Meadows, for me, and a fine home for my household and a fine occupation for my dear and highly capable wife.

54
UNCLE KHAZKL

During the course of the entire winter, I was kept very busy in Yozefov extracting myself from the estate. It is a big task to move from an old place where one has become firmly entrenched over a long period of a dozen years. Aside from the livestock, that is, the roughly 200 larger and smaller animals, most of which had to be sold off, there were many other things that we no longer needed and sought to get rid of. My wife selected the best oxen, cows, calves and horses to bring to her new estate in Oshitz. When it came to these kinds of matters, my father-in-law was unfailingly gracious and generous; this was also true of my mother-in-law, dear Sheyndl, may she rest in peace, who was singularly goodhearted. They were not interested in these matters and did not mix in my wife's business. Hey, is she taking so many cattle out of our partnership? She wants them? So let her use them in good health.

When it came to the other inventory, we could not take much with us to the new property. The earth there was much easier to cultivate than in low-lying and damp Yozefov. We thus had no need for the tools, ploughshares, harrows and many other items, and had to sell everything off at half price. We had no shortage of customers. Richer peasants as well as some neighbouring Jewish estate-holders came by, looked around, turned up their noses, offered very low prices and drove off, or purchased something.

With March 15 rapidly approaching, I arrived at Oshitz for the first time late one Friday night. My wife, who had been there with the children for about two days, greeted me with a happy "*gut shabes!*" Tears of joy sprang to my eyes.

The Shtsutsin Meadows had been buried in snow all winter, and no human being had set foot on them. When spring came, it became clear to me that many preparations had to be made to facilitate the individual sales of the meadows when the time came. The first thing that I had to do was hire people to assist me with the work. Above all, I needed a real business manager who understood how to handle the large task of selling individual portions of so many hundreds of acres of meadow to hordes of peasants. The task of becoming my business manager in the Shtsutsin Meadows fell to my wife's uncle, my father-in-law's brother-in-law, Yekhezkl Birnbaum, or, as he was known, "Uncle Khazkl."

He was an easygoing, reliable and intelligent man. In his younger years, he had been a leaseholder and estate proprietor like all of his brothers-in-law, sons-in-law and sons of old Reb Yisroel Kelkiover. However, he had ambitions to own his own estate, and take after his other brothers-in-law, and together with a relative as a partner, he purchased the estate of Ruzshe, which he had been leasing. This ruined him, and dragged him down from his station in life. He eventually left the estate without any assets. On top of this, he was what they call a proud pauper, and would not accept any help from his wealthy brothers-in-law. He was left completely destitute. From the whole estate, he barely managed to salvage a half-collapsed inn, about six acres of fields, and three or four cattle. This affluent estate-owner became the village's poor tenant innkeeper who sold the peasants their quarts of vodka.

If he had not displayed such a stubborn pride in the face of his wealthier brothers-in-law, they would never have allowed him to fall so far. They would have helped him acquire another estate the way they would help any poorer brother-in-law like Uncle Shimen Sandhaus. But, again, Khazkl was a proud pauper. I always loved him for it, and when it turned out that I needed a business manager, I chose him for the position, although there were others who were perhaps better suited to the job. Uncle Khazkl had one distinct advantage over the others: he knew Polish well, could read and write, and had very nice handwriting. During the couple of years that he had been struggling with his own estate until he finally managed to unload it, he had had constant dealings with lawyers, courts and civil servants to the point that he had become something of a lawyer himself. This knowledge came in very handy in a business as large as the Shtsutsin Meadows, where we had dealings with large numbers of local and foreign peasants, and often with the courts. I paid Uncle Khazkl a salary of 15 gulden a week—a generous sum in those days—and this really helped him get back on his feet.

Soon after Passover, we began to survey the Shtsutsin Meadows and divide them into "*jolkes*," which had never been done under the old Countess's previous management. A "*jolke*" in Polish refers to a section of land that contains 0.75 of an acre and thus 1,200 square fathoms. The *porits's* officers had not been meticulous, and had had *jolkes* of 2,000 fathoms or many hundreds of fathoms smaller. It was chaos and you could not make heads or tails of it. We decided to measure out equal *jolkes* over the entire area, but smaller than the norm, at 1,000 fathoms.

The surveying of the Shtsutsin Meadows proceeded in a remarkable manner, which is worth describing here because the average Jew has little or no concept of such matters. As I have already written, I rented the Shtsutsin Meadows from Count Mitshelski at the cost of 13 gulden per acre. It had been agreed to during the contract negotiations that the Count was to have an engineer survey the meadows and have a map drawn up, at his own expense. I was to pay an annual fee, 13 gulden per year, for how ever many acres were surveyed. However, the honourable Mr. Count pulled off a cheap trick that does not behoove a generous Polish *shliakhtsits*. Because he wanted to save money—it would have cost him several hundred gulden to do the survey—he simply paid some young engineer 50 gulden to copy out an old map lying in the local government office. This old map showed 650 acres of meadows. In truth, some 40 acres were missing because over the years, portions of meadow that lay near the Shtsutsin Manor had been ploughed and turned into grain fields. I did not know about this at first, and when I did become aware of the situation, Mr. Count did not want to own up to his swindle and I was not prepared to take legal action against him.

So, the Count had given me a map showing 650 acres of meadows and I had to divide it equally into *jolkes* of 1,000 fathoms each. Who can do this sort of work except for an engineer? And he would have had to have been paid the standard rate of one gulden per *jolke*, which would have set me back at least 1,000 gulden. This is where Reb Yitzhok Mordkhe Bernstein came to my aid, and rescued me from my dilemma. Who was this Reb Yitzhok Mordkhe Bernstein? It will certainly be of interest for readers to become acquainted with this fine man, a type of person that is hard to find these days.

55
YITZHOK MORDKHE BERNSTEIN

The Oshitz farm, which I had rented when I left Yozefov, was surrounded by a lot of forest that had initially belonged to two brothers-in-law, and was later divided between them. The primary overseer, who was appointed by the government as *"leshnitse"* (forest warden) was a close relative, Reb Dovidl Bernstein. This Reb Dovidl had about as much connection to the forest as you or me. He was one of these old Hassidim who spent weeks or months with the Rebbe, and when he did happen to be at home, it was to pour over the Talmud or Zohar. He didn't know the first thing about money and didn't understand a word of Polish, and yet he was the government-appointed overseer of this enormous forest, over 1,500 acres. The entire enterprise was managed by his amazingly capable wife, "Bobbe Henele." She attended to everything although she also had a large number of children. She married them off, provided them with dowries, and all from the small salary they were paid. Meanwhile, her husband sat and studied all day long with his Hassidic rebbes. In their old age, the couple went to the Land of Israel, but Bobbe Henele could not endure having nothing to do and abruptly returned to her forest. Reb Dovidl remained in the Land of Israel and passed away there. When they left for the Land of Israel, the post of *leshnitse* was passed on to their eldest son, Reb Yitzhok Mordkhe Bernstein.

Reb Yitzhok Mordkhe was a fine scholar, possibly much more so than his old father, but much less of a Hassid. Still, for duty's sake, he would occasionally make a quick trip into the nearby town of Dembitz to Rabbi Alter, whom I have already described. He was a specialist in the area of forestry, and he introduced many practical innovations. He was particularly expert in replanting young trees in stretches where the old growth was being logged. He also had in-depth knowledge of mathematics relating to forest and field surveying.

During the division of the forest between the two brothers-in-law who had inherited the Yashtshombke fortune, as well as on other occasions that large tracts of forest were sold, there were often several engineers at work surveying the forest and fields and making maps of various scales. Reb Yitzhok Mordkhe, the forest warden, would shadow them and not leave their side. The result was that he mastered the art of field and forest surveying as thoroughly as any engineer. He was often summoned when some field had to be surveyed or divided, and this brought him a tidy side income. I had known him from before when we had been together in Dembitz at the Rebbe's. Since my arrival in Oshitz, where we were neighbours with our homes in the same manoryard, we had become close friends. It was a pleasure to spend time with him and his household.

Reb Yitzhok Mordkhe proposed that he survey the entirety of the Shtsutsin Meadows and divide them into *jolkes*. He planned to do the bulk of the work at home; when he was finished, we would head out to the meadows and over the course of just three days, measure everything out on site. At that time, my grasp of field surveying was very limited, and I failed to understand what he was saying.

"What do you mean you'll do the work at home? How can it be possible to sit in your house here in Oshitz and survey meadows that are three miles away, all the way in Shtsutsin?" He smiled when he heard my doubts.

He asked me to bring my map of the Shtsutsin Meadows, which was several ells [0.78 meters] long and about three ells wide. With the help of his son, he placed it on a specially designed table made of long boards, and tacked it into place. He had all of the necessary instruments and devices that engineers use. Then he took several rulers out of a drawer that were three or more sided, selected one, and said to me,

"I shall survey all of the Shtsutsin Meadows with this!"

The three-sided piece of wood that he handed me was about twelve inches long and there were different lines and numbers on each side.

"This is a '*Masstab*' [ruler,], and it is used by engineers to measure out all of their maps as well as the fields or forests." Each side had another ruler: one side measured 1,000 lines per meter, a second had much denser lines at 2,000 lines per meter, and the third divided into 3,000 lines per meter.

Truth be told, the whole project remained something of a mystery to me, despite his explanations. But Reb Yitzhok Mordkhe enthusiastically got to work, and soon became completely engrossed. For full days as well as evenings he sat with the big map. He held a ruler in one hand, and a pencil or compass in the other, measuring and calculating and then recording markings, various figures and symbols on the map. He worked like this for about two weeks until he explained that he was finished; the following week we would be able to drive out to the Shtsutsin Meadows and then, over a period of several days, finish the practical work of dividing up the 1,000-fathom *jolkes*. The big map had been broken down into ten large sections, and was full of markings, figures and numbers. He had also created ten additional maps using a larger ruler as well as three special booklets for the venders where each *jolke* had its own number and its exact length and width were recorded, and there was also a place to record the name of the buyer and the price received. There were a lot of "*klines*" (wedges), that is, not full, regular *jolkes*. They were narrow but long, or short and wide. They ran alongside the ditches or bridges that bisected the meadows. These *klines* comprised hundreds of fathoms and their price was determined accordingly.

All of this was accomplished by Reb Yitzhok Mordkhe—a Jew who had never gone to school and had never seen a math textbook in his life—and in the best way possible: his system turned out to be practical, efficient and useful. During the period that he was busy with his calculations and map preparations, I purchased lumber from a forest and had it cut down and turned into meter-long posts. These posts were sharpened at one end so that they could easily be hammered into the ground; the other ends were evened out on both sides with an axe so that the numbers of each *jolke* could be posted. Even the smaller *jolkes* had a special number, both on the maps and in my vendors' books.

The following week, bright and early on Monday morning, I found myself at the Shtsutsin Meadows with Reb Yitzhok Mordkhe. My business manager, Uncle Khazkl, had already arrived several days earlier. He had prepared about 20 quick and skilled young boys. The work progressed as smoothly as a dream. Two workers dragged a thin wire chain that was ten fathoms in length, which was subdivided into full and half fathoms. The measuring began at the end of the meadows that lay at the village border and had a high dike. Reb Yitzhok Mordkhe, with one of his smaller maps in hand, would lead the way and call out "forty fathoms!" The two boys, the chain holders, would rapidly count out four lengths with the chain. Two other boys were waiting with heavy mallets in their hands to hammer in one of the posts that another worker was holding ready, and drive it into the soft ground to a depth of half a meter. Another worker who could write then immediately dipped a paintbrush into black paint and recorded the number of the *jolke,* as it appeared on the map and in the sales books, on both sides of the post. The work progressed systematically and at a rapid pace. As soon as the total length of one section was completed, the same process was repeated for the width. In this fashion, section after section was measured out. By Friday morning, we had finished virtually the entire task of dividing up the meadows. Only the *klines* remained, the irregular, corner bits and pieces that required a lot of labour and were thus put off for two weeks.

To this day I possess limited expertise in the art of field surveying, and I very much doubt that I have managed to offer an accurate description of Reb Yitzhok Mordkhe's skilled and painstaking work.

When everything was finished and I asked him about payment for his services, he would not hear of it. As he explained to me earnestly, he did it out of pure friendship and, even more, "out of love for the thing itself": it was a great delight and an honour to survey the great Shtsutsin Meadows using his own method, and he was convinced that he had completed the task as well as possible, like the most capable engineer. This was his satisfaction, and his reward. With some effort, my wife finally managed to convince his wife to accept a fine milk cow from our stall.

56
MY BUSINESS VENTURES
IN THE SHTSUTSIN MEADOWS

Notwithstanding all of my extensive preparations and all of the jealousy that people felt about my business ventures, thinking that I would become enormously wealthy from them, the whole thing turned out to be a dismal failure. But I continued to put on a good face so that no one found out.

There were many root causes for this failure. A lot of it had to do with the business itself. I overpaid for it. The property had a whole lot of acres that could not bring in even five gulden, and could not be gotten rid of; we had to cut the grass and on them and make hay, and this did not generate any money. I have already mentioned that the *porits,* Count Mitshelski, swindled me whereby I had to pay him annually for some 40 acres of meadows that did not exist. On top of this, the lease conditions for the meadows were very bad. The business also suffered from my having been a "*porits*," and an inexperienced young man. The meadows were low-lying and the ditches were in very poor condition: they did not draw away any water into the nearby Bren and Ribnitsa Rivers, and when it rained heavily, many meadows were inundated with water and ruined. The ditches had no bridges over them and this resulted in even greater flooding in the lower-lying meadow. I suffered doubly during major floods, when the best and most expensive meadows were tamped, and covered in sand and mud. As for me, I realized, all too late, that I did not behave appropriately in the situation. The Oshitz Farm, where I resided and my wife ran the agricultural business, also turned out to be a very poor venture that required me to invest a tidy sum of money. Moreover, my wife and six children were frequently ill and required doctors and trips to the spas, and these expenses amounted to a small fortune.

Most importantly, I was already several thousand gulden in debt at the time, although I was considered to be well-to-do and my credit was always good. I had to take out loans that had to be repaid promptly, and meeting these obligations required borrowing more money, which forced me further into debt. In order to maintain my credit, I had to live a little more lavishly than my means allowed, and offer a pretense of affluence.

After four years of leasing the Shtsutsin Meadows, I was about 15,000 gulden in debt, and the dam had to burst. I left for America. My father-in-law and wife then settled with my debtors. This was at the onset of 1898.

57

MY FATHER-IN-LAW
AND HIS ENEMIES

Here in the Golden Land, I have also experienced a great deal, and have come into contact with all sorts of people. It would be a fascinating project to describe the jobs that I held in America until I became Yiddish writer, as well as the people that I had the opportunity to meet. Each one was unique in his own way. But I am going to leave all of this until a later time, when I hope to be in a position to tackle it.

At this point, I feel that my life story in the Old Country remains incomplete unless I add a chapter—and a long one at that—about my father-in-law and his enemies, and the disputes that dragged on between them for years. This hatred wound up ruining them all, and bringing some of them to the verge of penury.

This chapter of history began some 60 years ago. These sorts of things do not happen among today's generation, are thus worthy of being inscribed into the annals of history.

* * *

This is an episode that played a vital role in the life of my father-in-law, Reb Mordkhe Dovid Shtiglitz and that naturally also had a major impact on me and my family.

As I have already described, my father-in-law had a father-in-law named Reb Yisroel Rider. In his later years he became known by the name of his most recent estate as Reb Yisroel Kielkover. During his youth, Reb Yisroel had lived in the village of Rida, not far from the town of Radomishla, some four miles from Tarnow. Later he had leased the large estate of Kielkov from a wealthy Radomishla man. The estate was located near the *shtetl* of Rzokhov, not far from the towns of Pshetslav, Melitz and Radomishla. The Kielkov Estate was immense, with very fine fields running along the Vistula River. It was also connected to a brewery, a distillery, and a *brave* establishment where large numbers of cattle were fattened up every year. Reb Yisroel Kielkover (no one called him Rider) prospered and become wealthy. Both he, and especially his wife Bobbe Rivke, were major philanthropists.

At that time, the *shtetl* of Rzokhov, which lay just on the other side of the Vistula River from Kielkov, was small and contained about 50 or fewer Jewish families. Almost all of them were poor and a large proportion of them somehow earned their livelihoods from Reb Yisroel, the bighearted Kielkov proprietor. He provided them not only with grain, potatoes and vegetables, but also with liquor for Kiddush and Havdalah. Every Friday afternoon over the course of many years, all of the older children of the town would flock across the Vistula River and come to the Kielkov Distillery for liquor. Every child had an empty quart-sized bottle tied around its neck. Bobbe Rivke, no matter how busy she happened to be, never refused this "great mitzvah"; with her own hands, she would fill the bottles of liquor for Kiddush and Havdalah. And if a pauper from Rzokhov happened upon the bright idea of sending two children instead of one after the liquor—even when she knew all of the children well and knew who each one belonged to—she never made a big deal out of it and never said anything. She simply filled both bottles. In addition, each child would receive ten kreuzer each Friday afternoon "for the trip." This went on over a period of several years. When a poor father had to marry off a child or simply needed a few gulden, he always knew that Reb Yisroel or his wife would provide what he needed. His hopes were never misplaced.

In his old age, Reb Yisroel Kielkover became ill. Half of his body became paralyzed, and after three years of torment, he passed away at the age of 70. Naturally he had to be buried at the old cemetery in the nearby *shtetl* of

163

Rzokhov. Why was this the case? First, the village of Kielkov belongs to the *shtetl* of Rzokhov. Second, Reb Yisroel had been the primary provider for all of Rzokhov for so many years. But things did not go as smoothly as that. Before Reb Yisroel could be buried, many hours had passed and violent battles took place. People actually hit each other, and it brought terrible shame upon the honourable deceased.

As I have already stated, the *shtetl* of Rzokhov consisted almost entirely of poor people. Their leader was a young man and estate holder of a nearby property called Yankl Leiman. As soon as he found out that Reb Yisroel Kielkover had passed away and that he would shortly be brought into town for burial, he hurried to Rzokhov. He soon called a meeting of all of the town's Jews and ordered a tavernkeeper to supply several casks of whiskey, beer, and other alcoholic beverages as well as a whole lot of fine refreshments. Everyone attacked the spread, eating a lot and drinking even more, until they were half drunk.

Then their leader, Yankl Leiman, made a proposal: whereas the town was dirt poor and whereas aside from the half-collapsing *beys-medresh*, they had nothing, not even a bathhouse or poorhouse, the time had now come for the town to be put right and get everything that other Jewish *shtetlekh* had. Since Yisroel Kielkover had died and left such vast assets behind and the family was already wealthy enough that they did not need his inheritance, the *shtetl* ought to demand a sum of at least 3,000 gulden. And because everyone knew that assurances and pledges mean nothing in these kinds of circumstances, his opinion was that they should refuse the deceased burial until the entire 3,000 gulden was paid in full in cash. Was everyone in agreement?

Of course, not a single Rzokhov Jew was opposed. What a great boon to the *shtetl*! This would generate a little income and everyone had his own personal benefit in mind. 3,000 gulden at one shot in this poor *shtetl*! Another two "ringleaders" from the *shtetl* said a few words and proclaimed that Yankl Leiman was right, and that he had the good of the *shtetl* at heart. They asked everyone to stand firm, hold fast and not give in on a single penny.

* * *

In Kielkov, where the deceased Reb Yisroel lay, no one knew anything about this discussion. All of his sons and sons-in-law had gathered alongside the other family members, waiting for a few Jews from the Rzokhov *Chevra Kadisha* to "perform his last rites" and transport him into town to the city's cemetery. They waited for an hour and then a second, and not a single Jew from Rzokhov appeared. Then the mourners began to suspect that something was not right, and that the "Rzokhov Paupers" were up to no good.

Two of the sons-in-law headed out to the *shtetl* and soon returned with the news that all of the Rzokhov Jews were half-drunk and were still in the midst of still more drinking, and that their leader Yankl Leiman was demanding payment of 3,000 gulden before the Chevra Kadisha would come anywhere near the body. These words cut everyone to the bone. What the heck was this: the "Rzokhov Paupers" had the nerve to make a demand like this? For years that had lived, and earned their livelihoods, almost entirely off of the Kielkover Manor, and now, at this time of distress, they had become as arrogant as this!

A dispute within the family ensued about what to do. Some wanted to bring the body to another town, to Melitz, Pshetslav or even—the simplest solution— to Radomishla. Let the "Rzokhov Paupers" stew! The women, however, and especially the widow, old Bobbe Rivke, would not hear of it. They absolutely wanted the burial to take place in the Rzokhov Cemetery, where so many great zaddikim and even a prophet lay buried.[4] Conceding that the women were right, the men agreed.

My father-in-law along with two or three other sons-in-law—there were three sons and seven sons-in-law in all—were hot-tempered and very stubborn people. They were beside themselves that "a rat like Yankl Leiman" would do this to his own people. If the *shtetl* needed a few hundred gulden, the beneficiaries were people with Jewish hearts who would see to it that things were taken care of. They did not have to be louses about it! My father-in-law and the others did not want to wait any longer. The dead body was loaded onto a wagon, covered with old clothing, and brought to the *shtetl* of Rzokhov. They would see who was stronger when they got there: they, the entire Kielkov clan, or "Yankl the Louse" with his Rzokhov Paupers.

When they arrived in town, no one made any move towards the wagon to unload the body and begin its purification. Everyone was gathered in the *beys-medresh*, where they were several bottles of booze and cookies to snack on, and anyone could help himself to his heart's desire. Meanwhile, negotiations began with Yankl Leiman and his two or three assistants.

Initially the family, with my father-in-law as representative, held fast in their demands: first, the dead had to receive his burial, and after the Shiva they would see what needed to be done for the poor *shtetl*. But Yankl Leiman refused to budge: 3,000 gulden cash, and not one cent less. Meanwhile, with the shorter fall days—it was Heshvan—night fell, and it became evident that there would be no burial that day. So the family decided to take the body off of the wagon where

---

4   There is an old legend that centuries ago, today's small *shtetl* of Rzokhov had been a great Jewish community and world centre of Jewish life. The legends spoke of great zaddikim and even a Jewish prophet called "Zechariah the Prophet." Because these zaddikim and this prophet did not have tombstones to mark their graves, it was an old custom that continues to this day not to erect any headstones. The Rzokhov Cemetery thus has no tombstones at all. The newer gravesites have small wooden indicators that state who is buried there, but when the boards rot away, no information remains.

it still lay, and place it in a corner of the *beys-medresh*. The Rzokhov citizens were not bothered by this, but they also did not help to lift the corpse from the cart. The family had to do it.

During subsequent negotiations with Yankl Leiman, my father-in-law and Uncle Khazkl, two strong Jews, got so incensed that it came to blows and before they could be restrained, they had landed a few good blows on Yankl Leiman. After the scuffle, the family—with the approval of the womenfolk—decided to bring the body to Radomishla, a distance of about three miles along (poor) Polish roads. They sent for fresh horses in Kielkov with the intention of traveling all night and arriving at dawn. However, now the Rzokhov Jews intervened and refused to allow the body to be moved.

"Before," they shrieked and bellowed, "the body came to our town, you could have brought him wherever you wanted. But now he is ours and will remain ours!"

More fighting ensued. Slaps, blows and punches flew in all directions and because it had since grown dark, it so happened that each side also took a beating from its own members instead of its opponents. There was quite the display of heroism—with later boasts of "boy, did I give it to them!"—in particular from Uncle Reb Yekhiel Moyshe Feffer from Melitz, who had been a "*flisiak*"[5] on the Vistula River in his youth.

People on both sides intervened and eventually, they reached a compromise. Yankl Leiman greatly relaxed his initial demands, and the family had no choice but to conciliate as well. A compromise of 1,600 gulden was reached. Initially Yankl Leiman insisted that he wanted the money up front in cash, but when he was shown that this was impossible because none of the sons or sons-in-law had brought that much money with them, he finally agreed to take jewelry as collateral. He refused to accept promissory notes, although the beneficiaries

---

5   The *flisiak* undoubtedly belongs to the Jewish jobs that have long since vanished and remain completely unknown to today's reader. In the olden days, large stretches in Galicia, as well as in other Slavic lands, were covered with dense and tall forests. The trees were cut down at a rapid pace, in particular during the winter, and brought down to the shores of the larger rivers, where they were bound into long "rafts" and floated downriver until they reached their destinations: Thorn and especially Danzig. There they were sold as building lumber or ship material (as masts or the like) to German merchants. The lumber industry was very large and lay entirely in Jewish hands. Merchants made or lost fortunes. These lumber "rafts" floated for weeks or months until they reached their destinations, depending on the height of the water. A "raft," which consisted of several smaller ones, was manned by 40–50 gentile workers with a Jewish overseer supervising everything. This *flisiak* headed the whole enterprise and he determined the merchant's fate: whether the "rafts" would arrive in peace or be torn apart by the stormy, roiling waters.

The life of a *flisiak* was very difficult and lonely, buy also very "romantic." It required a lot of physical strength, courage and patience to be a *flisiak* on the stormy Vistula, which often placed his life in great danger.

were certainly good for the money. The jewelry, valued at 2,000 gulden, was produced in the middle of the night. Bobbe Rivke and my mother-in-law's jewelry was brought and handed over to Yankl Leiman with the promise that it would be redeemed immediately after the Shiva and he would receive his 1,600 gulden in cash.

First thing the next morning, when the Rzokhov Jews had slept things off and sobered up, old Reb Yisroel Kielkover was buried after he had endured a whole 24 hours of shame that he had certainly not merited.

58
CRIMINAL PROCEEDINGS

The Shiva week passed and Yankl Leiman and the other Rzokhov Jews were preparing the coffers and strategizing how to spend the 1,600 gulden, which they would be receiving in the next day or two from the Kielkover beneficiaries.

"Naturally 3,000 gulden is more than 1,600, and it would certainly have provided more funds and allowed is to erect all of our long-planned community buildings. But, brothers, when things turn out the way they did, with us unable to beseech the beneficiaries to fulfill any more of their holy obligation, we have to be satisfied and see what we can do with this not insignificant sum of money." This was the gist of Yankl Leiman's message and those of some of his cohorts as they addressed the entire *shtetl*.

However, my father-in-law, who was acting as family representative, was in no rush to part with the 1,600 gulden and redeem the pawned jewelry from Yankl Leiman. The payment dragged on because of a difference of opinion among the beneficiaries as to what to do. One group maintained that the entire 1,600 gulden had to be paid out as soon as possible to get the whole thing over and done with. The second, more vociferous "party"—my father-in-law, Uncle Khazkl and especially Moshe Lind, the youngest son and the estate's primary benefactor and current owner, were furious and screamed that the "Rzokhov Paupers" should not receive a single kreuzer; let Yankl Leiman show what he is made of!

Yankl Leiman did not know about this internal dispute between the beneficiaries. He lost patience and dispatched a Yiddish letter with the *shames* of the Rzokhov *beys-medresh* stating that if my father-in-law did not come and redeem the pawned jewelry during the space of one week, he would auction it off. My father-in-law received this messenger, the *shames*, very cordially with a nip of whiskey, and gave him a whole gulden "for his troubles." This poor *shames* had, after all, traveled an entire mile from Rzokhov to his destination on foot. But he had him tell Yankl Leiman not to be a fool, and that if he wanted to sell the jewelry, he could go right ahead. Either way, he would soon be hearing from my father-in-law.

Two or three days later, my father drove to the regional capital in Tarnow, the result of which were criminal charges of blackmail against Yankl Leiman and two of his lackeys. Investigations, statements and testimonies from both sides ensued. During the court case, the defendants had the best and most industrious representative possible: the Jewish lawyer and brilliant speaker, Dr. Adolf Gold-hammer. It was thanks to him that the defendants received relatively small sentences: Yankl Leiman received three months of "hard labour" and his two assistants received six weeks and a month respectively. The jewelry naturally had to be returned, and the Rzokhov Jews were left with their collapsing *beys-medresh* and without a bathhouse or a poorhouse, possibly to this very day. All of this because Yankl Leiman wanted to take things too far and show what he was made of in such an extreme manner.

Although Bobbe Rivke and her youngest son, Moshe, continued to run the large Kielkov Estate, their considerable support of the Rzokhov Jews, with a couple of exceptions, came to an abrupt end. The Rzokhov Jews were not permitted to appear at the manor and the poor things had to make Kiddush over their challahs and not over Kielkov liquor like before. If the eternally generous old Bobbe Rivke, who could not abide the sight of a long face, wanted to help one of them out, she had to do it in secret. Her youngest son, Moshe, who was a generous and benevolent man in his own right, avoided giving anything to the Rzokhov Jews at all costs.

I recall that while I was boarding with my father-in-law at the Zgursk Manor some ten years later, a Rzokhov Jew once appeared. My kind and generous mother-in-law, received him, gave him a little grain and a couple of *"sixer"* coins, and sent him on his way. My father-in-law met him leaving the yard. He would not even look at him, but he—a man with a temper—raged at my mother-in-law and shouted:

"I have told you more than once that I do not want any Rzokhov Jew on my property!"

The Kielkov and Leiman families remained bitter enemies as long as they lived. But they had no contact and no one did anything bad to the other. This continued for about 20 years until my father-in-law got into another altercation with Yankl Leiman and left him destitute until the end of his life.

59

PIKOLOVKA

My father-in-law was not one of these people with a short memory who soon forgets that someone has done him wrong or committed some crime against him. I never heard him mention the name of his enemy, Yankl Leiman, or even talk about the horrible grievance that he perpetuated against old Reb Yisroel Kielkover and his family. But it lived on in his heart. He waited for some twenty years until the day came when he was able to avenge his old enemy.

The story goes like this:

As I have already described, my father-in-law leased the large, roughly 1,000-acre estate of Zgursk near Radomishla from the debauched *porits* Broniovski. After about a decade, the Bayer family came and displaced the royal Lubomirski family, and took possession of all of Broniovski's estates. My father-in-law's lease agreement had come to an end at just that time, and because he was not on good terms with the new *pritsim*, he was forced to give up the Zgursk Estate and find another business venture. Large and thriving estates did not often become available. My father-in-law searched, but was unable to find what he wanted. He had always especially desired an estate connected with a distillery and a stall to fatten up cattle (*brave*). With no such business on the market at the time, he considered his options and moved to the city. He settled in his birthplace of Radomishla, where he had a house with several barns and about ten acres of fields right behind the city.

So he relocated to town and my mother-in-law, who refused to sit idle and needed something to occupy her, ran the farming operation, albeit on a very small scale in comparison with the previous, large estate of Zgursk. The livestock—the horses, oxen, cows, and other cattle—were sold at good prices. The other inventory—the equipment and field implements—were brought to Radomishla and stored in the barns around the house.

He nonetheless continued to search for a real estate. Tarnow and Krakow estate dealers presented him with various business propositions, and I accompanied him to visit them on several occasions. But nothing came of any of them. Each estate had its own shortcomings and for the time being, my father-in-law remained in town.

* * *

Yankl Leiman, archenemy of my father-in-law, had transformed himself during the years since Reb Yisroel Kielkover's funeral, and had acquired a good reputation and nice manners. In his younger years, he had resided on a small estate near the *shtetl* of Rzokhov. He had made a good living there, but remained a very simple man, like all village Jews. It so happened that after he became a widower with several children in tow, he married the daughter of a respected estate holder from the village of Rzemien, also near Rzokhov. This new wife was an intelligent, modern woman and she began to educate and refine the very simple Yankl Leiman. She knew how to run a respectable house, and he followed her example. His reputation spread and the whole region began to consider him an important personage as well as a trustworthy person. People would bring him their dowries or funds for orphans and widows and request that he use the money for loans and pay modest interest rates on it. His star was rising when he managed to obtain a nine-year lease on the large estate of Pikolovka, near Pshetslav.

The Pshetslav *porits*, Count Ray, had a large family to support and several estates around Pshetslav as well as near Tarnopol. He managed almost all of this estates on his own steam, with a very few exceptions. In the Pshetslav area, Pikolovka was the only estate that was routinely rented out to a Jewish estate holder. Pikolovka, together with Morovka Farm, consisted of about 700 acres of very fine fields, as well as a distillery. It was located right by the Vistula River, and just on the opposite shore lay the *shtetl* of Pshetslav, which was a lot livelier than the *shtetl* of Rzokhov a mile further away. Moreover, the estate was a mere quarter mile from the Dombi train station on the Dembitz-Tarnowbrzeg line, which was a major advantage for any estate. In short, Pikolovka was a property with a great many advantages, and was virtually the best one in the entire region.

Yankl Leiman, who by this time was being called Pikolovker, paid Count Ray an annual lease fee of 7,000 gulden. Although the estate was probably worth a lot more, Yankl still did not manage to prosper there. First, he entered the business without enough of his own funds for an estate of that size, with a distillery and large numbers of animals to put on *brave*. He soon found himself appealing to the Jewish usurers in Radomishla, Melitz and Tarnow, and he was constantly "wheeling and dealing" with them and paying high interest. Second, he was a big spender. His wife liked to play the role of "lady," and they ran the manor in the opulent style of a *porits*, with many servants in the house as well as in the enterprise, *melamdim* and teachers for the children, and with one son studying in Tarnow. All of this cost a small fortune, a lot more than Pikolovka could bring in.

The owner, Count Ray, who lived very nearby in Pshetslav, was a Polish *szlachcic* from the "old school" and a rather miserly person to boot. He was not at all fond of his Jewish estate holder's opulent lifestyle. He really disliked him and decided that when the nine years of the lease were up, he would not renew the contract. Count Ray was born and raised in Pshetslav, knew every Jew in the region intimately and spoke a very passable Yiddish. Incidentally, he was also the son of the old Count Ray, who was the leader of the unfortunate insurrection of 1846, when he was killed by peasants; a lot of legends about him were in circulation among the Jewish population, as I describe in the *Morgen Zhurnal*.

170

It is possible that if Count Ray had not been aware that my father-in-law was staying in Radomishla without a business and that he and Yankl Leiman had been bitter enemies for many years, and if he had not known the root cause of the hatred, everything would probably remained the way it was and he would have renewed Yankl's contract. This would have been the case because no Jewish estate holder would touch an estate where another Jew was currently residing. To take away someone's tenure and rent away someone else's business was considered a very cruel act in those times and no one would have dared to do it. However, when it comes to enemies and one is seeking revenge, laws and prohibitions, and mays and may-nots, fall to the wayside. Moreover, my father-in-law, as well as my mother-in-law, had very solid reputations among the area's *pritsim* as very hardworking people who understood how to run large estates.

* * *

Count Ray dispatched a letter to my father-in-law and invited him for a visit. He wanted to speak with him about an important business proposition, but because he did not want anyone to find out about the encounter, he proposed that both parties meet in a certain hotel in Krakow on a specified date. When my father-in-law received the Count's note, he soon understood, or instinctively sensed, what it pertained to. He knew that Yankl Leiman's lease contract was going to be up a few months later, and if not Pikolovka, what business could the Count have with him, unless it was to lease him another estate? Who knew?

When my father-and-law and the Count met in the Krakow hotel, the latter, who was an experienced businessman, got right to the point without a long introduction.

"Would *Pan* Shtiglitz like to rent Pikolovka from me?"

"Probably yes, but what about the current proprietor?" my father-in-law answered back without even mentioning Leiman's name.

"I don't want him in any case. If *Pan* Shtiglitz does not wish to take Pikolovka, I shall take it over myself."

It did not take long for both parties to come to an agreement. My father-in-law would pay the same lease fees as Yankl Leiman—7,000 gulden a year—but the *porits* added a few concessions, including 200 fathoms of wood annually for use in the manor and the distillery, which were worth upwards of 1,000 gulden per annum. My father-in-law gave him 1,000 gulden as a declaration of the sealed deal. The lease contract was to be closed on January 1, and, at that point, my father-in-law was to provide him with an additional 6,000 gulden as a yearly surety for the estate. Both sides promised to keep the whole matter top secret, at least until January 1 when the contract was signed.

My father-in-law thus lived the greatest and happiest day of his life: he had acquired a property as vast and superb as the Pikolovka Estate. And, above all, he had managed to exact revenge on his old enemy and strip him of his livelihood.

171

However, having "sworn to heaven and earth that there would be no secrets on this earth," the secret leaked out within the space of two weeks, and the whole region heard the news: Mordkhe Shtiglitz had rented Pikolovka! Some people who were enemies and detractors did not say "rented" but "rented away from." Whatever poor village or *shtetl* you entered, there were circles of people including village gentiles talking over and discussing this important event. They gossiped and recounted the old hatred of the renowned Kielkover Family. In one form or another, the origin of their hatred was brought up, and people detailed, with much embellishment and exaggeration, the events surrounding the funeral of Reb Yisroel Kielkover in Rzokhov twenty years previously, and the enormous and needless dishonor that was inflicted upon him.

As is the norm with these sorts of conversations, two factions soon emerged. One side agreed that my father-in-law acted correctly: revenge is sweet, and "the dog deserves the stick." The other side maintained that it was "simply an unheard of outrage" that a Jew, and a father with children, have his livelihood torn away, and have the business where he had been situated for years rented away from him. This is not done in these parts! And revenge is certainly not a Jewish value!

* * *

In Pikolovka, in the home of Yankl Leiman, this news struck like thunder on a sunny day. The man in question, Yankl Leiman, initially wandered around in a state of utter confusion, may we all be spared such suffering. First, his pride was wounded, for his old enemy Mordkhe Dovid, had triumphed over him and taken such enormous revenge. Second, and most importantly, he was aware of his own status. Although he was not an educated man, he did possess enough practical intelligence to understand all too well that if forced to leave Pikolovka, he would be left forever destitute. As long as he remained on the large estate, the game would continue with him in a position to wheel and deal: take out a new loan to pay back another, more insistent debtor and "shut him up." Leaving Pikolovka would be "as bitter as gall" because all of his debtors would attack him at once and tear him to pieces; he would not even be in a position to take on a much smaller estate. And for this he had to thank that vicious Mordkhe Dovid, who refused to forget the silliness of twenty years ago.

* * *

Yankl Leiman was no great Hassid, and he had become more enlightened since his marriage to his second wife. He had never visited a Hassidic *rebbe* in his life. However, when he was faced with the crisis of having Pikolovka rented away from him, he suddenly remembered that there were Hassidic *rebbes*, and he went to them for help.

He traveled to the great Hassidic *rebbe*, Rabbi Yechezkel Halberstam in Shinievo, son of the world-renowned *zaddik* Reb Chaim Halberstam, or the *Divrei Chaim*, of Sanz. Together with his more articulate wife, Yankl Leiman presented the *rebbe* with a *kvitl* and a *pidyon* and described to him the great wrongdoing that Mordkhe Dovid Shtiglitz had committed against him, which would surely force him into dire poverty. The Shiniever Rebbe took this all very seriously. After all, this had to do with the loss of tenure, stripping a man of his business and depriving him of his livelihood! The Rebbe ordered a letter to be written to my father-in-law in his name, which he signed, ordering him to immediately cease and desist from the entire venture, forget the 1,000 gulden that he had given Count Ray, and help Yankl Leiman get the estate back. There were also a couple of lines at the end threatening that if my father-in-law did not comply, his future would be bleak indeed. No good would come of this for him.

When my father-in-law received this letter and had it read to him—his own knowledge of *loshn-koydesh* was limited and his letter writing ability limited to penning a short Yiddish note—he simply shoved it into his pocket and went on with his business. He certainly had no intention of following it. Like Yankl Leiman, he wasn't much of a Hassid. For duty's sake, he would occasionally make his way to Dembitz, and to Belz in his old age, where he played the part and paid out handsomely. However, he never traveled to the Rebbe in Shinievo, and did not consider him as "his" *rebbe*. This explains his indifferent reception of the letter.

Yankl Leiman and his wife returned to the Shiniever Rebbe, who meant his words seriously and ordered a second, sterner letter to be written to Mordkhe Dovid Shtiglitz. But my father-in-law was very stubborn. He did not have the option, or the desire, to back out of the agreement. The second letter had as little effect as the first.

The lease contract was signed by both parties on January 1, and Pikolovka thus officially changed hands. On March 15, 1896, Yankl Leiman was to leave the estate and my father-in-law was slated to take it over.

60

The Takeover of Pikolovka

Time did not stand still. The two and a half months from New Year's until March 15 passed rapidly. Yankl Leiman was unable to get another estate as his financial circumstances did not permit a major business venture, and he shipped some of his livestock and all of the equipment to his father-in-law in Rzemien. He acquired an apartment in nearby Rzokhov, the *shtetl* that he had to thank for all of his current woes. It is not hard to imagine how embittered and desperate the poor man must have been during the entire period that he was leaving Pikolovka, without great hopes for a better future.

* * *

On the day of March 15, a large portion of our family gathered to participate in the takeover of Pikolovka. We understood, both intellectually and instinctively, that the transition would certainly not go smoothly, and we wanted to have the presence of as many people as possible.

At about 9 o'clock in the morning, about twenty of us—including me and my business manager, Uncle Khazkl—gathered in Shmaye Vigoder's tavern by the Vistula River, right near the Pikolovka Manor. After we had eaten a hearty breakfast and tossed back a couple of glasses of whiskey to give us courage, all of us—with the exception of my father- and mother-in-law, who stayed at the tavern—headed out on three wagons to Pikolovka to take over the estate. We had with us half a dozen gentiles: forest guards with loaded rifles and a high-level forest warden, whom the *porits*, Count Ray, had sent for our assistance, protection, and defense.

When we arrived at the Manor, we found a large number of people, maybe 100 in all, just like on fair day. This included the entire Leiman clan, virtually all of the Jews of Rzokhov who were Yankl's friends and enemies of my father-in-law, as well as a fair number of Jewish bums from the surrounding villages who had come running to the spectacle.

All of us were Galician Jews and we had, thank God, never experienced a pogrom and thus had no concept of what the aftermath of what one might look like. However, whoever was at the Pikolovka Manor on March 15, 1896, had a pretty good idea.

All of the buildings—the living quarters as well as the workshop structures— were open and totally empty, with their doors and gates forced open. Most of the windows in the large rooms and stables had been broken or smashed in. The large kitchen was full of bricks, ash and wood. All of the cooking and heating ovens had been broken and dismantled.

Yankl Leiman was not present. He did not show his face so that he would not be held responsible for the vast damage that was being done. Only his wife was there, and with a bitter, mocking smile, she observed all of the Jews present doing as much damage as possible: everything but ripping the bricks out of the walls. Our side could have intervened, especially with the forest guards and their loaded rifles, but our leader Uncle Khazkl held us back.

"By all means, let them do what they want. Yankl will pay for it anyway and it will help them blow off steam." Uncle Khazkl was a very savvy politician with a good understanding of human nature. He had been through a lot in his lifetime.

When we arrived at the manor, we found the large rabble already half drunk and tossing back more booze on this freezing cold day. As soon as they saw us driving into the manor, they came rushing over with a noisy caterwauling. To this day, I don't know where they got that many tin utensils; they must have been prepared in advance or brought from home. In any case, almost all of these Jews, who looked like wild and evil ghouls to me, held some tin pot or bowl in their hands and were banging on them with a stick as loudly as they could. It was enough to make you deaf. They also yelled and shrieked as if possessed.

We just smiled and did not respond. We entered the manor and got out of our wagons. The horses stayed harnessed because we had not yet officially taken over the estate—the *porits*'s commissar arrived later in the afternoon—and had nowhere to put the horses. We did not want to start anything with these people, who were evidently just itching to provoke us into a fight. We were outnumbered several times over, and our "strategist and politician," Uncle Khazkl, continued to restrain us, although some of us really wanted to shut them up.

The caterwauling went on for about a half hour until they got tired and stopped drumming. Then they all entered the open apartments, and we could see through the open windows that they were starting new attacks. We stood or walked around the large courtyard, avoiding being too close to the apartments, and waited for the Commissar who had not yet arrived.

Suddenly they all rushed into the courtyard like a bunch of wild animals, and about a dozen of them entered a stall. They soon came out with a *"noshidle"* (a kind of rack used to dispose of manure). On it lay a bit of manure covered with a sack, and they yelled, *"tsdoke tatsl mimoves* (charity saves from death): Mordkhe Dovid has kicked the bucket!" Uncle Khazkl had to use everything in his power to restrain us from attacking them and beating them up for all they were worth. This spectacle of the stand with the *"tsdoke tatsl mimoves"* amused them greatly and they repeated it several times. They only stopped when they entered the courtyard so that they could warm their insides with a bit of whiskey from a good-sized barrel that they had with them. Just as war cannot be fought without gunpowder, you also need a little whiskey.

* * *

We were still standing outside freezing, although we also did not lack for whiskey of our own. I began to lose patience and I decided, come what may, I had to express my opinion to these people, who were, after all, fellow Jews, and tell them what I thought of them. I waiting for a moment when Uncle Khazkl was busy in another corner of the large yard, and in the company of a single gentile aged about twenty, I sped over to the apartments where the large crowd was assembled in order to warm myself and take a break from the constant

175

screaming, as well as to help myself to some whiskey and bread with herring that were standing on an old broken-down kitchen table. In the space of about a minute, I found myself among them.

They were so surprised at my sudden appearance that they just stared at me and did not say a word, although I had expected a substantial "welcome," or a whack or yank. I headed over to Mrs. Leiman, a lady in her forties of very nice appearance, all dolled up at the height of fashion. I bowed to her and said that as she was still the Mistress of the House, I was requesting her permission to address the gathering. It seemed that my behaviour garnered a positive response. Without so much as a word, she nodded that yes, I could speak.

"My dear Jews," I began, placing myself in a corner of the large room in order to protect myself against nasty blows from someone in their group, "I am now going to tell you a story about our great king, King David, may he rest in peace. The second Book of Samuel states that he once had a sick child. It was dangerously ill. David did everything in his power: not eating, not drinking, dressing in sackcloth with ashes on his head, and continuously praying to the Master of the Universe. But none of this helped and the child died. His court attendants were terrified to disclose the death. They said to each other, 'if the King tormented himself to this extent and took such extreme measures when the child was still alive, what will he do now that the child is no longer with us?' The expressions on the court attendants' faces told the King that his child had died, and he posed them a brief question: 'Has the child died?' Having no other choice, they revealed the terrible truth. He then tore off the sackcloth and ashes from his head, washed up, and sat down at the table and ordered a fine meal fit for a king. The court attendants were surprised when they saw the King's strange behaviour, but they did not dare ask him about it. Wise King David understood, however, that they were confused by him, so he assembled them and said: 'As long as the child was still alive, I fasted and prayed to God to allow him to live. But now, with the child no longer with us, all is lost. My fasting and prayer will not be able to help him any more. I shall go to him, but he will never return to me.' The same, my friends," I raised my voice several notches, "holds for Pikolovka. Your yells, screaming, and violence and all of your other acts of foolishness are no longer of any help. Pikolovka is dead to the Leiman Family, and cannot be brought back to life. You have all made a terrible mistake in doing so much damage here today. You don't know who will pay for it, and it might very well be Mr. Leiman himself. The best advice that I can offer you is to leave in good health and return to your homes and leave Pikolovka to God's mercy."

I spoke roughly along these lines and could see that my words had a certain effect, in particular the story about King David. It is possible that from here on in, everything would have gone much more smoothly and quietly. Some of individual village Jews had begun to back out and head home.

176

But Uncle Khazkl had noticed that I had "vanished" from our camp and had figured out that I had entered the "enemy camp." When he heard me speaking so loudly, with the voices carrying through the window, he forgot all about his strategic planning and together with everyone on our side and our half-dozen gentile guards, he stormed the open apartments in order to rescue me from "enemy" hands. If not for the gentiles, our side would surely have been cut down. As soon as our side set foot into the large rooms, a fight broke out. The Rzokhovers were in the majority, about five to one. The gentiles, with their sticks and rifle butts, chased all of them out and expelled them outside. We, together with our guards, were now left inside. Things might have escalated into another brawl but, to our great fortune, with the time close to three in the afternoon, there arrived the Count's Commissar to hand us over the estate.

Jews are always in great awe of a *porits*. As soon as they spotted the Commissar, they began to back out of the courtyard. On those that remained— members of Leiman's family—the Commissar expended minimal effort: he ordered his forest guards to simply chase them out of the yard. Mrs. Leiman did not stick around for honour's sake; as soon as she laid eyes on the Commissar, she picked herself up and drove off.

A short time later, the entire Pikolovka courtyard had been cleared out by our "enemies" and we were left the sole victors. The commissar walked around the rooms and other manor buildings and surveyed the damage that they had done, with a single word coming repeatedly out of his mouth: "*variati!* (crazies)" He extracted a piece of paper from his pocket, ordered me to sign it and went on his way.

This concluded the takeover of the Pikolovka Estate, where my father-in-law lived for a full nine years and made a lot of money. This extraordinary event and the circumstances associated with it serve as a "cultural snapshot" of a segment of Galician Jewry from two generations ago.

61

PUNISHMENT OR COINCIDENCE?

A few years later, my father-in-law was again destined to have everyone talking about him, this time because of a lot of trouble that he got into because of his bad temper: he killed someone! He did it accidentally, and the injured man only died about 24 hours after the fact, but no one—not even him—could deny that he was the only one to blame, and that he caused a person's death.

Everyone for miles around and in all of the surrounding cities, *shtetlekh* and villages talked about it, and there was ongoing discussion with differing opinions. The more enlightened people asserted that this was a common occurrence, although a very unfortunate one, and that one person accidentally killing another is a regular fact of life. Most Jews, and even peasants, held this viewpoint. The ordinary masses, however, were firmly convinced that this was a divine punishment for my father-in-law's previous sin of snatching Pikolovka away from Yankl Leiman and turning him into a pauper. Hassidim were elated; they were certain that this was a "miracle" by the old Shiniever Rebbe, Rabbi Yechezkel Halberstam, who had predicated several years earlier that my father-in-law's future would be bleak, and that his end would most certainly not be a happy one. Who knows? Who can say whether this was simply an accident or a divine punishment?

The sad story went like this:

It was summer and harvest time. Work was progressing at a feverish pace. Bundles of grain were being transported from the fields to the granaries. The sun was setting and the farmhands were bringing in the last wagonsfull of grain. Suddenly clouds appeared, and because my mother-in-law was afraid that grain bundles still in the fields would get soaked, she asked the farmhands to make one last trip. Almost all of the farmhands did as she asked. They knew her well and were well aware that she would reward them for the additional work with liquor or a few kreuzer. Only one farmhand would not carry out the *"pani's"* request: he acted like he had not heard and began to unharness the horses to bring them to the stall.

At that precise moment, my father-in-law arrived. When he saw what was going on, he sharply told the farmhand that he was immediately to go for more bundles like the others. This guy was stubborn and replied that he had worked enough for the day and would not be returning to the field. They exchanged words until my father-in-law lost his temper and raised a hand. The farmhand grabbed on to my father-in-law's long beard in defense. To free himself from the man's hands, my father-in-law gave him a kick with his right foot, and the farmhand dropped in a dead faint. It turned out that he had a hernia and the kick had caught him in just the right spot.

Two doctors were summoned but there was nothing they could do. Within twenty-four hours, the unfortunate farmhand had passed away. He was buried at my father-in-law's expense.

* * *

If this unlucky incident had happened to another leaseholder who did not have enemies who wanted to do him in, it could have been quietly "erased." It would simply have come down to money in the form of several hundred gulden: the widow would have received a couple of hundred, the court official might also have benefited, and mum's the word. Things were altogether different for my father-in-law. His enemies rejoiced and got right down to their denunciations, running off to the widow to explain to her that this was an opportunity to become wealthy and to insist on at least 20,000 gulden for her deceased husband.

My father-in-law was no fool, however, and he did not wait for his enemies to denounce him and have him arrested by gendarmes. The same night that the man died, he headed off to Tarnow and voluntarily turned himself in to the regional criminal court. This was a very practical move because it shortened the investigation and it only took six weeks for the case to come to trial. His defense was that he had killed the farmhand in self-defense because the man had been holding him by the beard when he had kicked him. The twelve jurors—all Christians—accepted this defense and came to their verdict: "guilty of second degree murder." The court sentenced him to two years of hard labour. In the end, he only served one year because his sentence was reduced. The whole unfortunate incident cost him about 10,000 gulden.

* * *

This is the long, but very interesting, story of my father-in-law and his enemies, as well as of my life in the Old Country. I have not embellished anything or taken sides. I have merely depicted things based on what I heard from reliable sources many years ago or that I had the opportunity to experience myself and in which I thereby played a minor role. It seems to me that these sorts of events and characters no longer exist today. Circumstances have completely changed and so have people.

MARGOSHES FAMILY GENEALOGY
compiled by
Rabbi Eliezer Lippa Gartenhoyz
(from the Margoshes family)

1) Our ancestor, the well-known rabbi and benefactor, his Excellency [Gaon] Rabbi Joseph Margoshes, may his memory be a blessing, is buried with honor in the holy community of Lvov, near the grave of his father, the well-known rabbi, Eliezer Margoshes, may his memory be a blessing, a trustee of the [Council of] Four Lands. Written on the gravestone of our ancestor, Rabbi Joseph Margoshes, is the following:

Grandson of our Rabbi Ephraim Fishl, president [of the Council] of Four Lands and president of [the supporters of] *Eretz Yisroel*.

The grave of our ancestor R. Fishl is by the head [of the grave] of our ancestor, Rabbi Joseph Margoshes.

2) Our ancestor Rabbi Ephraim Fishl son of Rabbi Zvi, may his memory be a blessing, was head of the rabbinical court and a leader of [the Council of] Four Lands] and president of [the supporters of] *Eretz Yisroel*. He died in Lvov in 5413 [1652/3]. This is engraved on his monument:

Confusion and trouble, in which the light was taken.

In the week of [the Torah portion] "for God took him," his soul left in purity.

A glorious noble, leader of Israel, head of the rabbinical court and leader of the community and the province, criterion and cornerstone.

Woe, woe for the captain of the ship, the mouth that emitted pearls of great wisdom, head of the exile of *Ariel* [Israel], supervisor of charity and master of [the charities of] *Eretz Yisroel*.

His hand was open to the poor who ate his bread. He was known in the gates, his name was as poured forth oil,

Our teacher and rabbi, his Excellency the Rabbi Ephraim Fishl son of our teacher, Rabbi Zvi, a wise man [who] is [thus] greater than a prophet, he scattered and gave charity and loans to the poor along with the rest of [his] good deeds.

Like a sapphire and diamond in his body, his soul was on high.

The reputation of his pleasant deeds will rise like a pleasing scent and like the incense [of the Holy Temple, so that God may] conceal him in the shelter of his wings forever.

3) The aforementioned R. Zvi was the son of his Excellency, Rabbi Ephraim Fishl, may his memory be a blessing, head of the rabbinical court of Brisk. He was cited in the *Bach, Orah Hayyim*, chapter 276, and in the *Derisha*, on *Yoreh De'ah*, chapter 16, and in the *Perisha*, on *Orah Hayyim*, chapters 25–27 and in *Even ha-'Ezer*, chapter 129, note 60, and in *Sefer Meirat 'Enayim* on *Hoshen Mishpat*, chapters 69 and 120. He was the son-in-law of our teacher, Rabbi Solomon Luria, may his memory be a blessing. His wife's name was Valentina.

4) The wife of the aforementioned Rabbi Ephraim Fishl, Mistress Gitl, daughter of R. Mordecai died on Thursday, second day of the new month of *Heshvan*, 5403 [1652]. See *Mazzevet Kodesh*, part one, number 61 and part two, number 118. He was the father-in-law of his Excellency Rabbi Abraham Shrenzils Rappoport, author of the book of responsa *Eitan ha-Ezrahi*, for his Excellency the author of *Eitan ha-Ezrahi* was the son-in-law of the aforementioned R. Mordecai.

5) The aforementioned R. Mordecai was the son of his Excellency, the magnate R. Isaac, head and leader of the congregation and the province. This Rabbi Isaac and his son Rabbi Mordecai, and Rabbi Nahman, husband of the distinguished and famous woman, Mistress Rosa, who was known as "Golden Rosa," donated and built the synagogue of Lvov in the middle of the city, which the priests took from them and, through their efforts, they returned the synagogue as is well known. Engraved on his epitaph:

Here is buried the pure spirit, our teacher, the Rabbi Mordecai son of our teacher, the Rabbi and Magnate Isaac. His great Torah became a perennial sacrifice in its [proper] order. He also scattered his money to nearby and far away [recipients]. He was a noble of the Torah, head and leader of the congregation and the province. He was occupied with the needs of the community in faithfulness, and established the yeshivot of the congregation as in the beginning. He exerted himself with redeeming captives in a proper way, sent his money to the poor of *Eretz Yisroel* constantly in order, and engaged in fasting for a long time. He donated a house for the hospital and also donated the dome to expand the synagogue which he had built. He built the guest house and donated much money for dowering brides. The greatness of his deeds of kindness and charity cannot be estimated. In this merit may his soul be bound up in the bond of life and his spirit and soul rest in the shelter of Shaddai. May his merit stand for us and all Israel. Amen.

There is also found in the book *Mazzevet Kodesh*, *Yizkor* [section], which [the author] copied from the minute book of the old synagogue in the midst of the city the following:

May God remember the soul of the pious and humble rabbi, our teacher, Rabbi Mordecai, son of our teacher, Rabbi Isaac, because he was occupied all his days with the needs of the community in faithfulness. On him was placed [the burden of] all the needs of the province. He took his life in his hands to return the small Temple [synagogue] to its original glory, with half of the open space of the faithful city. He was occupied with the great commandment of redeeming captives and was kind to the poor of Jerusalem. He endowed a large sum the interest of which went to the poor, and to dower poor but worthy brides, and for loans to the poor at their time of need [to redeem] pledges, to clothe the naked and to support Torah education to the sons of the poor, and to distribute [alms] to the poor on all three Pilgrimage festivals. He donated out of the goodness of his heart the dome in order to expand the small Temple, the new synagogue which we possess as an inheritance. Therefore may the Master of Mercy conceal him in the shelter of His wings...

There is also found in *Sefer Mazzevet Kodesh* the text of the gravestone of his brother, Rabbi Nahman:

I will arouse a murmur of woe
For here is buried the container of manna
The Glory of the age, faithful shepherd
A holy, generous and merciful man
The great sage and noble, our teacher Rabbi Nahman [text reads: Isaac]
Master of [the charities of] *Eretz Yisroel,*
Officer and commander and leader, chief spokesman before kings, officers and ministers,
His mouth and tongue spoke to nobles with wisdom and understanding.
Pure and upright, Torah was not missing from him for he was great in Torah with a good name.
He uplifted the causes of deeds of loving-kindness in abundance.

The righteousness of his expenditures will remain forever.
He also brought guests to his house.
In this merit may his soul be bound in the bond of life.
Amen.

6) The aforesaid Rabbi Mordecai was the son-in-law of his Excellency the
Rabbi of all the children of the Exile, our teacher Rabbi Joseph Katz, the head
of the rabbinical court of Krakow, author of the book of responsa *She'erit Yosef*.
His wife, Mistress Rebecca was the daughter of his Excellency the author of
She'erit Yosef (this is found in the book *Dor Yesharim*, however the matter is
not clear to me. Possibly it was his father, Isaac, who was the son-in-law of his
Excellency the author of *She'erit Yosef*. I believe I saw the gravestone of Mistress
Rebecca in Lvov, and there the name of his father was not inscribed as is to be
found in the book *Dor Yesharim*, only what he found at the end of the book of
responsa *Eitan ha-Ezrahi*. Perhaps [this difficulty centers on] Rabbi Isaac who
was the son-in-law of the [author of] *She'erit Yosef*. Also the chronology proves
this. More investigation is needed.

His Excellency the author of *She'erit Yosef* edited and published the book
Agudah, and was the father in law of Rabbi Moses Isserles. For Rabbi Moses
Isserles' wife was the sister of our ancestor the author of *She'erit Yosef* (see the
genealogy of Rabbi Ephraim Zalman Margoliot of Brody, may his righteous
memory be a blessing.)

His Excellency Rabbi Joseph Katz, author of *She'erit Yosef* was the son of the
well-known Excellency Rabbi Mordecai Gershon Katz, from among the exiles of
Vienna. This is the text of his epitaph in the book *Mazzevet Kodesh*:

In this cave [is buried]
A precious man of God, the noble Torah scholar, our teacher Rabbi
Joseph son of Mordecai Gershon Katz, who was head of the rabbinical
court and the Yeshiva here in our congregation for more than fifty years.
He was exceedingly modest, more than any man.
He taught Torah in Israel and enlightened our eyes with the responsa
She'erit Yosef as well as commentaries on *Ḥoshen Mispat* and *Mordecai*.
He died on the second day of Shvat, in the year "Count the heads of
the sons of Gershon."

Next to him is buried a worthy and significant woman, his wife, Mistress
Rebbitzen Shprinza, daughter of the honorable magnate, leader and official,
Master Moses Eberles, may his righteous memory be a blessing.

All her days she occupied herself with deeds of loving-kindness and visits to
the sick. She was her husband's crown.

She died on Sunday, fourth of Tevet, 5335 [1575].

Above her is buried her grandchild, the young boy Gershon son of Moses her son. Near them is buried his Excellency Rabbi Tanhum son of His Excellency Rabbi Joseph Katz. All his days he was a judge and supervisor. He died on the fourth day of the month Shvat, 5378 [1618].

7) His Excellency our teacher Rabbi Mordecai Gershon Katz, son of the holy man, his Excellency Rabbi Hayyim Katz, may his righteous memory be a blessing.

8) His Excellency, our teacher Rabbi Hayyim Katz, brother of His Excellency Rabbi Akiva Katz of Oben, leader and executive in the city of Prague, may his memory be a blessing, son of his Excellency, our teacher Rabbi Isaac Katz, head of the rabbinic court in the districts of Galata and Pera in the capital city of Constantinople, son of his Excellency Akiva Kohen Zedek, pure Sephardi, head of the rabbinical court of Salonika, may his memory be a blessing, who was among the exiles of Spain and was accepted as head of the rabbinical court of Salonika.

9) The wife of his Excellency the author of *She'erit Yosef*, Mistress Shprinza (above, number 6), daughter of the magnate executive and leader in Krakow, the honorable Moses Eberles.

10) Rabbi Moses Eberles was the son of the wealthy Rabbi Abraham Eber of the Altshuler family of Prague, may his memory be a blessing. He was enormously wealthy. Around the year 5380 [1619/20] he left his birthplace, Prague, and took all his wealth and property to come and live in the city of Krakow.

This Rabbi Abraham Eber stemmed from the pious of Provence who were exiled on Friday, the tenth of the month of Av, 5066 [1306]. This Rabbi Abraham Eber was very great in Torah but even more in fear [of God]. He had his wealth as a heritage from his fathers. He donated and did [deeds of] kindness. He was a modest elder and a faithful shepherd of the community. He died at a good old age and there his rest is with honour.

11) The wealthy Rabbi Moses Eber was son-in-law of his Excellency, our teacher Rabbi Eliezer Treves, head of the rabbinical court of Schlettstadt. His wife's name was Mistress Hannah.

12) His excellency Rabbi Mordecai Gershon (see number 7) was son-in-law of his Excellency Rabbi Isaac Kloyber, may his righteous memory be a blessing. His Excellency Rabbi Isaac Kloyber was the father of the mother of our teacher Rabbi Solomon Luria, may his righteous memory be a blessing [who was] of the lineage of Rashi.

GLOSSARY

Alfas: halakhic compendium of R. Isaac Alfasi
Aliyah: call to read a passage of the Torah
Apikoyres (pl. *apikorsim*): heretic

Badkhen (pl. *badkhonim*): wedding jesters
Balesbos (pl. *balebatim*): householder; gentleman
Baleboste (pl. *balebostes*): lady of the house
Bal-musef: prayer leader during the Musef prayer
Bar-mitsve (*Bar Mitzvah*): age 13
Beys-medresh (*Beit Midrash*): prayer and study house
Bekeshes: long coats
Ben: son of
Beys-din (*Beit Din*): Rabbinical court
Blat Gemara: a page of Talmud
Bokher (pl. *bokhrim/bakhurim*): young man of marriageable age

Calpac: a sable hat
Challah: special Sabbath and holiday bread
Chanukah: wintertime festival of lights
Chevra Kadisha: Jewish burial society
Choshen Mishpat: fourth part of Joseph Caro's *Shulkhan Arukh*
Cohen: descendant of the Biblical priestly class

Dayan: judge
Dikduk: Hebrew grammar
Din-toyre (*Din Torah*): trial before a Rabbinical court
Dreidl: spinning top that is part of the customary gambling game during Chanukah

eyshes khayel: woman of valour; ideal Jewish wife
Eretz Yisroel: the Land of Israel

185

Frum: religiously observant, pious

Gabe (pl. *gaboim*): Rebbe's manager
Gaon (pl. *gaonim*): genius in Jewish scholarship, luminary, Excellency
Gan eydn: the Garden of Eden, paradise
Gartl: belt worn by Hassidim
Gemara: Talmud
Get: Jewish divorce
Halakha (pl. *Halakhot*): Jewish law
Haluka: support for poor Jews in the Land of Israel
Haskalah: the Jewish Enlightenment
Havdole (*Havdalah*): ceremony to mark the end of the Sabbath
Hovevei Zion: "Lovers of Zion" organization

Jubkas: simple overcoats

Kabbalah: the teachings of Jewish mysticism
Kabbalas Shabbos (*Kabbalat Shabbat*): Friday night services
Kahal: Jewish community
Kehilah: Jewish Community
Kest: Room and board provided by the family of the groom to enable him study without having to worry about making a living
Ketubah: marriage contract
Khalitza (*Halitza*): Lit: Removed Sandal. Ceremony of release from the Biblical obligation of Levirite marriage to enable a widow to remarry.
Khazan: cantor
Khevre (pl. *khevres*): associations
Khevre mishnayes: Mishnah society
Kheyder (pl. *khadorim*): traditional Jewish school
Khumesh: Five Books of Moses
Khupe: wedding canopy. Fig: the wedding ceremony
Kiddush: benediction over the wine
Klal-Yisroel: the Jewish People
Klezmer (pl. *klezmorim*): musicians
Kloyz: small synagogue or house of study
Kol Nidrei: opening service for Yom Kippur, the Day of Atonement
Kvitl: a slip of paper with a request for a Hassidic rebbe

Lekhaim: [to make a] toast
Loshn-Koydesh: Hebrew

Maariv: evening prayer
Maggid: preacher
Mekhutn (pl. *makhatonim*): in-law
Maskil (pl. *maskilim*, adj. *maskilic*): proponent of the Jewish Enlightenment
Melamed (pl. *melamdim*): kheyder school instructor
Meylets (*melits*): rhetorician, stylist, translator, orator, advocate, in particular in the Hebrew language

Mincha: afternoon prayer
Minyan (*minyonim*): prayer quorum
Mishnayes: a volume of Mishnah
Misheberakh: prayer asking for God's blessings for the bride and groom
Misnaged: opponent of the Hassidim
Mitsve (*Mitzvah*): Jewish commandment, good deed

Nassi: president
Nigun (pl. *nigunim*): Hassidic melodies
"*Nusakh Ashkenaz*": the rite used Lithuania, Russia, and other areas not under Hassidic influence

Pan: Polish lord
Parobek (pl. *parobkes*): landless farm worker
Parshe (pl. *parshes*): weekly Torah portion
Peyes: ritual sidelocks
Pidyon (pl. *pidyones*): payment made to a Hassidic rebbe, usually for a kvitl
Pilpul: Method of study of Jewish law
Poskim: Decisors of Halakha (Jewish law)
Propinatsye: the exclusive rights to sell alcoholic beverages; proprinator: the person who hold these rights
Porits (pl. *pritsim*): lord, landowner

Rashi: Rabbi Solomon Bar Isaac, medieval Bible commentator
Reb: title equivalent to the English "Mr." In some cases, it also indicates rabbinic competency
Rebbe: Hassidic rabbi
Rebbetzin: Rabbi's wife
Rosh Beys Din: head of the Jewish court of justice
Rosh Hashanah: the Jewish new year
Rosh Kehilah: Head of the Jewish Community
Rosh khoydesh: beginning of the new month
Rosh Yeshivah: Head of the Yeshivah

Seyder (*seder*): ritual to mark Passover
Seyfer: holy Jewish book
Shabbes: the Sabbath
Shadkhen (pl. *shadkhonim*): matchmaker
Shaleshudes (pl. *shaleshudesn*): third Sabbath meal eaten late in the afternoon
Shames: beadle, assistant
Shas: the Talmud
Shayle (pl. *shayles*): questions on matters of Jewish law
Shatnez: halakhically forbidden blend of wool and linen
Shavues (*Shavuoth*): Spring festival
Shekhinah: Divine Presence
Sheygets (pl. *shkotsim*): gentile man; servant
Sheyner yid (pl. *sheyne yidn*, diminutive: *sheyne yidlekh*): man of learning, virtue

187

Shidekh (pl. *shidukhim*): matchmaking, the process of arranging a match

Shikse (pl. *shikses*): gentile woman; servants

Shirayim: scraps left on the Rebbe's plate that are coveted by his Hassidim

Shiva: Seven days of mourning after a death

Shtetl (pl. *shtetlekh*): small market town with a sizable Jewish population

Shtreiml (pl. *Shtreimlekh*): festive fur hats

Shoykhet: ritual slaughterer

Shul: synagogue

Siddur: prayerbook

Siyum: completion of the study of a unit of Torah, Mishnah, or Talmud, usually involves a celebration.

Spodik: tall fur hat worn by Hassidim

Sukah: outdoor booth

szlachcic: Polish noble

Takef: influential or powerful person

Talis (*Talit*): prayer shawl

Talis-kotn (*Talit katan*): undergarment with tassels at the four corners

Tfilin: phylacteries

Tish: Get-together of Hassidim at the rebbe's

Tosephos (*Tosephot*): discourses on the Talmud

Treyf: unkosher

Tsitses (*Tzitzit*): ritual fringes

Velt-shadkhen (pl. *velt-shadkhonim*): international matchmaker

Yibum: Levirite marriage

Yahrzeit: anniversary of the death

Yeshivah: institution of advanced Jewish learning

Yiddishkayt: Jewishness, Jewish identity and practice

Yikhes: lineage

Zaddik (pl. *Zaddikim*): righteous man

zikhroyno livrokho: may his memory be a blessing

Zmire (pl. *zmires*): Sabbath songs

INDEX